FAMILY

FAMILY

*The Making of an Idea,
an Institution, and a
Controversy in American Culture*

Betty G. Farrell

Pitzer College

Westview Press

A Member of the Perseus Books Group

Copyright © 1999 by Westview Press, A Member of the Perseus Books Group

Published in 1999 in the United States of America by Westview Press, 5500 Central Avenue, Boulder, Colorado 80301-2877, and in the United Kingdom by Westview Press, 12 Hid's Copse Road, Cumnor Hill, Oxford OX2 9JJ

Library of Congress Cataloging-in-Publication Data
Farrell, Betty G.
    Family : The making of an idea, an institution, and a controversy in
American culture / by Betty G. Farrell.
        p.   cm.
    Includes bibliographical references and index.
    ISBN 0-8133-1545-X (hc.) — ISBN 0-8133-1546-8 (pbk.)
        1. Family—United States.   2. Family—United States—History.
3. United States—Social conditions.   I. Title.
HQ536.F385   1999
306.85'0973—dc21   98–49325
                                                                            CIP

The paper used in this publication meets the requirements of the American National Standard for Permanence of Paper for Printed Library Materials Z39.48-1984.

10   9   8   7   6   5   4   3   2   1

Contents

Acknowledgments

This book has been long in the making. Its roots are in my first studies of family sociology with Sam Kaplan, a teacher and friend whose breadth of interest in sociology, history, literature, politics, and culture has always served as a lesson to me about the narrowness of disciplinary boundaries. As an early participant in the Newberry Library's program in Family History and Demography, I had the opportunity to work with Daniel Scott Smith and Tamara Hareven, among other historians who were instrumental in revitalizing interdisciplinary interest in family studies. Lee Rainwater, Theda Skocpol, Ann Swidler, and Rae Blumberg have all served as important scholarly mentors at various points in the course of my professional career. Janet Farrell Brodie, Moune Charrad, Britta Fischer, Rena Fraden, Maureen Mahoney, and Joanna Worthley have been the best kind of scholarly colleagues and friends—supportive and encouraging, good critics, always there, always ready to read another draft. At Pitzer College I have been fortunate to find a congenial environment for pursuing wide-ranging interests. Over the past eleven years, I have had many bright and engaging students in my classes whose good questions about contemporary family life have helped sharpen the lines of inquiry in this project, and I have a fine set of colleagues, past and present, with whom I have enjoyed working—in particular, Don Brenneis, Jose Calderon, Susanne Faulstich, Paul Faulstich, Jim Lehman, Stu McConnell, Peter Nardi, Dan Segal, Susan Seymour, Ann Stromberg, Jackie Levering Sullivan, Jack Sullivan, Rudi Volti, Lora Wildenthal, and Michael Woodcock. Being part of the consortium of the Claremont Colleges has its distinct advantages; Elazar Barkan, Robert Dawidoff, Ranu Samantrai, and Helena Wall are also my good colleagues who can be found at close hand. My special thanks go to my Pitzer colleague and walking companion, Lucian Marquis. Lucian pushes everyone to read more, to think more critically, and to draw a broader set of connections between ideas. His intellectual example of thinking about the points of intersection between politics and culture sets a high standard for the rest of us. Lucian Marquis and Jane Slater Marquis together provide the kind of sociability and opportunities for conversation that nurture and sustain a sense of community. Claremont is a better place in which to live and work because of them.

A book about families is also rooted in personal experience. My own family has been supportive of this project and of me in countless ways. I want to thank my parents, Kenneth and Mary Farrell; my siblings, Janet, Deborah, Bob, Patricia, and Lisa; my in-laws, out-laws, niece, and nephews. Deborah Farrell provided very helpful comments on an early draft of the manuscript. Jedediah Farrell Brodie and Nathaniel Farrell Brodie have particularly kept me on track about the issues concerning children and adolescents in American society. I don't hold them responsible for the mistakes of interpretation I may have made, but they have taught me a lot about what it means to grow up during the past twenty years. Finally, and in no small measure, gaining access to a new family has brought many of the issues and themes of this book alive. Thanks to Marty, David, Linda, Andrew, Marc, Sandy, Jake, Joshua, Lisa, all the cousins, and especially to Zach and Neela for such a generous welcome. Richard Taub has been the most sympathetic and completely honest critic a person could hope to find. His ability to keep work and the rest of life in balance has been a good lesson to me, one that made the final stages of this project both more intellectually focused and far more enjoyable.

While working on this project, I received helpful research assistance from graduate students at Claremont Graduate University—Desirée Dreeuws, Laura Abeyta-Paulus, and David Parker—and, at the University of Chicago, from Kelly Daley. Pitzer College has a generous sabbatical leave policy that allowed this book to be written in many different settings: San Francisco/Berkeley, Los Angeles/Claremont, Cambridge/Somerville, Chicago, and Santa Fe—all places with great libraries and bookstores, rich social networks, and appropriate diversions to complement the essentially solitary task of writing. I am grateful to have had the opportunity to think about American families from this rich and diverse set of geographic vantage points.

Betty G. Farrell

1

Introduction

Q: What did Eve say to Adam on being expelled from the Garden of Eden?
A: "I think we're in a time of transition."

The irony of this joke is not lost as we approach the end of a century and anxieties about social change seem rife. The implication of this message, covering the first of many subsequent periods of transition, is that change is normal; there is, in fact, no era or society in which change is not a permanent feature of the social landscape. Yet, on the eve of the twenty-first century, the pace of change in the United States feels particularly intense, and a state of "permanent transition" hardly seems a contradiction in terms at all. To many, it is an apt description of the economic fluctuations, political uncertainties, social and cultural upheaval, and fluidity of personal relationships that characterize the times. For a large segment of the population, however, these transitions are tinged with an acute sense of loss and nostalgia. Moral values, communities, even the American way of life seem in decline. And at the core of that decline is the family.

In a nationwide poll conducted by the *Los Angeles Times, May 26, 1996,* 78 percent of respondents said they were dissatisfied with today's moral values, and nearly half of that group identified divorce, working parents, and undisciplined children as the key problems. Only 11 percent of the respondents believed that their own behavior had contributed to the moral problems in the United States, and a resounding 96 percent believed that they were personally doing an excellent or good job of teaching moral values to their children. Conversely, 93 percent thought that *other* parents were to blame for the inadequate moral upbringing of their children. The sense of loss and decline many Americans feel today is filled with such contradictions. Americans want their families to offer unconditional love yet also to enforce and uphold strict moral values. They want flexibility, mobility, and autonomy in their personal lives but yearn for traditional communities and permanently stable families. When the substance of the debate over families is this ambiguous and contradictory, it is important to look more closely at the underlying issues in this time of transition.

For most people in most eras, change seems anything but normal. Periods of social change can evoke much social anxiety because the unknown is inherently unsettling and because many people are stakeholders in the status quo. Those who seek change generally want to effect a shift in the relations of power, either for themselves or for others. But such shifts are always unpredictable, and they can seem treacherous to those who hold the reins of power as well as to those who feel their social, economic, or political power eroding. The groups with eroding power are the ones most likely to resist, through active strategies and passive resistance, the ideas, values, symbols, and behavior associated with change. This describes such groups in the contemporary United States as militias who see minorities, foreigners, and new cultural values as a threat to the American way of life; whites who see blacks, Latinos, and Asians as challenging their privileges and claim on limited resources in a zero-sum game; pro-life advocates who see pro-choice supporters as threatening traditionally defined family roles; and antigay proponents who see gays and lesbians as subverting the gendered social order. Although social structural forces are ultimately responsible for the realignment of prestige and power among social groups in any society, these forces are always complex, abstract, intangible, and invisible. So those who symbolize or represent the forces of the new—women, minorities, immigrants, the poor, and other marginalized groups—tend to be singled out and blamed for the disruptions and upheaval associated with change. Social psychologists identify this process as scapegoating, the act of displacing generalized anxiety onto a conveniently visible and available target. Scapegoats have been identified in every era, but in periods in which the pace of change is particularly fast and a sense of unsettling disruption is acute, those social newcomers who challenge established values and behavior can all too readily become the targets of the rage, fear, and ambivalence of people feeling the earthquake tremors of social change.

Popular Perspectives on the Family

The family values debate has been generated against just such a backdrop in the late-twentieth-century United States. Fundamental changes in the expectations, meanings, and practices defining American family life have characterized much of the twentieth century, but especially the final thirty years. Consequently, concern about the family has moved to the center of the political arena. Threats to the family, on the one hand, and salvation through the family, on the other, are the two most prominent themes in the recent family politics discourse. That the American family is broken and in need of repair is a common assumption of many social observers. Its complement is that families are worth fixing because making them strong (again) is the key to solving most of society's ills. Neither of these assumptions has been subject to much critical scrutiny, nor has the historical image of the strong, vital, central family institution of the past on which they rest. Longing for order is one of the impulses behind the current turn to family politics in the United States, and feminists, gays and lesbians, single-parent mothers, absent fathers, pregnant teenagers, and gang-oriented youth, among others, have all at one time or another been made the scapegoats for family decline in the United States.

Longing for a more orderly, mythic past is most commonly associated with the conservative position on the family politics spectrum, and it would be easy to caricature the nostalgia for a family modeled on the classic 1950s television sitcom as the sum total of this side of the family values debate. But if we assume that concerns about The Family, writ large, are only those of conservative politicians attempting to manipulate public sentiment, we would overlook the vast reservoir of social anxiety about contemporary family life that is also being tapped by many others from a variety of political and social perspectives: working mothers who are consumed with worry about childcare; white Christian men who, by the tens of thousands in the late 1990s, attended Promise Keepers revivals that focused on renewing their traditional roles as husbands and fathers; adolescents seeking the emotional attachment of family ties among peers and in gangs when it is found lacking in their own homes; committed gay and lesbian couples fighting for inclusion in the legal definition of family even as they retain a skeptical stance toward this fundamentally heterosexual institution. Why such concern about the family? One reason is that the metaphor evoked by family is a powerful one. A family is defined not so much by a particular set of people as by the quality of relationships that bind them together. What seems to many to be the constant feature of family life is not a specific form or structure but the meanings and the set of personal, intimate relationships families provide against the backdrop of the impersonal, bureaucratized world of modern society.

The core sentiments of family life that define the nature and meaning of this social institution for most Americans are unconditional love, attachment, nurturance, and dependability. The hope that these qualities are common to family relationships accounts for the shock with which we react to reports of violence, abuse, and neglect occurring inside the sanctuary of the private home. In popular culture, as in real life, stories of families beset by jealousy, envy, lust, and hatred rather than by the ideals of love, loyalty, and commitment provide an endless source of titillation and fascination. Family stories are not only the stuff of life we construct through our daily experience but the narrative form used to entice us as consumers into a marketplace adept at presenting all sorts of products as invested with emotional qualities and social relationships.

The widely promoted "Reach Out and Touch Someone" advertising campaign developed by AT&T in 1978 was a prototype of this genre (Arlen 1979). In this set of ads, a powerful multinational company hoped to pull at the heartstrings and the pocketbooks of the consuming public by promoting itself as the crucial communication link between family members separated by great global distances. The copy in the print advertisements told heartwarming personal tales of mothers and sons, uncles and nephews, and grandmothers and grandchildren reunited by AT&T's implied commitment to family values, albeit at long distance phone rates. The family metaphor works as an advertising ploy because there is widespread sentimentality in American society about family life. What makes families so compelling for those of us who actively choose to live in them, as well as for those of us who just as actively reject them as oppressively confining, is that families reside at the intersection of our most personal experience and of our social lives. They are institutions we make, yet they are in no small part also constructed by cultural myths and social forces beyond any individual's control.

A desire for the kind of care and connection provided by the ideal family cuts across class, race, and ethnic lines in the United States. A commitment to family seems to be so widely shared across groups of all kinds in the hybrid mix that makes up American culture as to be nearly universal. It therefore comes as some surprise that the qualities many accept as natural components of family ties today—unconditional love, warmth, enduring attachment—were not the same expectations most American families had until 150 years ago. The historical variations in family life challenge the claim that the family, even within the same culture, has had the same meaning or has offered the same timeless experiences to its members.

Assumptions about American family life in the past are widely shared. These include the beliefs that families were large and extended, with most people living in multigenerational households; that marriages occurred at an early age and were based on permanent, unwavering commitment between spouses; that the ties between kin were stronger and closer than those experienced today; and that family life in the past was more stable and predictable than it is currently. These assumptions about the family of the past have collectively produced an image that one sociologist has called "the Classical Family of Western Nostalgia" (Goode 1963). It is the image upon which politicians and advertisers, among others, routinely draw as they explain contemporary social problems by reference to family breakdown or as they tap consumer desires by associating a product with positive family values and warm family feeling. The family is a potent symbol in contemporary American society because it touches our emotional needs for both intimate personal attachments and a sense of embeddedness in a larger community.

How and why have families come to have the meaning they do for us in contemporary American life? How do our expectations and understandings about the family as an institution differ from those of the past? Is there truth to the fears that family values are weaker today than in the past—that children are more vulnerable, adolescents more intractable, adults less dependable, and the elderly more needy? These general questions provide the framework for this book. By exploring the changes and continuities in key life stages in American families over time, my goal is to provide a fuller context for assessing the kinds of concerns that have dominated the family values debate—or, more broadly, the turn to family politics—of recent decades. In both popular culture and political discourse, sentimentality and nostalgia about the family have often prevailed, and a social and historical context for framing the issues has largely been missing. It is important to challenge the popular understanding of the family as an institution that is biologically based, immutable, and predictable with a more culturally variable and historically grounded view. Because families are central to the way we talk about ourselves and about our social and political lives, they deserve to be studied in their fullest scope, attached to a real past as well as a present and future.

Academic Perspectives on the Family

Assumptions about the nature of the family abound not only in popular culture but in social science as well. The disciplines of anthropology, sociology, history, and psychology all have particular orientations to the institution of the family that define their theoretical positions and research agendas. Among sociologists and anthropologists, for example, a starting premise about the family has been that it is one of the central organizing institutions of society. Its centrality comes from having the capacity to organize social life quite effectively by regulating sexuality, controlling reproduction, and ensuring the socialization of children who are born within the family unit. Many social science disciplines start with the question "How is society possible?," and they recognize that the organization of individuals into family units is a very effective means of providing social regulation and continuity. Through the institution of the family, individuals are joined together and given the social and legal sanction to perpetuate their name and traditions through their offspring. Whole societies are replenished with future generations of leaders and workers.

In the early twentieth century, the anthropologist Bronislaw Malinowski made the argument that the most universal characteristic of family life in all cultures and all time periods was the "principle of legitimacy" (1974: 51–63). He had noted that the rules for sexual behavior varied widely across cultures but that control over reproduction was a common feature of every social order. Every society made the distinction between those children (legitimate) born to parents who had been culturally and legally sanctioned to reproduce from those children (illegitimate) whose parents were not accorded this sanction. The function of the principle of legitimacy, according to Malinowski, was to ensure that a child born into a society had both an identifiable mother and father. The father might, in fact, not be biologically related to the child, but his recognized sociological status as father was the affiliation that gave the child a set of kin and a social placement in that social order.

In addition to being the only sanctioned setting for reproduction, families are important sources of social continuity because they are most often the setting in which children are cared for and raised. The power of social forces is such that parents normally can be counted on to provide long-term care for their dependent children because the emotional closeness of family bonds makes them *want* to do so. Families are therefore particularly effective institutions because they press people into service for their kin by the dual imperatives of love and obligation. Although it is possible that food, shelter, physical care, and emotional nurturance could be provided through alternative means by the state or other centrally administered bureaucratic agencies, it would require considerable societal resources and effort to ensure that these needs were effectively met for a majority of individuals in a society. What families seem to provide naturally, societies would otherwise have to coordinate and regulate at great cost.

To argue that families are effective or efficient as social institutions is not, however, to claim that they are necessary or inevitable. One common fallacy that some sociologists have promoted in studying the family at the societal level is the equation of its prevalence with the idea that it is functionally necessary. The assumption that societies "need" families in order to continue, based on the observation that some form of family exists in all known societies, ignores the range of variation in or the exceptions to this institution. Individuals and subgroups within all societies have constructed alternative arrangements to the traditional family of parents and their children. But the very fact that they are considered alternatives or experimental social organizations suggests how powerful the dominant family norm continues to be.

Another assumption that is shared across several social science disciplines is that family harmony and stability constitute the basis for order and control in the larger society. From this perspective, the family is a microcosm of the larger society, and social regulation in the domestic sphere helps promote order and control at all social levels. Individual social analysts might alternatively celebrate or lament the kind of control, regulation, and social order that was understood to begin in the family and radiate outward to the larger society, but the assumption that society was built on the foundation of the family was rarely challenged.

As a microcosm or a miniature society of the rulers and the ruled who are bound together by reciprocal rights and obligations, the family helps maintain social order first by its capacity to place people in the social system. It does so by providing them with identifiable kin and establishing the lines of legitimate succession and inheritance that mark their economic, political, and social position in society. Because individuals are located in an established social hierarchy by their birth or adoption into a particular family group, the nature of power and access to resources in a society remain largely intact from one generation to the next. Thus, one meaning of the family as a central institution of the social order is that it reinforces the political and economic status quo. Families ensure that the distribution of resources both to the advantaged and disadvantaged will remain relatively stable, since the transmission of wealth, property, status, and opportunity is channeled along the lines of kinship (Farrell 1993).

In another important way, families help to regulate the social order. Family life, according to both law and custom, prescribes roles for men, women, and children. Although these roles are really the products of social and cultural forces rather than biological imperatives and are therefore highly fluid in times of change, they appear to most people to be prescribed by stable and immutable rules governing everyday life. The meaning of "traditional" family life is that people are conscripted into established roles. Everyone knows his or her place and tends to keep to it by the pressures of community norms and social sanctions. But such traditional family roles exact a toll, as well. What promotes social harmony and order to the advantage of some produces severe constraints on others. Women and children, whose roles in the family have traditionally been subordinate to those of men, have sometimes resisted such prescriptive expectations and have led the charge for social change in both overt and covert ways. It is not surprising that in times of rapid social change the family has been identified as an inherently conservative institution, one that not only helps to perpetuate the status quo but is perceived as being oppressively restrictive to many of its own members.

Sociology of the Family: The Rise of a Subdiscipline

Given its centrality to the important societal tasks of establishing long-term continuity and maintaining social order, the family has always been of general interest to sociologists. But it has held a special place in the history of American sociology, which emerged as a discipline in the late nineteenth century. Because in this era industrialization and urbanization were transforming the United States, the first American sociologists were particularly concerned with the social problems associated with dislocation: crime, delinquency, poverty, and divorce. The question of what would provide for continuity and social order in the modern era had particular resonance and meaning for that generation of social analysts. Family disorganization and dissolution seemed to be problems of great magnitude that threatened to unravel the social fabric. Whether family breakdown was the cause or the consequence of the other kinds of change associated with the transition to a modern industrial society was often ambiguous in early sociological analyses of American society. Even as the changing role of the family in the modern era became the subject of debate, the implicit assumptions about its importance for continuity and social order continued to be the basis on which much social theory and policy was formulated.

Over the course of the first half of the twentieth century, sociologists came to reassess the place of the family as a key social institution in American society. Some argued that the instrumental tasks previously provided by the family were increasingly taken over by other institutions and that the modern family was characterized by its loss of functions. With the development of more specialized political, economic, legal, educational, religious, and welfare institutions in modern industrial society, there seemed to be substantial evidence to support this claim. Schools were now available to provide education, businesses to provide jobs, and churches to provide moral guidance. All of the activities formerly conducted within the family were now taken over by other organizations and agencies (Ogburn 1933; Ogburn and Nimkoff 1955). Other sociologists, however, placed a different interpretation on the shift in the family's functions. Although concurring that the total number of instrumental tasks performed by the family had decreased, they argued that the private nuclear family had become vastly more important as the arena providing for the socialization of children and the emotional sustenance of its members. From this perspective, the family could be understood as playing an important integrative role in modern society. The modern nuclear family, with its strong conjugal ties and weak attachment to the system of extended kin, appeared to be particularly well adapted to an industrial society, which required much flexibility in terms of geographical and social mobility (Parsons and Bales 1955).

Although there continued to be expressions of concern that any change in the family meant a loss of social order, American family sociology in the first half of the twentieth century gradually shifted from emphasizing the societal role of the institution to focusing on the dynamics of family relationships and the internal division of labor. Sociologists noted a shift from "institution to companionship" and argued that the family should be studied as "a unity of interacting personalities" (Burgess, Locke, and Thomas 1945). This reinterpretation of the family's social role is highlighted by two public discussions of family issues that spanned the first half of the twentieth century. In 1908, all seven sessions of the annual meeting of the American Sociological Society focused on "the problem of the family." No other social institution seemed so closely connected to the major social dislocations of the era. By 1948, however, the first National Conference on Family Life sponsored by the White House took as its focus the changing stages in the family life cycle: "the founding family," "the expanding family," and "the contracting family." Family change was now no longer understood as the source of massive societal problems but as a predictable life cycle event requiring individual readjustments. With this shift in focus, the era of a more social psychological approach to family studies was well underway in American sociology by midcentury.

Although much was made of the claim that the family still fulfilled the important function of providing for emotional support in an increasingly individualistic society, social observers continued to be worried that American families were no longer as strong as they once had been. In their studies of Middletown in 1924–1925 and again in the mid-Depression year of 1935, Robert and Helen Lynd cited the decline in parental control over children and a rising divorce rate as evidence of family breakdown and more general social crisis (1929; 1937). Since the family was assumed to be the basis of social order in society, all changes that affected this institution were of concern to social scientists and casual observers alike. If men, women, and children no longer knew their roles or kept to them and if marriage could no longer be counted on to last a lifetime, then the very foundation of the social order seemed subject to erosion. If the traditional policing functions of the family no longer held, social chaos appeared inevitable.

The first major reassessment of the idea that the family was the necessary source of stability and social order came in the midst of a general revision of American sociology in the late 1960s and early 1970s. In this era, a new critical sociology emerged to challenge the dominant theoretical orientation of the discipline in the first half of the twentieth century, which had stressed the need for societal consensus, order, and stability. New questions challenged old assumptions: If the family provided for social order, in whose interests was that order maintained? Who benefited, and who did not? A new critical perspective emerged about the nature of power and privilege that served to bolster the forces of continuity and social control. Instead of providing a necessary social function, it was argued, the family could better be understood as the source of repressive conformity. In this context, the critical voices of feminists, gay rights activists, and minority scholars began to level a new critique against the notion of a monolithic family with its prescribed roles and social functions (Poster 1978; Thorne and Yalom [1982] 1992). Annual conferences on the state of "The Family" now broke up in acrimonious debate over the issue of constructing a singular definition for this institution that in reality had such a plurality of forms.

Since this turning point in the history of American sociology, a politics of the family has emerged and has increasingly taken center stage in political and public policy debates. A conservative political backlash movement of the late 1970s and 1980s developed its platform around the politics of nostalgia for the traditional family, even though the defining characteristics of that tradition were rarely articulated or subjected to critical scrutiny. At the same time, much of the liberal criticism of the family as an oppressive institution was eroded by the immensely popular appeal that family life has continued to hold for most Americans. In the 1990s, a concern for revitalizing family values has become a staple of public rhetoric, a rallying cry not only of the religious Right but of a wide range of social commentators of all political persuasions. A concern with the stabilizing influence of family organization and family values has resurfaced and, in fact, has never seemed so widespread.

In an era in which alternatives to family life are more widely accepted than ever before, a majority of Americans still choose to marry and, within marriage, to have children. The United States continues to have one of the highest marriage rates of any advanced industrial society in the world. Although a high rate of marriage places a large proportion of the population at risk of divorce, it also suggests that the promise of marriage and family life holds great significance for most Americans. Even gay rights activists, who launched a successful campaign of political mobilization on the critique of the traditional nuclear family in the 1970s, have made the extension of the boundaries of legal marriage to include gay and lesbian couples a key issue of the 1990s. One of the many paradoxes of the past thirty years is that the family continues to hold such significance for so many, even as a consensus about its specific definition, form, or content becomes more difficult to reach.

The current state of family sociology is ambiguously divided between two perspectives and approaches. On the one hand, a societal-level or macrosociological perspective is still needed to account for the prevalence and functions of families in the larger social order. Perhaps because institutional analysis of this kind has been associated with a conservative theoretical perspective in sociology, macrostructural study of the family has declined in the discipline today. The micro-level analysis of family roles and interaction, on the other hand, has gained in popularity as the emotional importance of family life has increased. Investigating the ways in which images of the family affect both private and public life, as well as tracing the diversity of family structures and functions, are among the central projects for American family sociology in the 1990s.

Social Historians and the Rediscovery of the Family

Although sociologists routinely considered the family to be one of the central institutions of society, worthy of investigation at the general level, American historians only rarely focused on it as a primary subject of investigation during the first half of the twentieth century. The main exception was a sweeping compilation of three centuries of American family patterns by historian Arthur W. Calhoun. His three-volume work, *The Social History of the American Family, From Colonial Times to the Present* (1917), provided the most authoritative reference source of the era on family history in the United States. This work has been a key source of many of the popular beliefs about families in the past that are still prevalent today.

Calhoun argued, for example, that colonial marriages occurred early (often by age sixteen for seventeenth-century daughters), that family size was large (with ten to twelve children being common and "twenty to twenty-five children not rare enough to call forth expression of wonder" [1917, vol. 1: 89]), and that households were made up of extended kin. Drawing on diaries and letters of prominent individuals and families and a range of secondary literature written in the late nineteenth and early twentieth centuries, Calhoun generalized such findings as being typical of American family patterns. His analysis was that changes in the family were the result of the forces of nineteenth-century industrialization and urbanization. Because this argument so closely fit the model of change that dominated both the disciplines of American history and sociology in this era, there was little motivation on the part of scholars to challenge Calhoun's sources as too narrow to support his generalizations. The family patterns he presented as indisputable facts would be substantially overturned by later historical investigation. But many of the assumptions implicit in Calhoun's interpretation of the American family have proven much harder to dislodge from popular consciousness.

A new historical interest in the study of family life began with the growth of the fields of historical demography and social history in the 1960s and 1970s. As was also true of sociology in this era, many historians began to raise new questions about the theoretical assumptions and accepted methodologies within their discipline. Social historians, women's historians, and family historians, in particular, led the way in shifting the subject of historical inquiry. No longer were the rich and powerful the only subjects worthy of study. The poor, the working class, minorities, women, children, and others who had formerly been ignored or forgotten were now taken as legitimate subjects of historical investigation. Lives lived in the private sphere of the family were newly defined as interesting and worthy subjects of study, rivaling the history of great men and political events.

New techniques in historical methodology made it possible to trace ordinary lives in the past. Where once historians had relied on the traditional written sources of diaries and letters to reveal general information despite their upper-class bias, now demographic data proved to be a valuable source of information about many facets of the everyday life of more ordinary people. The patterns of households, family groups, and communities could be reconstructed using the technique of "family reconstitution," a detailed compilation of individual demographic data reorganized into the collective units of households and families to reveal marriage, fertility, and mortality information (Wrigley 1966). Such data proved valuable in refuting many of Calhoun's original contentions about the formation, size, and structure of American families. The new demographic data challenged the standard sociological assumption that all families responded to the structural changes of industrialization and urbanization in patterned and predictable ways. The study of demographic characteristics of households and families also raised new questions about the nature of family life. Even though size and structure of Western families have been relatively consistent over the past several centuries, no such claim could be made about the meanings, sentiments, and values applied to family life. Shifts in the demarcation of public and private life and changing attitudes toward familial relationships have fundamentally altered the experience of living within families (Anderson 1980; Gordon 1973). This area of inquiry continued to provide a rich vein for historians to tap through the end of the twentieth century. The contributions of American family historians will be cited throughout this book, but it is worth noting here that they have led to a substantial reinterpretation of Calhoun's conclusions about American family patterns.

At several points, the interests of sociologists and historians who study the family overlap. Both share a concern with the ways in which changes in the family radiate out to the rest of society and, conversely, with the ways in which families respond to the shock of major social structural change from the outside. Analysis of the relationship between social change and family patterns is central to both disciplines, since it helps account for the way in which societal continuity is maintained and social order upheld or overturned. Similarly, scholars in both disciplines share an interest in tracing the shifting boundaries between public and private life, the pulls between individualism and attachments to larger collectives, and the changes in values and attitudes that characterize significant tensions in

American culture. The family is an important subject of interdisciplinary inquiry because it is an institution at the center of these debates.

But sociologists and historians have sometimes followed different, even incompatible, routes in their quest to explain family experience and family patterns. In the interest of developing broad models of social behavior, sociologists have often generalized too readily about the family as a monolithic social institution without appropriate attention to the nuances of individual and group variation and historical change. In the interest of documenting specific family experiences, firmly rooted in time and place, historians have often missed the opportunity to draw more general conclusions about trends or patterns. The insights from each discipline have rarely been combined to generate a broader and richer program of family studies.

As we approach the end of a century of academic family studies, popular interest in and concern about the state of contemporary families has not abated. Discourse about family life today has great currency as the subject of magazine articles, television talk shows, and political debate, but this discourse is rarely informed by the academic literature, just as academic study is not always framed around the family issues people care most passionately about. One goal of this book is therefore to bring what we know about the social history of American families more directly into the realm of public discussion. This is not an empty exercise, since assumptions about families of the past routinely structure the way we think about families of today. It is important to know the past, historians often remind us, to understand the present. We might also add that it is important to know the past in order to develop explanations of contemporary social patterns that can account for the great complexity and variability of human behavior. The construction of informed dialogue and effective social policy to address the many real and pressing problems that families face today requires no less.

Framework of Analysis

Four essays about key life stages in American families make up the core of this book. Childhood, adolescence, adult married life, and old age are the platforms on which this overview of U.S. family history rests and the subjects of Chapters 2 through 5. The myths about each life stage are easily summarized: in the traditional American family children had a more protected life, adolescents were under stricter parental control, married adults made life-long commitments to each other and to their families, and older people were well integrated into family life and consequently less lonely and isolated. Against this idealized image of the stable family of the past many Americans measure—and find wanting—family life today. The reservoir of social concern about seemingly new problems in each of these life stages is, in fact, historically deep. Longing for order in the face of continual change is the source of the family politics that have become increasingly strident during the past thirty years.

In contrast to the romanticized and static image of the family that drives much of the family values debate, one key premise on which this book is based is that change has been a permanent feature of American family life since the era of first settlement. Social observers and political leaders have helped foster the belief that the family is the bedrock institution of society—in particular, that it will provide order when everything around it is in flux and that a stable family life is the basis of all social stability. In fact, no society is as predictably stable as our myths would have it; American family values and family behavior have been changing throughout their history. This book presents an account and an explanation of these changes.

If social change is inevitable, the source of that change is primarily social structural. A second key premise on which this book is based is that although changes in values, ideologies, and the modes of interaction that structure family life are often dramatically visible in American history, they follow from the major economic, political, and demographic changes that have transformed American society since the late–eighteenth century. Broad theoretical models of societal transformation—"tradition to modernity," "feudalism to capitalism," "Gemeinschaft to Gesellschaft," or what one historian has called the "conceptual sledge hammer of the classic sociological dichotomies" (Smith 1978: 286)—do not capture the nuances of change in people's everyday lives or the capacity for individual accommodation or resistance to those large-scale changes. But there is no doubt that a shift as dramatic as the one, for example, that transformed the basis of making one's living from agriculture to commerce and industry had some profound and unforeseen consequences in the realm of personal relations and family life. In attempting to use "the scalpel of historical analysis" rather than an overly broad theoretical framework to explain American family patterns, I still hope to keep those larger processes of social change fully in view. They constitute the crucial backdrop against which individual experience takes its form and meaning.

Although I highlight changes that have characterized American family life over time, I am mindful of important continuities as well. The most striking continuity is the importance that the family holds for so many people. The reasons that the family is important have varied historically, but there is no doubt that it has been a central institution, one on which people have pinned all manner of beliefs, values, and prejudices, as well as fears about and hopes for the future. Families reside at the intersection of private and public experience. We are all experts, since most of us have lived within one or more families at some point in our lives. Families can house both our highest hopes and our greatest disappointments, and their fragility or resilience therefore carries great personal meaning, in addition to social significance. The novelist Amos Oz has called the family "the most mysterious, most secret institution in the world." Its mysteries and secrets are not fully revealed in the social and historical record, but in reconstructing some of the patterns of family life we can begin to understand why it has continued to play such a central role in American culture, as an organizing social institution, a lived experience, and a powerful metaphor.

2

Childhood

In the seven months between October 1997 and May 1998, the communities of Pearl, Mississippi; West Paducah, Kentucky; Jonesboro, Arkansas; and Springfield, Oregon, were linked by a common event: They were all sites of a murderous rampage by a child who, armed with guns more befitting a solider at war than a schoolboy, opened fire on his classmates, teachers, and, in some cases, parents. On June 5, 1998, two other news items appeared side by side on the same page of the *New York Times* recording more tragic events involving children. In one, a father admitted to having used a sledgehammer to kill his two 5-year-old twins when he "just lost it" because they were moving too slowly while getting ready for day care. A blurb in the adjacent column reported that a Dallas jury had returned a guilty verdict in the case of an eleven-year-old boy who, with his seven- and eight-year-old accomplices, had sexually assaulted, beaten, and killed a 3-year-old girl. The seven- and eight-year-olds were too young to face criminal charges; the eleven-year-old, a fourth-grader, could receive a sentence of up to forty years (*New York Times* June 3, 1998, A12; June 5, 1998, A15).

These stories have the power to shock and horrify, even in a society that has become inured to reports of violent crime. They carry greater weight than do other kinds of personal tragedies because they involve children. On the one hand, a child murderer seems profoundly shocking even among people resigned to adult violence because children are presumably innocent by nature. Intense social anguish has followed on the heels of these crimes perpetrated by children, as the survivors and other members of the distraught community, the general public, and social commentators speculate about the causes of the tragedy. An inadequate home life? Inattentive teachers and school officials? Corrupting media influence? Declining moral standards? The availability of guns in a culture of violence? All of these explanations have been offered as to why some children seem to defy the very nature of childhood by engaging in the most violent acts. Because it is commonly assumed that children are inherently good, a murderous child is a deeply disturbing anomaly that must be explained, interpreted, and analyzed in order to be contained as a social threat.

On the other hand, adults, unlike children, are assumed to be dangerous. But any adult—particularly a parent—who harms a child evokes special horror for having violated the implicit trust that the vulnerable young must place in their adult caretakers and protectors. Child victims are often mourned publicly even more than are adult victims, many of whom may be upstanding citizens, community leaders, or key economic providers for their families whose loss has objectively greater social, political, and economic consequences than that of a child. The loss of a child, however, stirs powerful sentiments, symbolizing as it does both the tragedy of unrealized human potential and the culpability of adult negligence.

These two images that are seemingly so contradictory—the dangerous child who is capable of the most horrific acts of violent crime and the vulnerable child who requires but does not always receive vigilant adult protection and nurturance—coexist uneasily in shaping contemporary American perceptions of children and ideas about childhood. Are children more vulnerable and at risk today than ever before? To what extent have changes in the American family been responsible for simultaneously increasing threats to children and producing threatening children? These questions touch a social nerve for all adults—parents and nonparents alike—because they point to social conditions that shape the next generation and hence the future. Murderous children and murdered children are only the most extreme cases, of course. Between these endpoints on the continuum of modern childhood lie a whole set of other social concerns about American children: babies suffering from the inherited effects of AIDS or fetal alcohol syndrome; young children and adolescents affected by the growing public health epidemic of youth violence (Prothrow-Stith 1991); driven, hurried, over-scheduled "children without childhood" (Elkind 1981; Postman 1982; Winn 1983; Medrich 1982); consumer market-targeted and media-saturated youth. All of these concerns seem hallmarks of our time, uniquely modern problems. To help put these concerns about children into historical perspective, I focus on four themes in this chapter: changes in the ideology of childhood; the demographic and social parameters that have shaped children's lives; the shifts in caretaking arrangements that children in the United States have experienced; and the relations between children and the state. Only by looking at the ideologies, social conditions, family structures, and social policies that have shaped American children's lives over time can we begin to make sense of whether children's lives today are more precarious than in the past.

The Ideology of Childhood

Given the frequency with which children are cited as the country's most precious national resource, the United States would seem to be unambiguously child centered in its commitments and ideology. Even the characterization of children as a national resource should give some pause though, suggesting as it does that children are a commodity, however much a valued one. Yet, at the same time that many adults claim child-centeredness, the troubling statistics about the growing number of children in poverty, being abused and neglected, and among the homeless raise serious questions about the level of national commitment to children's welfare (Children's Defense Fund 1995; U.S. Advisory Board on Child Abuse and Neglect 1995). These contradictions, among others, challenge us to think critically about the rhetoric used in relation to children and how and why it differs from the actual conditions of their lives. How adults think about children—what ideologies about childhood prevail in particular cultural contexts and historical moments—is a critical component in understanding the institutional forces that shape children's lives.

What we do know with certainty about children is that they need adult care for a very long period of time—longer than the young of any other species—if they are to survive to adulthood and to develop with full physical, social, cognitive, and emotional capabilities. Any society that does not provide adequate care for its children can not be sustained over time. Thus, the physical condition of dependency among children and the social importance of providing for their care would seem to imply that it is natural, universal, and inevitable for adults to think of children as vulnerable and innocent vessels on whom the effects of culture and society are imprinted from the moment of birth. But even the universal fact of physical dependency does not account for the wide variation in ideologies about the nature of children and the state of childhood. Childhood is a physiological stage of human development, but it is also a socially defined and culturally constructed stage of life that varies by time and place.

Children in America have not always been seen as innocent beings and potential victims, in need of the most vigilant adult attention. This ideology is relatively new and still considerably ambiguous. For although most twentieth-century American parents consider their own children to be vulnerable and worthy of adult protection and care, they are much less sympathetic toward other people's children. From the lack of support for public education and universal health care to the many indications of a widespread lack of concern about the quality of life for children in poverty, ideas about family privacy and individualism that are widespread in U.S. culture have also infused the way Americans think about children. The origin of the sentimental beliefs about the sanctity and preciousness of childhood that dominate public rhetoric but have come to be applied privately and locally rather than generalized to all children is the starting point for this analysis. In sketching out the history of the idea of childhood as it has developed in American culture, I mean to suggest that Americans should adopt a more critical stance toward the notion of "the best interests of the child." Which interests get defined as "best"? by whom? based on what prevailing ideas about human nature? and with what consequences (Mnookin 1985; Purdy 1992; Fineman 1995)? Ideas about children, as they have been articulated by adults, have had a significant impact on shaping the experiences and life chances of American children.

The relatively distant American past of colonial New England provides the sharpest contrast with current notions of innocent and vulnerable childhood. The seventeenth-century Puritans subscribed to a doctrine of natural human depravity. Salvation, they believed, was a state that had to be achieved through a long and arduous process in which parents actively and vigilantly socialized their children. Some historians have speculated that such seventeenth-century child-rearing customs as putting out, the process of sending one's own children out to be apprenticed to nonrelatives while taking other children into the household in their place, was explained by this ideology of children's natural depravity. Recognizing that the bonds of love and attachment to their own children threatened the kind of strict discipline that would ultimately lead to adult salvation, Puritan parents, some have argued, developed the institutional response of putting out to remove their children from the temptation of overly indulgent parental care (Morgan 1966). Others have suggested alternatively that family crisis or economic need in colonial America was a far more common cause of putting out than the fear of spoiling children (Wall 1990: 97–111, 212, n. 103). Yet, whatever the cause, putting out was a system that affected even very young children and thrust them into the demanding world of work outside a relatively protected environment. A court in seventeenth-century Plymouth Colony, for example, ruled in favor of a master who claimed that his young servant, Joseph Billington, repeatedly left his service to return home. The court ordered Joseph to return to his master's employ and to remain there, and it further ordered his parents to be placed in the stocks if they allowed their son to come home again. At the time of this ruling, Joseph Billington was five years old—a vulnerable, small child by twentieth-century standards, but clearly not so by the measure used in the seventeenth century (Wall 1990: 124).

The psychodynamic relations between parents and young children in colonial New England—in particular, the Puritan theological injunction to break the will of the child for his or her own good, or "better whipt, than damned" in the words of Cotton Mather (Mintz and Kellogg 1988: 15)—also contrast with contemporary perspectives. The demographic facts of large families and short birth intervals must have created the basis for a very different set of family relations than the conditions of the twentieth century have produced (Demos 1970; Greven 1970, 1977; Wells 1982). Close living quarters and many helping hands in the household may have meant constant attention to the needs of infants, but as new siblings took their place in the family order and as parental concerns about the dire consequences of spoiling the child became more pronounced (Greven 1973), children by the age of two may have encountered an environment of harsher discipline than most American adults today would agree is ideal for raising children.

In his landmark book, *Centuries of Childhood* (1962), Philippe Ariès provocatively argued that medieval society lacked the concept of childhood as a separate or unique stage of life. Only in the seventeenth century, he claimed, did themes of childhood emerge in painting and literature through depictions of children's distinct style of dress, play, and speech. Based on evidence drawn from paintings, literary references, and diaries—the kinds of historical sources that have traditionally reflected an upper-class bias— Ariès argued that the "discovery" of childhood helped produce a new set of feelings and attitudes about the family as a more child-centered institution in the seventeenth century. By the eighteenth century, these social relationships intensified as the family became more withdrawn from the larger society, taking on its modern guise as a private fortress in a sea of external social relations.

Ariès's argument about the historically variable nature of childhood has been both contested and refined over the past thirty years. One debate among family historians, building on Ariès's thesis that childhood itself is a relatively new concept, has centered on whether or not parents and children related to each other differently in the past, in particular with parents reserving their emotional investment in infants and young children because of the high rates of infant mortality (Pollock 1987). Although this premise seems questionable, much evidence in the historical record supports the idea that parent-child relationships during the colonial period were more emotionally distant than most twentieth-century Americans would recognize as innate or natural. A ritual of extended mourning did not mark the death of young children in seventeenth- and eighteenth-century America, for example, and parents routinely named their children after older siblings who had died, a custom that may offend contemporary sensibilities about the uniqueness and individualism of even very young children (Smith 1977). Another Massachusetts court case from 1661 provides a glimpse into the complex mix of emotional and pragmatic considerations that characterized parent-child ties in colonial America. In this case, a widow who had apprenticed out her only son moved into the master's home to care for him for three weeks when he became seriously ill. Upon becoming sick herself, she returned to her own home, leaving her son to the care of the master's mother over the next ten weeks. Although the widow had reason to fear that her son was sick enough to die and although she thought the master was overly harsh in his treatment of her child, she clearly expected compensation for any prolonged care of her son (Wall 1990: 124–125). As this case suggests, a fine line between affection and pragmatism characterized the parent-child relationships in colonial America.

There are some indications of regional variations in colonial child-rearing ideas and practices. The Chesapeake gentry families of the eighteenth century, whose distinctive culture was built on the development of a slave-holding plantation economy, were more likely to emphasize the father's paternal influence in family life and to adopt a child-rearing style of affectionate indulgence and tolerance for children's autonomy. Quakers in the Delaware Valley, unlike their Puritan New England neighbors, did subscribe to a belief in childhood innocence, and they sought to create a controlled family environment in which children would be protected from the corruptions of worldly influences (Lewis 1983; Levy 1988). Yet, even with these variations, it is still clear that seventeenth- and eighteenth-century adults saw children through a very different lens than the one most Americans currently use. The socioeconomic context from which family life took its meaning, as well as the larger size of families and households in colonial America, gave children an instrumental role and significance that they lack today. As necessary laborers in the domestic economy and as the future caretakers of aging parents, children were useful additions to the family unit. That quality of usefulness meant that, beyond infancy, children were not understood as being particularly fragile, innocent, or vulnerable, as they have come to be seen since. Instead, the defining characteristics of useful children were sturdiness and an early capacity for responsibility, all the qualities that gave them the appearance of little adults roughly by the age of seven.

By the time of the American Revolution, the distinctive regional variations in family values and practices of the colonial period had largely given way to an emerging national culture in which the affectionate, antipatriarchal family played a central role (Reinier 1996). The shift in beliefs about children and the nature of childhood took root first among the middle class in the early nineteenth century, spreading to encompass working-class children by the early twentieth century. Not surprisingly, middle-class children were redefined as vulnerable innocents in need of full-time care and devoted attention in the same era as their mothers were being redefined as the guardians of virtue and morality, the ideal keepers of the domestic sphere. Nineteenth-century America was the context for the emergence of an ideology of domesticity that still reverberates in family life today, but only a relatively small group of privileged middle-class children were the first recipients of the nurturing attention of newly idealized mothers. As middle-class women were defined by and enclosed within the sanctuary of the private home—an ideological shift that enhanced their domestic power in the short term but resulted in the long-term exclusion from resources and power in the economic and political spheres (Welter 1966; Cott 1977; Ryan 1981)—middle-class children were sentimentalized and redefined as needing their mothers' full-time, loving, but vigilant, attention.

Not all parents could live up to this ideal. Many, by economic or geographic necessity, continued throughout the nineteenth and into the early twentieth century to define their children as little adults, particularly in their capacity as paid and unpaid laborers in the family economy. Those children growing up on the western frontier plains, for example, were always crucial workers in their farming and ranching families (West and Petrik, 1992: 26–37). And class differences, which sharpened as the United States industrialized during the nineteenth century, drew clear distinctions in the life experiences of children. With the decline of the apprenticeship system in the early industrial era, working-class children provided a cheap source of labor in factories, as well as contributing to the family income through a substantial amount of piecework at home. Even very young children could be engaged at home in such tasks as making buttons and artificial flowers, pulling bastings, cutting and gluing boxes, caring for younger siblings, and running errands. Young urban children scavenged on city streets for wood chips, coal, or dropped food items while their older siblings collected rags, nails, and pieces of rope to be sold to junk dealers (Reinier 1996: 138). A Polish immigrant growing up in Chicago in the first decades of the twentieth century recalled in an oral history interview that "no one in my neighborhood ever had to buy any fuel, any oil, or any wood" (Nasaw 1985: 97). The historical evidence suggests that working-class children were active in their scavenging efforts, and most were neither closely watched nor carefully protected, whether at work in factories or fields, on urban streets, or in their own homes.

Despite the enormous variation in children's life experiences in the nineteenth-century United States, it was ultimately the middle-class model of the vulnerable and defenseless child who required a mother's full-time care that gained dominance as the cultural norm, if not the behavioral reality, by the middle of the century. The power of this new ideological construction of childhood was such that it began to spread across the sharp divides of social class and geographic variation in children's worlds, even when it did not fit their actual experience. Between the 1870s and the 1930s, working-class as well as middle-class children began to be sentimentalized and reinterpreted as innocent and vulnerable, a process that involved a significant cultural shift from a belief in the economic usefulness of children to one in which children were understood as economically useless but morally and emotionally priceless (Zelizer 1985).

Sociologist Viviana Zelizer has identified several key indicators of this significant shift in the way Americans thought about children by the early twentieth century. The battle over child labor was waged in terms of competing ideologies about the moral worth of work for "useful children" versus the exploitation of "vulnerable children." Social structural changes certainly contributed to the removal of many children from the industrial workplace in the early twentieth century. The development of industrial capitalism, for example, increased the demand for a more skilled workforce, and, over the course of the nineteenth century, immigrants replaced children in many unskilled and semiskilled jobs. But, along with these structural factors, a growing cultural sense of children as unsuited for most paid work, other than in the exceptional cases of child actors (whose activities were considered more fun than work) and newspaper deliverers (whose tasks were considered wholesome work), separated the young from the productive economy and relegated them to the "domesticated, nonproductive world of lessons, games, and token money" (Zelizer 1985: 11). Child labor aroused the sympathy of Progressive Era reformers, even as part-time work for urban children, wedged between their school and family time, continued to flourish as an acceptable opportunity to earn valued spending money (Nasaw 1985).

A number of paradoxes accompanied this reinterpretation of priceless childhood in the early twentieth century. Child life insurance was introduced to cover the high costs of an elaborate funeral in the case of a child's early death; high court settlements were awarded in cases of accidental death, not so much to offset the loss of a child's labor power as to compensate, at least symbolically, for the parents' emotional loss; and a market developed for the adoption of blond, blue-eyed infants because they were now considered the most priceless children of all. These institutional developments had the paradoxical consequence of redefining the economic value of children's worth, ultimately setting a price on priceless children. The end result, one with which we still live today, is that there has been an unintended commercialization of childhood along with its sentimentalization. Increasingly excluded from the sphere of economic productivity by the early twentieth century, children were nevertheless defined in economic terms by a wide array of institutions and agencies, and today they continue to be enticed into the market as significant consumers at younger and younger ages.

While the new ideology about childhood was spreading in the first three decades of the twentieth century, the Depression and World War II intervened to ensure that many children did continue to experience the role of the "useful" child to midcentury. As Elder (1999) and Clausen (1993) have shown through their longitudinal studies of children who came of age in these decades, many experienced a foreshortened sense of childhood as they contributed to the family income or assumed responsibilities that were defined as unchildlike for earlier and later cohorts. Despite the growing dominance of an ideology promoting the innocence and vulnerability of children in the twentieth century, not all analysts have argued that this earlier exposure to the adult world was harmful. Some have suggested it as one cause of the remarkably familistic values and behaviors of those middle-class Americans who came into adulthood in the immediate postwar era of the 1950s (Cherlin 1992). At least one explanation for this cohort's notable patterns of young age at marriage, high fertility (resulting in the baby boom), and low rate of divorce has been attributed to the early responsibility that they assumed as children of the Depression era.

By many historical accounts now available, the 1950s and early 1960s should be seen as a unique social and economic period in U.S. history, rather than as the benchmark against which to measure current family experiences (May 1988; Skolnick 1991; Coontz 1992). As the war economy of the 1940s was converted into a new growth industry based on durable consumer goods and a service economy in the 1950s and as veterans' benefits fueled massive suburban community development, the social world in which white, middle-class women and children found themselves was increasingly homogeneous and contained. A newly revitalized ideology of domesticity that located women's and children's roles in the home and men's roles in the public world emerged in the postwar decades and became the standard against which nonwhite and non-middle-class mothers and children were judged as well. Even when they did not fit the actual life experience of many people in the United States, the ideologies of proper womanhood, childhood, and middle-class family domesticity had a remarkably powerful capacity to extend beyond their original reach. This era was, not coincidentally, the one in which television grew up and presented its narrowly homogeneous view of the world through the frame of the family sitcom (Taylor 1989). Normal childhood and family life have been measured ever since against the picture seen through this lens, a fictive construction against which contemporary social reality is often judged and found lacking.[1]

The forces of social change that lay just beneath the surface at midcentury and that began to be seen and felt by the mid-1960s had a profound effect on ideas about children and childhood. Whereas previous cohorts of adults had worried about rebellious children (to be dealt with through the legal system), deprived children (to be dealt with through social services agencies), and sick children (to be dealt with through the medical system), a new concern about child victims began to be more pronounced in popular consciousness and national policy debates during the 1970s (Best 1990). Indeed, the concern with the prevalence and extent of child abuse arguably reached the level of a national obsession in the 1980s. Adult fears about child abduction, kidnapping, and molestation—at their height in the 1980s and 1990s—have fueled contemporary concerns about children as an especially threatened and vulnerable group. Every day, newspapers and television reports seem to confirm that ours is an especially difficult and unsafe era for children.

Concerns about child abduction actually had deep historical roots by the time the furor about an epidemic of missing children swept across the United States in the late twentieth century. The first ransom kidnapping of a child to receive widespread national attention occurred in the famous 1874 abduction case of four-year-old Charley Ross, known to a generation of Americans as "the Lost Boy" (Fass 1997: 21–56). In several ways, this highly public and never-resolved case defined the threat of stranger abduction and heightened awareness of childhood vulnerability forevermore in American culture. It showed that neither parents nor the police could ensure children's safety in their homes or communities. It revealed, in the shocking demand for ransom in exchange for Charley's safe return, that the preciousness of childhood now carried a price. In the power of this story to sensationalize and titillate the American public, it "provided the occasion for Americans to discuss an array of social issues: family and parenting, sexuality and gender, policing and law enforcement, criminality and insanity, community norms, and the role of the state" (Fass 1997: 257). This case of child abduction was one of the first times, but by no means the last, that American adults would rally around children and childhood as embodying all their anxieties about the modern world in the throes of social change.

The definition of children as victims crossed another milestone in 1962 with the development of the medical concept of "the battered child syndrome," and the subsequent emergence of a highly successful campaign in the 1970s and 1980s to shape public conceptions of this social problem on a new scale. The initial publicized fear that thousands of children were routinely being subjected to physical and emotional harm by neglectful parents and to abduction, molestation, and ritual abuse by strangers was not borne out by supporting evidence. The subsequent shift from a concern about an epidemic of child victimization to the rhetorical claim that "even one child harmed is too many" suggests how successful the campaign to redefine children as victims (or potential victims) has been. At a cultural juncture when many Americans were experiencing generalized anxiety about the direction and consequences of social change, threats to children emerged as a powerful, yet manageable, symbol of that change. In the place of broader anxiety about the future and the pace of social change, children—as visible symbols of the future—could serve as a specific focus of the concern. When the dangers facing children get defined as those caused by individual deviants—kidnappers who lurk around playgrounds, sadists who poison children's Halloween candy, and the like—structural explanations of and solutions to a broader array of complex social problems affecting children and families are effectively muted.

Although there may be genuine reason for concern about dangers to children in the modern era, it is also clear that the current notion of childhood vulnerability is a powerful idea that lobbyists can manipulate as a political issue. Where the institutionalized neglect of children through inadequate health provisions, underfunded schools, and the decline of affordable housing fails to elicit an immediate call to action, the threats of child abduction and abuse often do. The sentimentalization of childhood that is so much a part of the contemporary ethos—the idea that childhood is the repository of a natural innocence that is constantly threatened by predatory adults—turns out to have great political resonance and the power to mobilize widespread public response. It should not be surprising, then, that threatened children appear on both sides of intensely debated social and political issues: as the "murdered babies" versus the "unwanted children" in the abortion debate, as the "future beneficiaries" versus the "impoverished victims" of current budget cuts and efforts to restructure government priorities and programs. In this context, reports of murderous and dangerous children seem particularly anomalous and horrifying. Having so thoroughly incorporated the idea that children are by nature innocent and harmless and vulnerable to exploitation, Americans are especially susceptible to the shocking discrepancy between the child victim and the child victimizer.

The ideological constructions of childhood that have prevailed in American history matter not only because they have shaped the way most Americans see and understand the world but because they are the foundation for the set of institutions, programs, and policies that adults construct with real consequences for children's lives. The history of the ideology of childhood in America is one that reveals a profound ambivalence: Americans publicly proclaim their child-centeredness but remain more committed to the idea of the innocence and vulnerability that characterize the state of childhood than to improving the lives of actual children. It is important to investigate the physical conditions and life chances that children in the United States have faced over time, then, to provide an antidote to the sentimentalization of childhood that has taken such firm root as an ideology since the mid-nineteenth century.

Demographic Patterns in the
History of American Children

In the broadest sense, the experience of being a child is determined by the demographic conditions that define an era and a place. Birth and death rates set the broadest parameters for a child's life chances, and marriage and migration rates determine much about the family and community context in which children's experiences are shaped. Demographic indicators of childhood experience are one important measure of the impact of the external world on family life.

Three critical periods define American demographic history: the seventeenth and eighteenth centuries, together constituting the patterns of early America; the period between the American Revolution and World War I, during which dramatic changes in demographic experiences and expectations took place in the United States; and the contemporary era, since 1920, in which adaptations to the significant improvements in health and life expectancy continue to reshape the nature of American family life (Wells 1982). Within each of these periods, class, racial-ethnic, regional, and gender differences have also sharply differentiated the lives of American children.

Children in Early America

In seventeenth-century America the most dramatic difference in childhood conditions for white children was the result of residence in New England or the mid-Atlantic Chesapeake region. Far better demographic conditions and overall life chances prevailed in New England in the earliest years of settlement, whereas Chesapeake Virginia and Maryland remained an unhealthy place for both children and adults for another century. The combination of relatively low rates of child and maternal mortality and a high birth rate in New England meant that families there were both larger and more stable than their Chesapeake counterparts. These demographic patterns defined starkly different experiences for children in early America.

The sex ratio of two female immigrants to New England per every three males, a high life expectancy rate of fifty years or more at birth under the most favorable New England conditions (in contrast to an average life expectancy at birth of 35 to 45 years in 1650), and the Puritan cultural emphasis on organizing communities around family units all worked to promote long marriages and stable families in the seventeenth century. Marriages were contracted by men in their mid-twenties and by women in their early twenties in colonial New England. The average length of marriage was twenty-four years, most of which was devoted to childbearing. The high birthrate resulted in families with six to eight children, and a household size at any one point in time of five to seven persons (Wells 1982).

The Chesapeake region, by contrast, was characterized by high death rates, low life expectancy, and the resulting chronic instability of families. Indentured service and an imbalance in the sex ratio—with six men immigrating to Virginia for every woman in the early seventeenth century— meant a scarcity of wives and late ages at marriage for men. The precarious conditions of birth and death meant that long marriages were rare and that relatively small family sizes of four to five children, with only two or three surviving to maturity, were the norm. Family disruption, rather than family stability, characterized life for the children living in the seventeenth-century Chesapeake region, with remarriage ensuring that kinship networks and family relationships were dense and complex (Rutman and Rutman 1984; Smith 1980).

Where one lived in early America clearly mattered, given such demographic profiles and patterns of family structure. Yet over the course of the eighteenth century, these regional differences began to converge. Conditions improved for the white planter families of the Chesapeake, while life chances and health conditions worsened for New Englanders as greater population density and the introduction of new diseases and sanitation problems led to a higher incidence of infant and child mortality, especially in port cities (Hareven and Vinovskis 1978). Although this demographic record is dismal in comparison with that of twentieth-century Americans, seventeenth- and eighteenth-century white colonists still enjoyed some of the most favorable life chances of any population in the world. Native Americans in neighboring areas could not make the same claims, however. Far more severe demographic parameters constricted the life chances of the native population beginning with the first colonial encounters.

In contrast to the experience of white European immigrants to the New England and Chesapeake regions, Native American children experienced a different set of environmental conditions. Despite the great diversity in culture and institutions among the more than 240 North American groups present at the time of the first colonial encounters in the early seventeenth century, most Native American children experienced certain commonalities in their upbringing. Family life occurred within the context of kin and community. Social rites of passage marked the transition from one life stage to another in the process of growing up (Mintz and Kellogg 1988: 26–31; Szasz 1985). But these traditional patterns in children's lives were profoundly disrupted by the diseases and epidemics resulting from seventeenth- and eighteenth-century colonial encounters. Along the eastern seaboard and following white migration routes west and southwest, smallpox and other plagues relentlessly decimated Native American tribes. By the early twentieth century, Native Americans numbered 240,000—by best estimate only about 5 percent of the pre-Columbian population (Wells 1982: 127).

For all of the regional differences characteristic of this period, childhood in early America was predominantly defined by two important demographic facts: family size and parental longevity. Few children in early America lived in the kind of small families that have come to predominate in the twentieth century; the majority of children who survived beyond infancy lived in large families with nine or more other siblings.[2] Most children experienced early in life the death of at least one of their parents. Youngest children in New England and the majority of all children in the Chesapeake experienced the death of one or both of their parents before reaching maturity (Wells 1982). From the historical distance of the late twentieth century, we can only speculate about what this meant in terms of the level of attention and supervision children received from their parents, other adults, and their siblings. A strong argument could be made, however, in support of the notion that all children in early America had a very different and far riskier childhood than their twentieth-century counterparts, for whom the transitions from infancy through all stages of youth have become more predictable and routine.

Demographic data, coupled with evidence from material culture, have been creatively juxtaposed by several historians to suggest patterns in the psychological life of children in the past: How the lack of household privacy affected social relations, for instance, or what kind of parent-child bonds must have resulted from high infant mortality rates and relatively low life expectancy. What seems clear is that the vulnerability of children in early America far exceeded contemporary experience. In demographic terms, children in this era were far more susceptible to disease and early death than the majority of children in the United States today. They were less protected from the effects of a harsh environment and, within much larger families, perhaps less subject to adult scrutiny and supervision than in later eras as well. That is not to say that the lives of all children were the same in this period or that they improved at the same rate or in the same ways over the next two centuries. Where the shifts occurred and for whom became more significant in the nineteenth and twentieth centuries, periods of major demographic and social transitions.

Nineteenth- and Twentieth-Century Demographic Changes

The period of U.S. history spanning the American Revolution to World War I encompassed enormous changes in the social structural conditions that defined the lives of Americans. Over the nineteenth century, the combined forces of industrialization, urbanization, and immigration brought a new definition to social class lines, much broader ethnic diversity, and accelerated geographic mobility to the population in the United States. Children's lives became more distinct from adult lives in this period, and the differences among children also intensified, making it problematic to generalize about American childhood as a singular experience. Nevertheless, there were commonalities among clusters of children, depending on where they lived and the social and economic positions of their families, that shaped children's material lives. At least three such broad clusters can be identified in the nineteenth century (Clement 1997).

Children of white, middle-class professionals living in the urban centers of the North, children of the most prosperous northern and midwestern farm families, and children of southern white planter families were the groups who enjoyed the most extended period of youth, with all the material privileges and educational opportunities that their families' relative prosperity afforded them. These children led relatively sheltered lives in their domestic spheres under the supervision of attentive adults; they attended school during their youth; and they had access to prime career opportunities. The greatest difference among this group of children came about in the second half of the century as a consequence of the Civil War and its aftermath, with southern children experiencing far more poverty, homelessness, and parental death than their northern counterparts.

Urban working-class children of both American-born and foreign-born parents, as well as rural children living on small farms or on the frontier, had more truncated childhood experiences because of the necessity of contributing to the family economy. Rural children assumed adult tasks from an early age. Urban working-class boys and girls found employment in factories, home manufacturing, the street trades, and domestic service. Dangerous working conditions, life on the streets, and crowded housing conditions in cities and barrios were some of the environmental factors that contributed to the harsher conditions of life for working-class children than for their middle-class counterparts. Despite their many cultural differences, similar social and economic conditions shaped the social worlds of the children of Irish, German, Scandinavian, Polish, Italian, and Russian Jewish immigrants on the East Coast; of Chinese and Japanese immigrants on the West Coast; and of Mexicans who were incorporated into the American Southwest and southern California through U.S. expansion after 1848. In all cases, the necessity of contributing to the family economy curtailed childhood at a relatively young age and plunged children into the adult worlds of industrial, agricultural, and domestic work.

Black children experienced the most limited childhood of all groups in the United States in the nineteenth century. Both children and adults suffered demographically from the harsh conditions of slavery. In the early nineteenth century, blacks could expect to live ten to fifteen years fewer than whites in the same region (Wells 1982: 21). Estimates of the combined effect of stillbirths and infant mortality among blacks were approximately two and a half times the rates for whites, at nearly 50 percent. The black infant mortality rate has been estimated at approximately 350 infant deaths for every 1000 live births, most of them occurring before the end of the first month of the infant's life (Steckel 1986: 427–465). The heavy physical labor demanded of women, both during pregnancy and shortly after childbirth; poor prenatal care; attenuated breastfeeding; and nutritional deficiencies caused by a common lactose intolerance among West African blacks and their descendants coupled with a diet low in protein, iron, and calcium accounted for much of this extraordinarily high infant and child mortality rate (Berrol 1985; King 1995). Other researchers have recently suggested that a high incidence of Sudden Infant Death Syndrome in slave families was a contributing factor to the mortality rate of newborns. Young children who did survive the precarious first year of life often had to accompany their parents to work under minimally supervised conditions or were cared for collectively by one slave woman who was assigned child-care duties. And, in sharpest contrast to the ideology of innocent and vulnerable childhood that was emerging elsewhere in the nineteenth-century United States, slave children were generally put to work in the fields around the age of seven. Frederick Douglass noted in his autobiography, "We were worked in all weather. It was never too hot or too cold; it could never rain, blow hail, or snow too hard for us to work in the field. Work, work, work was scarcely more the order of the day than of the night" (Douglass 1892). A historian of American children has aptly called work "the thief who stole the childhood of [slave] youth" (King 1995: 21). A foreshortened childhood and harsher demographic conditions continued to distinguish the life experience of African American children after the Civil War, through Reconstruction, and well into the twentieth century.

One case in point is that of nineteenth-century Boston, a city with a well-developed black community before the Civil War, including black political representation and educational opportunities. But despite these advantages and being surrounded by prominent medical schools and hospitals, black neighborhoods in Boston were "cesspools for disease" that produced an extraordinarily high rate of infant mortality. In 1880, 392 out of every 1000 black infants did not survive their first year, compared with 274 per 1000 white infants. Twenty years later, the black infant mortality rate was still 220 infant deaths per 1000 live births, compared to a white infant mortality rate of 189 per 1000 (Pleck 1979: 35–36). A comparative study of white and black child mortality in 1900 found that the urban, industrial states—especially in the Northeast—presented more perilous conditions for black children than even the rural South. Overall, mortality among both black children and black adults was extraordinarily high and relatively unchanging through the early twentieth century. Demographers have noted that the black child mortality level in the United States in 1900 was "higher than India's in the 1980s, and more than twice that of China" (Preston and Haines 1991: 82–85, 210).

One of the most significant demographic changes to affect family life in the nineteenth century was the dramatic control over fertility led by white urban and rural women, a practice that spread to all groups by the early twentieth century (Wells 1982: 92–100). Between 1800 and 1900, the average number of children born to white women who lived to complete their child-bearing years dropped from 7.04 to 3.56. This sharp decline could only have resulted from the active attempt to limit fertility by women (with or without their husbands' consent and mutual participation in the use of birth control) and has therefore been cited as an example of "domestic feminism," evidence of a new consciousness and power by women in controlling their own reproductive lives (Smith 1974; Brodie 1994).

The cultural acceptance of contraception occurred first among middle-class women; working-class, immigrant women had to wage a longer struggle against the cultural norms that stressed procreation and limited their capacity to practice family limitation. The desire and the need to do so was strong, however. When Margaret Sanger opened the first birth control clinic in a Jewish and Italian neighborhood of Brooklyn in 1916, there were 464 visitors on the first day (Ewen 1985: 133–34). Black women as well were limiting their fertility by the early twentieth century. Giddings reports that "half of all married, educated black women had no children at the turn of the century and, even more revealing, one fourth of all black women—the majority of them rural and uneducated—had no children" (1984: 137). Over the course of the nineteenth century and accelerating in the twentieth, then, more control over fertility meant fewer children per family and, from the perspective of children themselves, growing up in a household with many fewer siblings than in early America. This demographic change coincided with the development of the new ideology about childhood, so that these fewer children were also understood as needing more individualized attention and care by protective adults, especially mothers.

In addition to the dramatic decline in fertility, life expectancy rates for Americans improved very gradually over the course of the nineteenth century and then more dramatically after 1920. In 1850, for example, life expectancy at birth recorded in Massachusetts was 38 years for males and 41 years for females (U.S. Bureau of the Census 1975: 56). By 1900, white males in the United States had a life expectancy at birth of 47 years, white females of 49 years, black males of 33 years, and black females of 34 years (U.S. Bureau of the Census 1975: 55). After 1920 there was a dramatic spurt in life expectancy rates for every group so that by 1970 these rates were 68 years (white men), 76 years (white women), 61 years (black men), and 69 years (black women).

This improvement in life expectancy had several implications for children. First, it should be noted that infant mortality rates were slow to change and remained high throughout the nineteenth century, with significant differences in the rates among children determined primarily by race and area of residence (Preston and Haines 1991; Wells 1982: 124; Hareven and Vinovskis 1978; Uhlenberg 1980). At the turn of the century—despite living in the richest country in the world with high levels of per capita income, literacy, and food consumption—18 percent of children in the United States died before reaching the age of five (Preston and Haines 1991). The rates were highest among African American children, children living in cities, and the foreign-born. But all children, regardless of race, ethnicity, social class, or region were at risk of contracting gastrointestinal, respiratory, and infectious diseases, the leading causes of child mortality. Only in the 1930s did the infant mortality rate for white children fall to 50 per 1000, or 5 percent, and only after World War II did children of color achieved that same rate. More widespread understanding of the germ theory of disease, leading to such preventative public health measures as improved sanitation, the spread of immunization programs, and especially the compulsory pasteurization of milk, contributed to the eventual decline in the infant mortality rate (Preston and Haines 1991).

Not until the last decade of the twentieth century did the infant mortality rate for the United States as a whole drop below 10 infant deaths per 1000 live births, a rate still high relative to that of other advanced industrialized countries of the world, particularly because of the racial and class discrepancies that continue to differentiate the life chances of children in the United States (U.S. Bureau of the Census 1997: 92). The steady increase in life expectancy, however, meant that gradually American children could anticipate having both parents survive through their youth. Wells notes that children born in the 1830s still had a fifty percent chance of losing one parent before they could be expected to marry and leave home. Only by the last decade of the nineteenth century did children's prospects improve for having both parents survive through their first twenty years (Wells 1982: 157). By the second half of the twentieth century, life expectancy had improved so substantially for all groups that "today children have a better chance to celebrate their sixtieth birthdays than many babies born before 1800 had of living to the age of one" (Wells 1982: 1, 157).

This demographic overview suggests that most improvements in the basic health and welfare conditions facing children in the United States have occurred recently, in the twentieth century. By some objective measure, then, children today could be said to be better off in terms of their life chances than American children in the past. But at least two qualifications are necessary. The first is that infant mortality and life expectancy rates should be read in relative terms, not just as absolute numbers. That infant mortality rates have vastly improved overall in the twentieth century is a triumph of modern technology, improved medical expertise, and activist public health efforts. But the large gap between the infant mortality rates of minorities and the poor, on the one hand, and middle-class whites, on the other, despite the technological and medical sophistication of the United States, gives less cause for celebration. When the capacity to improve the quality of children's lives is within reach but not achieved for social, political, or economic reasons, it is harder to claim that all children are, unambiguously, better off today than they were in the past.

The demographic parameters that have improved American children's lives also require some social context. The historical changes that have done the most to expand children's life chances and experiences—better health conditions, greater family longevity, and the ideological commitment to childhood as a valuable life stage—did not occur in a vacuum. At the same time as children's life chances were improving and a new understanding of childhood as a special stage of life was being forged, there were substantial demographic improvements in the life chances of adults as well. Greater life expectancy meant not only that children might expect to live to maturity with both parents surviving but that their parents could also look forward to reaching old age, with a substantial increase in the number of years they would spend outside of childrearing. One of the paradoxes of the modern era is that, just at the time that more focused maternal attention was being directed at American children, the demographic foundation for a new emphasis on adult marital relationships was also being laid. As adults could begin to look forward to an extended period as a married couple, after their childbearing and child-rearing years were over, children— precious and valued though they individually might be—receded, at least demographically, from the center of family life.

The demographic shifts of the nineteenth and twentieth centuries thus hold an important clue to the ambiguous status of children in the United States. Children's lives have improved by a variety of demographic measures in an absolute sense, but they have done so at the same time as adult lives have improved. The rhetorical emphasis on the preciousness of children and vulnerability of childhood came about in an era in which childbearing and childrearing were becoming a much smaller overall part of the adult life experience. Although children's lives may be said to be objectively better today than in previous centuries from a variety of demographic measures, then, it is also the case that childhood as a life stage has diminished relative to the much longer life stage of adulthood. In this sense, the demographic changes that have so improved children's material lives in the twentieth century have also served to undermine the centrality of childhood in the family life course.

The Living Arrangements of American Children

If demographic trends and material conditions set the broadest parameters for childhood, family structure is another important determinant of the nature and quality of children's lives. Although infant mortality rates have dramatically improved in the twentieth century, most commentators on the family assume that family structure has become less stable in the modern era and that this instability consequently acts as a more disruptive influence on children's lives today. In what kinds of family arrangements do children live, and to what extent have these arrangements changed over time? If the death of one or both parents was a common experience for children in early America, what has been the impact of greater adult longevity and of families now more readily disrupted by desertion, separation, and divorce than by death?

Contemporary observers are often surprised, because of the frequent proclamations about the breakdown of the American family, that the great majority of households in the United States are still made up of family units. In 1996, 70 percent of all households were designated by the U.S. Bureau of the Census as "family households," made up of married couples, with or without children, or of a single householder, either a male or female, heading a household with children or other relatives present. Although the number of "non-family households" has been growing over time (30 percent in 1996, up from 26 percent in 1980), this household type is still distinctly in the minority in the United States (U.S. Bureau of the Census 1997: 60). The great majority of these "non-family households" (25 percent of all households) are made up of persons living alone, a phenomenon that is a striking illustration of how powerful the norm of privacy is in American culture, at least during some period of the life cycle. Many of the persons who had been living alone at the time that the census was taken will make a transition into a "family household" by getting married, a change of status that, in 1996, some 90 percent of all Americans had experienced, at least once, by the age of forty (U.S. Bureau of the Census 1997: 107).

But whether or not one lives in a household with someone else related by blood, adoption, or marriage or in a household by oneself is not the key concern about changing family structure in the United States. At the heart of the issue for most social observers is whether or not children live with one parent or two, and what the caretaking arrangements for children are within those family structures.

Changes in the living arrangements of children under the age of eighteen have been most dramatic over the past twenty-five years. In 1970, 87 percent of all children in the United States lived with two parents. Although there were significant differences by race, with 90 percent of white children under the age of eighteen living with two parents compared with only 64 percent of black children (the proportion of Hispanic families in this category is unavailable for 1970), this was still the majority experience for all children. By 1996, however, 68 percent of all children lived with two parents, a striking decrease of 19 percentage points in twenty-six years. Seventy-four percent of white children, 63 percent of Hispanic children, but only 36 percent of black children were now recorded as living in two-parent families.[3] In each case, one-parent families were predominantly maintained by mothers, with only 5 to 6 percent of one-parent families of any race maintained by fathers (U.S. Bureau of the Census 1997: 63). What seems clear is that for a growing number of children in the late-twentieth-century United States, the experience of living in a single-parent, mother-child family or in a family formed by the remarriage of one's mother will be increasingly likely. Given the prevailing rate of divorce, only a minority of American children in the future can be expected to spend their full childhood living in a family with both biological parents (Sweet and Bumpass 1987: 262–263).

The Impact of Living in Single-Parent Families

Controversy about the consequences of living in a one-parent family can be traced to the publication of the Moynihan Report in 1965. In that year, Daniel Patrick Moynihan, then the assistant secretary of labor, produced a report entitled "The Negro Family: The Case for National Action" that noted a growing discrepancy between the rates of one-parent, "female-headed households" among white and black families. The report cited data from the 1960 census showing that, whereas 9 percent of white families with children under eighteen lived with a mother only, 21 percent of black children did so. Published at the moment that the Watts Riots and other dramatic instances of urban racial unrest were focusing national attention on predominantly black, inner-city communities in the United States, the Moynihan Report offered an explanation for the great social upheaval of the era in what it labeled "the tangle of pathology" of the black, "matriarchal" family, argued to have been one of the most harmful vestiges of slavery.[4] Considerable controversy surrounded the publication of this report, with its most vocal critics arguing that it succeeded in "blaming the victim" rather than helping to illuminate the systemic nature of racism that undermined black family life (Rainwater and Yancey 1967). One of the most lasting effects of this controversy, now just one chapter in the persistent and heated controversies about the politics of race over the past thirty years, was to halt much further social science research, with the exception of that of historians, and to mute public policy discussion about the state of the black family in the United States (Patterson 1997; Wilson 1987).

Over the course of the next fifteen years, until the concept of the "underclass" was identified and put on the social science research agenda, little attention was drawn to the dramatic growth of one-parent families characteristic of all racial-ethnic groups but particularly striking as a pattern of African American family life. Although the majority of children in the United States continued to live in two-parent families, there was a steady growth in single-parent families among all groups that was increasingly visible but rarely the subject of public debate.[5] By the 1980s, many within the black community began to raise renewed concerns about the deterioration of inner-city neighborhoods, the higher incidence of urban poverty, and family- and job-related behavior associated with these conditions.

Among such African American family patterns were a lower overall rate of marriage and a greater propensity to separate childbearing from marriage, although social scientists could point out that these trends were also growing among all low-income groups in the United States (Cherlin 1992: 91–99). During the past three decades, then, two trends in particular have contributed to the growth of single-parent, predominantly mother-child, families: a divorce rate that has reached historically high levels and an increase in the number of nonmarital births. In charting these trends, a growing number of studies have begun to sound a new alarm about the harmful consequences for children of living in a single-parent household.

There are two sources of data about children's experiences in families. Clinical, observational data have the advantage of being able to capture lived experience in rich detail, often by tracing a group of children over time. Yet these data are also based on small, nonrepresentative samples, often of children or parents who have sought out clinical help. Although this does not necessarily mean that these children or parents are more troubled than others in the population, it does raise questions about the extent to which researchers can generalize from their findings. Conversely, national survey data are representative and can therefore provide information about a broad spectrum of children. Yet surveys are, by their nature, more limited in the kinds of information they can elicit, and they generally measure change as snapshots taken at different points in time rather than by tracing the longitudinal patterns of the same group of people over time.

The problem with both types of studies is that they lack control groups, which makes it particularly difficult to sort out the effects of general societal change from the effects of specific family structure. For example, although there is common agreement in the developmental literature that children thrive on stability, consistency, and predictability in their lives, these are not the social conditions most characteristic of the late-twentieth-century United States. Are the problems some children face in the process of growing up, then, attributable solely to living with a single parent and her more limited access to resources, or are they related to a broader set of social stresses that a child growing up in a two-parent family in the same era of tumultuous social change might experience as well? To what extent are the problems associated with children from single-parent families in evidence before the disruption of the two-parent household? These questions would be of strictly methodological or academic interest if they did not have such current political resonance and policy implications. But, tapping into the widespread social anxiety about the deteriorating state of American childhood, the pace of social change, and the unpredictability of the future, studies that point to the harmful effects of single-parent families on children have generated an impassioned response, often in the form of hastily formulated policy proposals. The data therefore deserve careful attention.

All studies of the process of family dissolution note that it is nothing less than a wrenching experience for children and adults.[6] What is experienced as a devastating loss of attachment for adults (Weiss 1975) produces varied, often severe, reactions from children. Depending on their age, children exhibit surprise, confusion, fear, and anger at the breakup of their parents (Wallerstein and Kelly 1980; Wallerstein and Blakeslee 1989; Furstenberg and Cherlin 1991). The short-term effect—often lasting two to three years—is a "crisis period" in children's lives, during which the disruption of the household routine and changes in parental authority and supervision can undermine children's ability to recover or adjust to their new family circumstances. Most children and most adults do eventually recover emotionally after experiencing the disruptive process of divorce, although some clinical studies have suggested that a sizable minority of children continue to experience emotional and behavioral problems as long as ten years after the divorce (Wallerstein and Blakeslee 1989). Overall, the data from the clinical samples and observational studies suggest that two key conditions in children's postdivorce environment help to moderate the most disruptive effects of the family breakup: the custodial parent's ability to reestablish a predictable routine and orderly environment for the children and minimal conflict between the divorcing parents.

Divorce propels most children into a single-parent household, at least for a time, then into a stepparent family if the custodial parent remarries. Data from both observational and survey studies have raised serious concerns about each of these types of household structure. In the most comprehensive study to date, McLanahan and Sandefur (1994) reviewed the data from four nationally representative data sets with information on the longitudinal effects of family structure on children's well-being. Addressing the question of the effects, on the average, of growing up in a family without both biological parents (that is, in a single-parent family or a stepparent family), McLanahan and Sandefur point to lower educational achievement, a weaker attachment to the labor force, and the greater likelihood of early childbearing among girls as the most serious and enduring outcomes. These results, they argue, can be explained by the loss of resources—economic, parental, and community—that are experienced by children living with a single parent. By contrast, those children who live with both biological parents have access to greater resources, both economic and social, that provide them with the support and stability crucial to healthy child development.

In contrast to the growing literature on the consequences for children of divorce and remarriage, there is relatively little information about the effects of growing up in a single-parent family that is the result of the increase in the nonmarital birthrate. More media attention, however, has been focused on this subgroup, many of whom are teenage mothers with children, perhaps—as will be explored in the next chapter—because there is currently more consensus about labeling unmarried teenagers a social problem than there is about judging the many divorced adults in the population. Both types of family structure are identified generically as "single-parent families," yet they were clearly produced by different means. Whereas the "divorce crisis" is more culturally ambiguous and therefore more complicated to address, there is a growing political consensus about the need for welfare reform, particularly as it affects unmarried mothers and their children.[7]

Recently, a new critical perspective about the harm to children in single-parent families has emerged with a focus on the cultural meaning and social consequences of father absence in the lives of contemporary American children (Popenoe 1996). Arguing that nonmarital childbearing is on the rise in the United States and that its subtext is the cultural dismissal of the "good provider father" as an important and viable role for men, Blankenhorn (1995) has pointed to the many concentric circles of social problems that, he argues, emanate from the mother-child family structure. Children (and women) not only lose the security of the male income when the biological father is absent, but they lack the protection against crime and the power of authority that masculinity can confer. Men who are denied the opportunity to invest in their biological children through a permanent alliance with the mother also lose out, since they lack the order and meaning that marriage brings to men's lives and are subject to fewer curbs on the tendencies toward male violence. Although other reviews of the literature have cited more ambiguous findings about the harm to children caused by father absence (Furstenberg and Cherlin 1991), Popenoe, Blankenhorn,

Whitehead, and others who have recently focused attention on what they see as the diminished cultural script of fatherhood have succeeded in raising a new public concern about the long-range, societal impact on children of living in single-parent families from which fathers are excluded or have withdrawn.

On the face of it, there would seem to be little question that living with two biological parents, rather than with one who lacks the resources of a pair or with a stepparent with whom new relations of authority and family loyalties must be forged, promotes the greatest chances for achieving the kind of consistency and stability on which children thrive developmentally. But reconciling this insight with the realities of a high divorce rate and the increasing tendency of American women to separate the experiences of childbirth and marriage has produced little consensus in terms of implementing policy responses. One of the problems is that what appears to be best for children (i.e., predictability and routine) is not always possible, or even defined as most desirable, for adults to achieve. Because childbearing and childrearing have become a smaller part of the adult life course, children's special needs and interests therefore occupy adults for far less time than they did previously. When the cultural script for adults emphasizes change, growth, and individualism rather than the constancy and predictability needed by children, the opportunity for a cultural conflict of interests increases. Many would interpret this conflict of interests as a primary example of adult selfishness and an abdication of the traditional parental responsibility to sacrifice for the sake of the children. But the reality may be more complex, given how difficult it is for most parents to know how to reconcile the demands for personal stability with a social life that uproots many people through geographic mobility, economic restructuring, and a dizzying pace of social and cultural change. The kinds of social structural changes that have contributed to the growth of single-parent families—in particular, women's labor force participation and the greater economic independence that follows—have created new opportunities but also new dilemmas in reconciling the lives of American children and adults.

Thus, although many describe children as the country's most precious national resource, few agree on how to encourage the conditions that would nurture them best. Ultimately, interpreting the significance of what it means to grow up in a single-parent family depends on which competing perspective of family life one finds most compelling. At least two currently dominate the ongoing debate about family structure and children's experience.

According to one perspective, the nuclear family is the central institution in American society that shapes collective values. When family structure changes, then, as it has with the growth of single-parent families, there are significant social repercussions: growing rates of poverty, less stable neighborhoods, a higher crime rate, poorer school performance, and less effective socialization of boys (resulting in more violence) and girls (resulting in more premarital sexuality and pregnancy). In this view, the key to ameliorating the many different social problems that particularly affect children is to reinvigorate and stabilize the nuclear family and to encourage a cultural shift that puts children and two-parent families first. In general, the policy implications of this social perspective are to promote programs that encourage new constraints on the single-parent family structure (restigmatizing divorce and nonmarital childbearing, for example) and to encourage new cultural models for parenting, especially for fathers. Proponents of this perspective argue, overall, that cultural values are the driving force of behavior and that the two-parent family structure is the best crucible for shaping the kind of values that protect and nurture children (Blankenhorn 1995; Whitehead 1993).

According to the second perspective, the family is no longer the basic unit of society. To claim it is so is to overstate the family's power to direct and shape larger social forces, which are primarily economic and political in nature. Adherents of this view tend to accept single-parent families as a modern reality, even when they recognize that these families need help. To provide for children's well-being, they would promote the policies and programs that offer tangible forms of support (expanded earned-income tax credit and assured child-support benefits, for example). They adopt the view that employed, healthy, secure parents—whether they are single or married—will provide the best environment for the full development of children. Support to custodial parents is therefore the best means for ensuring child well-being (McLanahan and Sandefur 1994; Furstenberg and Cherlin 1991). Whereas proponents of the first perspective argue that such programs promote and encourage the formation of single-parent families by providing a system of incentives or rewards, adherents of the second suggest that the most important outcome is to support children, regardless of what type of family structure they live in.

So far, this debate has predominantly focused on the meaning of the single-parent family, and, with its opposing perspectives that can rarely find common ground, it is a debate that runs the risk of becoming a tug-of-war over cultural definitions of appropriate adult roles rather than over the welfare of children.[8] Because these two paradigms are based on such contradictory understandings of the family as an institution and the processes of social change, they have produced a public debate that precludes much real dialogue. Against the backdrop of implicit and explicit social approval of the two-parent family as the ideal environment for children, however, it is important to note that even a two-parent household does not necessarily ensure consistent patterns of parental caretaking. Social structural changes have played a significant role in reshaping work and family relations and therefore, by necessity, the nature of parental care of children. In the course of what has been called the "silent revolution of the twentieth century," the steady entrance of women into the labor force has fundamentally altered the nature of childcare arrangements, even within the context of the two-parent family.

Childcare Within the Two-Parent Family

The historical record clearly reveals that both the ideology and material conditions supporting a mother's full-time care of her children are relatively recent phenomena. Only in the nineteenth century did the family roles of male breadwinner and full-time female homemaker come to define the experience of the middle class in the United States. Before this era, families were at the center of the domestic economy, and both men and women worked to provide family support. The separation of spheres in the middle class that emerged in the nineteenth century had severe gender-based consequences. By the early twentieth century, the call for a "family wage," through which a single breadwinner could support a family of dependents, had spread to the working class as well (Bernard 1981). Yet when additional workers were needed for family support, children rather than wives were more often called on for their economic contributions. Labor force participation by women occurred first among the young and unmarried as the opportunities for factory work and clerical work expanded in the nineteenth and early twentieth centuries (Kessler-Harris 1982). Although the labor force participation rates of married women did vary by race, with black women far more likely to be employed than white women, the majority of all married women worked at home rather than in the paid labor force through the mid-twentieth century.

World War II brought more married women into the work force, but predominantly those who were older, with children already in school or grown up. In the period since the 1960s, however, there has been a steady increase in the number of women with young children who work outside the home at least part-time. In 1960, fewer than 20 percent of married women with a husband present and children under six years of age were employed; by 1996, the proportion had risen to 62 percent, with 60 percent of white wives and 76 percent of black wives in this category. Now, even 59 percent of women with husbands present and children one year old or younger are participants in the labor force (U.S. Bureau of the Census 1997: 404). Such a massive change in the employment patterns of mothers of young children has undoubtedly contributed to the generalized concern about children's vulnerability. Who cares for young children and who supervises adolescents when full-time mothers are no longer the norm, even in the two-parent household?

The ideologies of domesticity and of the private nature of family life have held such sway in defining the appropriate family roles of women and children since the nineteenth century that studies about the longitudinal effects on children of different care arrangements continue to be highly charged. Care within the family household by a full-time mother has been and continues to be the model of ideal care for all children. This attitude is not surprising, since the history of daycare in the United States has been closely associated with philanthropic gestures of custodial care, particularly designed as a last resort for immigrant and poor children who lacked appropriate parental care (Clarke-Stewart 1993). Only during the 1930s and 1940s, first as the Works Progress Administration (WPA) programs expanded and then as the mobilization of women into the labor force for the war effort dictated a need, did the Federal Government commit modest resources to build and run daycare facilities. The Lanham Act of 1942 briefly sponsored the construction of daycare centers at work sites, but with the stipulation that they not be permanent so that, after the war, women and children would be encouraged to return home. Ambivalence about working mothers was always close to the surface, however, even at the height of the war effort. Mayor Fiorello La Guardia of New York declared in 1943, "The worst mother is better than the best nursery," and the Women's Bureau concurred: "In this time of crisis, . . . mothers of young children can make no finer contribution to the strength of the nation than to assure their children the security of the home, individual care and affection" (Chafe 1986: 15).

In the post–World War II era, federally funded daycare has continued to be controversial despite the growing need for such services. As childcare came to be associated with opportunities for early childhood education rather than simply with the custodial care of poor children, it was embraced by more middle-class parents. Yet efforts to enact a national policy that would both expand and regulate childcare facilities have repeatedly met with resistance and defeat. In 1971, President Nixon vetoed the Congressionally approved Comprehensive Child Development Act, which would have created a national childcare system with uniform standards open to all children, on the grounds that "committing the vast moral authority of the National Government to the side of communal approaches to childrearing over against the family-centered approach would lead to the demise of the American family" (Bane 1976; Clarke-Stewart 1993: 36). Nearly twenty years later, the "Act for Better Childcare" (ABC) bill, which would have addressed concerns about daycare quality and more widespread accessibility, failed to be passed by the 1990 Congress.

Even provisions for improved childcare by working parents have been controversial as social policies, with much debate before the final passage of the 1992 Family and Medical Leave Act, guaranteeing parents the right to a leave, without pay but without job penalty, for a period of up to four months for the care of a child or sick family member. With the passage of this act, the United States joined the company of all other advanced industrial countries in the world in making provisions for some integration of work and family life, although with fewer and more limited benefits than any of these other countries.

As of 1995, 40 percent of children under age six were cared for only by their parents, who made accommodations for childcare by juggling shift work, making use of flexible hours, or caring for their children while at work. Among the 60 percent of children in some form of nonparental care, 21 percent were cared for by other relatives, 18 percent by nonrelatives, and 31 percent in organized childcare facilities, such as day care centers, nursery schools, or other center-based programs (U.S. Bureau of the Census 1997: 391). These options for childcare by working parents are relatively limited, constrained by availability, affordability, enormous variation in quality standards, and confusion about the consequences of these different care arrangements on children. Most childcare arrangements are still considered the primary responsibility of mothers. Despite the massive entry of women into the labor force, the "second shift" of work at home that includes childcare continues to be the province of women (Hochschild 1989). In one of the most striking examples of how norms and behavior do not always mesh neatly, the roles of the male breadwinner and female homemaker continue to prevail as cultural ideals, even though fewer than 15 percent of households in the United States fall into this "traditional" family model.

In a comprehensive review of the literature on the effects of different care arrangements on children, Alison Clarke-Stewart (1993) looked at the relative advantages and disadvantages of care at home, in the home of nonrelatives (family daycare), and in daycare centers. The data suggest that daycare centers promote the physical and motor development of children, particularly those from poor families; that the intellectual development of language skills, manipulative abilities, and perceptual abilities of children in daycare facilities matches or surpasses that of children cared for at home; and that the social interactions of children in daycare settings are more complex, mature, and assertive, although also less compliant and more independent, than those of children in other care arrangements (Clarke-Stewart 1993: 61–75). These differences are not permanent and generally disappear by the time children are in kindergarten or first grade. Clarke-Stewart suggests that the developmental advantages of daycare are primarily the results of children's capacity to get a head start in learning to operate in a new "culture," particularly one that involves a broader set of social relations than those found within the familiar confines of the nuclear family. But it is precisely such cultural skills that give many parents pause.

At what age is exposure to this larger social world appropriate for innocent and vulnerable children? As that social world comes to seem more and
more dangerous and unpredictable to many adults, anxieties about the
caretaking arrangements for children escalate. Recent controversies about
abusive daycare workers and unsupervised private nannies in the home
have only added to the dilemma for working parents.

The social changes that have affected the caretaking arrangements of
American children have been particularly unsettling in the last three
decades of the twentieth century. The question of which arrangements are
best for children is complicated by the politics of changing gender relations
and the social structural changes that have simultaneously contributed to
the growth of single-parent households and undermined the traditional division of labor in two-parent households. Although it was clearly a historical rarity for most American children to have the undivided and devoted
attention of a full-time, caretaking parent, with another providing full economic support, the belief that this arrangement is the best for children's
well-being has dominated U.S. ideas about childhood for the past 150
years, even though it has become more difficult for families to construct
that caretaking arrangement. The consequence is the perception—widespread and anxiety-provoking—that children are worse off today in terms
of their living arrangements than they were in the past.

The data in support of this interpretation are worth serious consideration because they do point to significant disadvantages for children in single-parent families. But to identify family or household structure as the single cause of children's heightened vulnerability in the late twentieth
century, rather than as one of the consequences of the many social and economic changes transforming American society, is to oversimplify the issue
of children's vulnerability. As I have argued, this issue is defined by two
competing and opposed paradigms about the family. Another such issue
has to do with an understanding of the family as a private institution or as
one that is inextricably embedded in a web of larger social relations. An
ideology of privatism about children and the family has often been at odds
with this societal perspective, and it has contributed to a cultural ambivalence about who should be responsible for the welfare of children.

Children and the State

All children need protection and care; but *by whom* (parents? communities? the state?), *for how long* (when does innocent childhood end and responsibility for one's own actions begin?), and *against which threats* (individual deviants or social structural problems)? These questions loom large
just behind the rhetorical claim of a widespread cultural commitment to
children, and they suggest some of the difficulties in assessing the state of

childhood in the contemporary United States. In addition to being members of particular families, children are future workers and citizens, a "national resource" for the larger society, which ultimately must depend on generational replacement for social continuity. Throughout much of American history there has been an uneasy relationship between the notions of private responsibility for and societal obligations to the family, with children precariously poised between the two positions.

Only in seventeenth- and eighteenth-century colonial America, particularly in New England, did an intense commitment to communal forms of social organization and social control forge a family system that was unambiguously community-based rather than rooted in an ideology of private individualism. Scholars of colonial America have noted the many ways in which the long arm of community control, through both formal and informal means, stretched into the homes and relationships of colonial residents. Family and community were reciprocally and intricately intertwined in this era, each the moral and functional equivalent of the other (Wall 1990). By the nineteenth century, however, the pervasive ideology of individualism rooted in both the political and economic transformation of the United States was mirrored in the rise of the private, bourgeois family, no longer seen as a reciprocal part of the community but as a fortress against the outside world and a private refuge from it. The essentially private nature of families and the inviolability of parents' rights in and responsibilities for their children have been staples of American social rhetoric ever since. But, as with many other family values that seem fundamental and unassailable, this one is riddled with ambiguities lurking just beneath the surface. Are children to be understood as the exclusive property of their parents or as individuals with separate rights of their own? Where does (and should) parental control over children end and that of the state begin?

However strongly most Americans subscribe to the ideals of family privacy and individual responsibility, there has always been community and state intervention in children's lives. Particularly since the nineteenth century, schools and child welfare agencies have been the primary institutions through which the state has attempted to monitor, regulate, protect, and control children in the United States. An overview of the development of these institutions since the early nineteenth century reveals both the limitations of an ideology of family privacy and the ambiguities that surround American notions of children and childhood.

Outside the family, school has historically been and continues to be the primary social institution that structures the experience of the majority of American children. Educating the next generation is a prerequisite for social continuity, so no society can afford to leave the important task of formal education entirely to the whim of individual parents. But when, why, how, and for whom a system of public education is constructed reveals how a society construes its collective responsibilities. In the nineteenth-century United States, various "learning communities for the young" were developed in concert with and in response to the social forces of industrialization, urbanization, and immigration (Finkelstein 1985). Whether schools acted as structures of opportunity or of regulation and social control has been the subject of much debate; it seems likely, however, that they were both. Schools were "networks of association and structures of authority" that touched the lives of most U.S. children in the nineteenth and twentieth centuries, although there were significant differences in the timing and impact of schooling depending on the class, race, ethnicity, and gender of the children in question.

By the 1830s, new views of children—especially of infants and young children—gave support to the idea that they should be shielded from all influences outside the family and guided primarily by a mother's moral care. Sunday schools and infant schools had been established for the working poor, with orphanages an institution of last resort for abandoned or destitute children. But most of these institutions were understood as supplementing, rather than replacing, the moral instruction ideally provided by parents within the confines of the home. The idea of the innocence and purity of young children was so powerful an ideological construction in this era that it has effectively shaped the institutionalization of formal schooling beginning at age six ever since. Until the rise of the Kindergarten Movement in the 1860s and 1870s, which defined a transition year for the young from the mother's care to a setting that would be an extension of domesticity in its emphasis on moral and personal development through play, children under the ages of six or seven were universally considered too young for compulsory public education. Fearing "sexual, social and mental precocity" in children, reformers argued that mothers could most effectively protect young children from the unhealthy and corrupt influences of the outside world (Finkelstein 1985).

By the late nineteenth century, the idea that school could provide a safer and more moral environment for young children than either the homes or the communities of their working-class, immigrant parents led to an increased use of early schooling as a moral training ground. The first public kindergarten in the West was established in San Francisco in 1878 by Kate Douglas Wiggin, who later became known as the author of *Rebecca of Sunnybrook Farm*. Borrowing the ideas about learning through play that had been developed by the German educator Friedrich Froebel, Wiggin was instrumental in extending the kindergarten experience to urban, poor children and in training a generation of kindergarten teachers in California (Ogden 1988). A kindergarten was the first program established by the settlement workers in Jane Addams's Chicago Hull House in 1889. Here, the children of working-class immigrants were to be trained in "elementary principles of hygiene and manners and the development of social instincts and inclinations through cooperative play and group activity." The potential social control functions of the school were extended to kindergartens throughout Chicago after the 1894 Pullman strike, with educators arguing that even very young children could be taught self-control, good manners, marching ("part of allegiance to country"), and the discipline of scheduling by the clock (Clement 1997: 109). Despite this new enthusiasm for an early start to education, only 10 percent of U.S. five-year-olds attended kindergartens in 1920, and not until 1946 did California begin to include kindergarten in the state's elementary school system (Ogden 1988: 15). A mother's care—particularly that of a white, middle-class mother—was still considered the best environment for a young, impressionable child.

For children between the ages of six and thirteen, however, school was readily interpreted by nineteenth-century reformers as a far better arena for socialization than the world of work, a "structure of persuasion" that would most effectively begin to broaden children's sphere of association from the narrow privatism of the family to the larger world of extrafamilial relations. Especially after the 1840s, as immigration made "cultural strangers" more visible in urban life, schools could also provide the kind of purified, homogeneous, and regulated environment that would reinforce middle-class moral values, behaviors associated with the work ethic, and social control that operated by persuasion rather than coercion. Female teachers were seen as the ideal instructors for extending the influence of mothers into the regulated setting of the school, and teaching emerged as one of the primary professional occupations for women after this era.

By 1850, 50 percent of children between the ages of five and nineteen from all ethnic and class backgrounds attended public school in the United States. Attendance increased over the second half of the nineteenth century in every region except the South, where blacks, in particular, faced restricted educational opportunities (Clement 1997: 81–121). Race, ethnicity, class, gender, and region determined the different rhythms of children's educational experiences within the schools. The more affluent stayed in school longer and with fewer interruptions. Urban immigrant children left school earlier than did the native-born, generally moving into the labor force as significant family workers after the sixth grade. Scots and eastern European Jews were the exceptions among immigrant groups in fully supporting the system of public education and in promoting longer school attendance and high academic standards by their children. Other immigrants, especially the Irish and Germans, fought the dominant Protestant and middle-class ethos of the public schools and were successful in establishing parochial schools or bilingual programs; southern Italians were the most distrustful of state-run school systems, with their children consequently the least likely to maintain school attendance. Urban black children attended school longer than did white immigrants because they faced more discrimination in the labor market, but they also tended to be in separate, physically inferior schools (Clement 1997, 1985). For all children, public education was designed to promote the values and behavior most congruent with industrial capitalism: punctuality, conformity to rules and regulation, and self-control. For middle-class children, it was assumed that school would simply supplement parental socialization to the same values and behavior. For the children of the working class and the poor, however, schools were increasingly seen as the most effective means of wresting children away from the lax supervision or bad influences of inadequate families and communities.

Compulsory education was only one aspect of the reach of the state into the lives of American children. Over the course of the nineteenth century, other institutions were developed and built to promote the moral reform and rehabilitation of needy or wayward children. In the second half of the nineteenth century many new child-oriented institutions were built in the United States: orphanages, reform schools, industrial schools, and juvenile asylums. "Child saving" became one of the most prominent occupations of Protestant, middle-class, women reformers beginning in the middle of the nineteenth century. Two organizations in particular reflect the extent to which private agencies and government programs began to reach into the sphere of family life in this era. That they more often reached into the families of the working class and the poor, with combined humanitarian and social control intent, served to differentiate family experience by social class even more sharply in this period.

The New York Children's Aid Society, founded in 1853 by Charles Loring Brace, sought to help poor, urban youth by removing them from their inner-city neighborhoods and placing them with farm families in the Midwest and West, where they would be in a safe environment and provided with care in exchange for their work. Brace was a critic of asylums and other institutional programs for youth because of their hierarchical structure and authoritarian tactics, which often required parents to relinquish all legal rights to their children until they reached adulthood. By contrast, the Children's Aid Society allowed all parties—the children, the receiving families, and the agency—to have a say in the children's placement status. Brace also repudiated the kind of discipline and conformity on which most other programs of this era were modeled, believing instead that individualism, independence, and self-sufficiency were the proper traits to be instilled in working-class boys and girls. The openness of the West would, in Brace's view, provide the most fertile ground for the development of a pioneer spirit and would diffuse the potentially dangerous concentration of the urban young as a revolutionary force in urban settings (Boyer 1978:

96–107). The effect of the New York Children's Aid Society program was legendary. In the thirty years between 1854 and 1884, it placed out 60,000 children (Clement 1997: 199), evidence that the boundaries of the private family were, in fact, highly permeable.

Another program with remarkable reach into the lives of working-class and poor children, this time based on an explicit moral judgment about the inadequacy of their parents, was the Society for the Prevention of Cruelty to Children (SPCC), which developed first in New York in 1875. Five years later, it had expanded to thirty-five cities across the United States. The child savers of the SPCC were concerned that children working and wandering on city streets were victims of parental abuse, and they worked through the courts to remove these children from parental custody by relocating them in orphanages or foster families (Clement 1997, 1985; Gordon 1988). Such programs were not simply evidence of the power of middle-class professionals to define appropriate family values and proper behavior for the working class and poor. Many were successful only because they also met the needs of poor families. Child welfare programs could provide parents with a more protected environment for their children in a time of economic crisis, as was the case for eleven-year-old James Peters, one of three surviving children in a family of twelve siblings, whose mother placed him with the Children's Aid Society when she took a job as a housekeeper to a physician in order to provide for her children as a single parent (Clement 1997: 205–206). In other cases, parents saw these programs as providing vocational training for their children. But the desire to use the programs to provide for their children in a way parents could not do themselves often conflicted with other goals and values in this increasingly bureaucratized welfare system.

The trend of private and state bureaucratic intervention into the lives of children continued to grow in the early decades of the twentieth century with the full-fledged child-saving efforts of the Progressive reformers. Of all periods in American history, the Progressive Era, dating from the 1890s to the 1920s, is the most revealing of the underlying ambivalence that has characterized public policies toward children. Reformers worried about and turned their attention to many of the most pressing issues facing children: child labor, maternal and infant health, and the dangers to children on city streets. But for all of the good intentions behind them, the programs and laws enacted had only limited success in ameliorating the lives of most U.S. children. In some cases, such as child labor laws, they were too limited or poorly enforced to reach the many children working on farms, in tenements, and in street trades. In other cases, such as the Sheppard-Towner Maternity and Infancy Protection Act—which was passed in 1921 and provided states with federal matching funds for nutrition and hygiene programs, prenatal and child-health clinics, and nurses making home visits both before and after childbirth—competing political interests worked against preserving a program that effectively met the health needs of children (Cohen 1985; Rothman 1978). Claiming that the act was "a Communist-inspired step toward state medicine that threatened the home and violated the principle of states' rights," a coalition of medical associations and conservatives organized to defeat it completely by 1929 (Ladd-Taylor 1994: 169).

Progressive reformers approached child welfare issues from a maternalist perspective. That is, they identified women's key role as mothers, and they threw their unqualified support behind those policies that would allow women to live up to their full-time, at-home mothering role—such as mothers' pensions—while remaining ambivalent about those that would remove women from the home—such as daycare (Michel 1993: 277–320). One consequence of developing a program for children's welfare based on this singular conception of women's roles was that it significantly limited the extent of government aid to children. Ladd-Taylor (1994) has suggested that the Sheppard-Towner Act and other pieces of progressive legislation affecting children were defeated by a backlash against "politicized motherhood." Opponents objected to the act not only on the grounds that it expanded the social welfare functions of the state but also because, by increasing women's authority over child health and welfare programs, it undermined men's responsibility and authority in the family (Ladd-Taylor 1993: 321–342). Children's needs were thus subsumed into the gender politics of the era.

Many Progressive Era reform projects had a similar kind of paradoxical effect. Acting sometimes in support of families and at other times out of distrust for parents' capacity to socialize and provide for their own children, Progressive reformers worked to expand the power of the state over seemingly private U.S. families. They did so in the belief that they were acting in the "best interests of the child," backed by studies from the new field of child development, which had just begun to chart the normal stages of development for healthy, well-adjusted children (Gravens 1985)—a normative model based on the experience of the middle class that would serve to divide children even further along the lines of social class and race. Childcare experts thus joined the growing ranks of other professionals in children's services whose influence was increasingly being felt within the private domain of U.S. families by the early twentieth century.

The following decades were also ones of limited policy initiatives and limited gains for U.S. children. One historian has described child welfare policies during the Depression and World War II as developing "haltingly, sometimes reluctantly, often inadvertently, and [leaving] a genuinely ambivalent legacy to the postwar period" (Ashby 1985). The Social Security Act of 1935 contained several provisions for children: Aid to Dependent

Children, an expansion of mothers' pensions; grants-in-aid for maternal and child-health programs for the poor; welfare services for homeless, neglected, and delinquent children; and medical care for disabled youth (Ladd-Taylor 1994: 198). Title IV of the Social Security Act provided relief to poor families and their children, but states could attach the moral stipulation that welfare benefits should be granted only to "suitable homes," a clause that primarily discriminated against the children of unmarried women and women of color. The effect was to punish children for the social position or behavior of their parents. The role of the caretaker was not even acknowledged in the original welfare program aimed at children and their families, and mothers were not provided with their own grant assistance until 1950 (Ladd-Taylor 1994: 199–200).

In pursuing a maternalist strategy of child welfare, reformers and policy makers adopted and effectively built on the ideology of childhood as a separate, special stage of life and of children as in need of physical and moral protection. By the 1930s, a "dramatic reorganization of child space and child time" had been effected, with schools and playgrounds redefined as appropriately child-oriented places, distinct from the adult settings of public streets and the world of work (Zelizer 1985: 49). The programs directed toward children did help expand the idea that government could and should address social problems through a variety of policies that intervened in family life. This idea expanded with the War on Poverty programs in the 1960s but has come to be sharply contested since the 1980s. Political debates in the 1990s about the limits of welfare benefits for dependent children and about the institutionalization of children who lack appropriate parental care are therefore not new but part of a long history of an ambivalent relationship between children and the state in the United States.

The most comprehensive review to date of the literature on child welfare policies offers a succinct summary of this history in its very title: *Broken Promises: How Americans Fail Their Children* (Grubb and Lazerson 1988). The authors argue that the needs of children in the United States have been compromised by the many contradictions between a private family ideology and the belief that state intervention is necessary and appropriate in the case of family failure. Americans express more sympathy toward needy children than toward needy adults—although more so toward their own children than to those of others, especially the poor. Consequently Americans burden children's institutions with the expectation of ameliorating all the social problems built into an economic system that produces massive social inequalities. Given these expectations, the public programs and institutions for children are chronically underfunded, and they are subject to the kind of public accountability based on cost-benefit criteria that is not always congruent with children's needs. Grubb and Lazerson suggest that advocates for children have been ineffective for a variety of reasons: parents, because they tend to seek private solutions to public problems; professionals, because they often antagonize parents with their claims to a superior expertise about childrearing; and humanitarian groups, because they act as general representatives of children rather than forming the kind of narrow, single-focus interest group that works most effectively in the political system. Although the White House Conferences on Children have been convened every decade since 1909, they have produced more rhetorical support for the welfare of U.S. children than policies that have changed the actual conditions of children's lives.

This historical summary suggests that ambivalence has been the predominant legacy of the relation between children and the state in the United States. The rhetoric of family privacy and parental privilege over children continues to be a powerful rallying cry, even as U.S. families at all class levels have become less private and more subject to the reach of the state and the economy. As concerns about children's vulnerability escalate, the inherent tension between public and parental responsibility for children is likely to become even more visible and contentious. The issue of parental rights over children is made much more complex, for example, in the era of new reproductive technologies and contested custody arrangements, as the distinctions between biological, adoptive, and surrogate parents shift in meaning and legal status and as the "best interests of the child" become more difficult to determine (Rothman 1989).

Conclusion

Is it harder and riskier to be a child today than it was in the past? Difficult as this question is to answer, it is one that is commonly posed by parents, professionals, politicians, and the general public. In many ways it is a question so laced with the ideological constructions of American childhood, family life, and cultural values that it defies a simple, definitive answer based on any clear-cut, objective criteria. As this review of the history of childhood has suggested, the status of U.S. children is highly ambiguous. Acclaimed as a national resource, children as a group are nevertheless consistently disadvantaged by their lack of access to the political, social, and economic resources of the society. Although they may be loved and valued by individual parents, they are not shown much "public love" in terms of the programs and policies designed to address their optimal physical, social, cognitive, and emotional development. Childhood innocence is a standard motif that has been captured in stories and pictorial images since the eighteenth century, yet those images can also be subverted, as when the innocent child is turned into an eroticized model in the modern advertising photograph (Higonnet 1998). Children never control their own images or histories. Consumer tastes for the sentimental and powerful market forces have been reshaping childhood as a life stage, even as improved demographic conditions made an extended childhood possible for the majority of the young.

In a number of ways, the evidence suggests that contemporary children do face more obstacles in the process of growing up than did their historical counterparts. With less parental and other adult supervision at home, middle-class children may simply have "caught up" with the more loosely structured caretaking arrangements that many working-class and poor children have routinely experienced in the past and present. Working class and poor children also have fewer community supports than they experienced in the past. The gap between an ideological belief in the model of full-time maternal care for children and the reality of adult American working lives has sharpened the sense of a crisis in the U.S. family, and the erosion of the two-parent family as both a norm and a behavioral reality has heightened that perception as well. Finally, the lack of a widespread commitment to finding collective solutions to children's needs, set against the problematic doctrine of family privacy, has fueled current political debates about children and the family without providing much clarity on the issues. The tendency for concerns about children to shift to issues relating to adults is not surprising, since both are members of the same family system. Yet, as this overview of the literature has suggested, children's interests and adults' interests are not always the same and may even conflict, producing much confusion over old and new cultural scripts for the family.

Looming over all the concerns and rhetoric about children and the state of childhood in the late-twentieth-century U.S. is the anxiety generated by rapid social change and an unpredictable future. Perceptions about children's vulnerability are intensified by the economic insecurities that affect all but the wealthiest Americans in the late twentieth century. For the first time in U.S. history, parents do not have the assurance that their children will be able to surpass them in terms of the standard of living achieved in adulthood. The pace of social change in the last thirty years of the twentieth century has been dizzying for many Americans and, for the middle class in particular, the social roles encompassed in the traditional family that have historically shaped life stages and experiences have been transformed. Despite the power of the rhetoric, however, the call for the return to traditional family values is meaningless without the kind of broadly based institutional policies and societal commitment Americans have been loathe to make in the past. Without a full analysis of the meanings attached to childhood and an understanding of why the changing family context in which American children live generates such impassioned controversy, Americans will continue to have a family politics that draws on the rhetoric of vulnerable childhood while ignoring the real dilemmas contemporary children face.

Notes

1. In 1998, it was still considered newsworthy to report that the real life of the Nelson family, on which the long-running television show "Ozzie and Harriet" had been based during the 1950s, did not fit the televised version. In a television documentary and subsequent report in the *New York Times* on June 18, 1998, it was reported that Ozzie Nelson, counter to his television persona, had been an authoritarian and driven man, concerned more about the television show than about his family relationships; that Harriet, unlike the "moral mother" she portrayed, had been a former showgirl who smoked and drank; and that Rick, the youngest son and a rock musician, was a more troubled person than he had appeared to be on screen. Similarly, an obituary for Robert Young, the actor who had starred in "Father Knows Best" from 1954–1960, reported that

> "he and the show's creators sought to portray 'what we thought would be representative of a middle-class American family, if there was such a thing.' Mr. Young once recalled, 'There probably isn't, but that was what we were looking for.'
>
> Mr. Young's portrayal of a strong and humorous father with no serious problems was all the more remarkable because he was privately battling personal demons, including alcoholism. He attended Alcoholics Anonymous meetings during the making of the show" (*New York Times*, July 23, 1998).

Even fifty years of experience with modern family life and considerable media savvy have apparently not dispelled the power of those early television sitcoms to frame the image of family life that resonates to this day.

2. Wells (1982: 21) cites this example, and it is one that shows what a difference it makes to look at family life from the perspective of children rather than of adults. Whereas only 35.9 percent of eighteenth-century parents had nine or more children, for example, 50.7 percent of children lived in families of this size. Only 2.6 percent of eighteenth-century children lived in families with three or fewer children. By the twentieth century, almost half of all children lived in families with no more than two siblings, and only 6.6 percent lived with nine siblings (Wells 1982: 242).

3. The percentages of Asian children living in two-parent families in the United States are not included in these data, although earlier data suggest that the rates for most Asian groups are higher than the rate for white children. For example, the distribution of children living in two-parent families in 1980 was 83.8 percent for non-Hispanic whites, whereas it was 93.4 percent for Asian Indians, 90.4 percent for Koreans, 88.6 percent for Chinese, 87.6 percent for Japanese, and 84.9 percent for Filipinos. Lower rates than for whites occurred only in the case of Hawaiians, with 68.1 percent, and Vietnamese, with 74.3 percent—the latter explained by the number of refugees in this population. In all cases, the proportion of two-parent Asian family groups greatly exceeded that of blacks (46.0 percent) in 1980.

4. Herbert G. Gutman, in *The Black Family in Slavery and Freedom* (New York: Pantheon, 1976), later refuted the argument that slavery caused the breakdown of the black family. According to his historical study, two-parent families were the norm among blacks in the period during and immediately following the Civil War.

It was the racial discrimination in the labor market that led to a weakening of black family structure in the late-nineteenth and early-twentieth centuries, a trend exacerbated in the black migration to northern cities in the twentieth century.

5. Between 1970 and 1996, the proportion of all single-parent households with children under the age of eighteen grew from 13 percent to 32 percent. The rate among whites grew from 10 percent to 26 percent; among Hispanics, from 26 percent (in 1980) to 37 percent; and among blacks, from 36 percent to 64 percent. (U.S. Bureau of the Census 1997: 63). The widespread influence during the 1970s of single community ethnographic studies, such as Carol Stack's *All Our Kin* (1974), which argued for the viability of extended networks of kin and acquaintances rather than the nuclear family model among poor, urban blacks, occurred in the context of this protracted controversy following the Moynihan Report's identification of black single-parent families as a "tangle of pathology." Stack described a pattern of resource sharing, in fact common among many people in poverty as a functional response to limited resources, as a black cultural phenomenon. What Stack, and many others who seized on this pattern as a counterpoint to the perceived racism of the Moynihan Report, identified as a strength of black family life, subsequent researchers have qualified or begun to challenge. McLanahan and Sandefur (1994: 30), for example, cite a forthcoming study that argues that the quality of parenting is lower in multigenerational black families than in single-parent families because of conflicts between grandmothers and mothers over child-rearing issues.

6. The most extensive observational research based on clinical samples has been done by Judith Wallerstein and associates (Wallerstein and Kelly 1980; Wallerstein and Blakeslee 1989) and by E. Mavis Hetherington and associates (Hetherington, Cox, and Cox 1978; Hetherington, Camara, and Featherman 1983; Hetherington and Aresteh 1988; Hetherington, Lerner, and Perlmutter 1988; Hetherington 1989; Cowan and Hetherington 1991). Furstenberg and Cherlin (1991) provide an overview of these studies, and, in some cases—such as Wallerstein and Blakeslee (1989)—a methodological critique. See also Seltzer (1994).

7. Linda Gordon (1994) has studied the historical construction of single motherhood as a social problem beginning in the early twentieth century. She notes the distinctions that have always been drawn between single mothers who were widows and those with absent husbands or no husbands, the latter being far more stigmatized.

8. The family debate in the popular press has focused more on men and women in their roles as "good family man" fathers or struggling single mothers than it has on children (see, for example, "Can We Talk? The Marriage Strategy," *Mirabella*, March 1995: 82, on a conversation between Blankenhorn and Coontz). The title of Barbara Defoe Whitehead's article in the *Atlantic Monthly* (April 1993), "Dan Quayle Was Right," seemed designed to provoke precisely the kind of responses that it did generate (*Atlantic Monthly*, July 1993, "Letters to the Editor"), almost all of which focus on the Dan Quayle–Murphy Brown episodes—a prime instance of the way image and substance tend to get confused in debates over the family. See also the responses to Whitehead's article in the *Journal of Marriage and the Family* 55, no. 1 (1993): 23–38 and vol. 55, no. 3 (1993): 527–556.

3

Adolescent Sexuality

If adults now worry about the vulnerability of modern children, they have more ambivalent and conflicted concerns about adolescents. Whereas young children appear in clear need of adult care and protection, adolescents can provoke a wider range of adult responses, from empathy and bemused indulgence to frustration, dismay, hostility, and even fear, as the young test the boundaries of their transitional status and challenge the limits of adult authority and social control. Occupying the space between childhood and adulthood, with a tenuous foothold in each sphere, contemporary adolescents are in a structurally difficult position. They are economically and politically quite marginal in contemporary American society, yet they are also increasingly exploited as a cultural force in a society that values and celebrates youthfulness and leisure.

Because adolescence is defined as a period of change and maturation, it is seen as natural for the young to experiment with developing independence and autonomy from the family of origin, and it is a key parental task to encourage such separation and maturation. But how much autonomy is both appropriate and tolerable, and how soon should parental control and guidance be relinquished? Even the most vigilant parents of contemporary adolescents recognize the uncanny capacity of the young to slip outside of family control and to be swept up in a powerful peer culture of their own. To some extent, this peer culture is allowed great autonomy from adult culture, with its own argot, style, and status symbols. But since the early twentieth century the young in the United States have been the harbingers of a modern sensibility, and consumer capitalism is adept at usurping their tastes and interests and making them part of the dominant culture. Adolescents are both insiders and outsiders; they occupy a marginal space in U.S. culture, neither dependent children nor fully independent adults. Have youth today slipped too much from parental and societal control? These questions currently have the power to generate much personal and social debate about how contemporary U.S. adolescents should and do relate to other family members and to the institutions of the larger society.

Perhaps no area of experience captures the current sense of crisis among youth as much as adolescent sexuality. Declining school performance, escalating youth violence, and alarmingly high rates of teenage suicide are all topics of heightened concern and discussion in the late 1990s (Uhlenberg and Eggebeen 1986; Furstenberg and Condran 1988; Cherlin 1992; Gaines 1991). But adolescent sexuality occupies a special place on this list of the social problems of youth because it uniquely involves the expression of attitudes and behavior that are legitimate and encouraged for heterosexual, married adults yet proscribed for children and youth.

The Dilemma of "Normal" Sexual Development

Psychologists point out that the capacity for erotic expression is a desired consequence of early childhood attachment and developing emotional maturation, and that one of the key tasks in socialization is for parents and other adults to help channel the forms that such erotic expression can take in the process of what comes to be defined as normal (i.e., heterosexual) sexual development of the young. Although there are different theoretical interpretations of the psychological and interpersonal dynamics through which this developmental task is accomplished, it is widely agreed that sexual identity has become a core feature of the modern adult personality. One of the defining characteristics of modernity in Western societies is the notion that sexuality defines fundamentally who we are (Foucault 1978; Weeks 1985, 1986).

Sociologists and anthropologists are also concerned with the ways in which sexuality is both nurtured and controlled within all societies. In an important theoretical discussion of the central role played by the family in this social process, Talcott Parsons argued that the social function of the incest taboo is to prohibit the child's expression of erotic attachment inside the nuclear family once the capacity for such eroticism has been generated there by the close bonds established between mother and child. In developing this argument, Parsons built on the theoretical insights of Lévi-Strauss, who noted that with the imposition of the single social rule of the incest taboo, a variety of developmental tasks and family functions was set in motion. First, sexual relations were prohibited between all nuclear family members except the mother and father. This meant that, within the family context, parents could solidify their authority and power and hence their capacity to rear their children effectively by reserving their own exclusive right to a sexual bond. In addition, parents could effectively control and channel the sexual capacity of their children, first by encouraging the early expression of emotional intimacy within the family and later, by propelling their young adult children into the outside world to find sexual partners through culturally appropriate and economically and politically strategic marriages (Parsons 1974; Lévi-Strauss 1974). Wealth and power could be consolidated within family lines by control over children's marriage partners. Class solidarity could also be preserved by shepherding the young toward appropriate partners.

This model of sexual development underscores the family's central role in the individual's development, first as the social arena in which a child develops as a sexual being and then as the key agency of social control over a young person's emerging sexuality. Although much of the social science literature has prescriptively assumed that there is a normal course of individual development and a normal process of family interaction through which adolescents move steadily toward adulthood, historians have challenged the assumption that the stages of development are universal or somehow naturally rooted in purely biological processes. The historical study of adolescence reveals that there are many more variations both cross-culturally and in any one culture over time in the definitions of what constitutes normal development than can be explained by the dictates of biology alone. A key area for study, then, is how, when, and why particular norms about and behaviors by adolescents have taken hold in any particular era.

In the late twentieth century, adolescents' appropriation of adult sexual behavior has come to epitomize trouble in the American family. In their new and seemingly unrestricted access to all forms of sexual expression, many adolescents are no longer subject to the kinds of effective constraints that formerly held youthful behavior in check and limited young people's claims to adult privileges. In the sexual arena, in particular, adolescents as well as adults have adopted the prevailing cultural expectations about the value of dyadic intimacy and self-expression. Access to sexual experience, however, has traditionally been seen as a marker of adulthood that has been normatively reserved for heterosexual, married couples. Since the 1970s, as adolescent sexual behavior began to imitate that of adults, there have been many problematic consequences in American society.

Early sexual activity coupled with emotional immaturity may profoundly affect an adolescent's further socioemotional development and capacity to develop affective attachments in adulthood (Feldman and Elliott 1990). Recent evidence that the sexual experience of many young adolescent girls has been with men in their twenties and older points to an imbalance of power that increases girls' vulnerability in sexual encounters (The Alan Guttmacher Institute 1994). In addition, the spread of sexually transmitted diseases, pregnancy, and early childbirth are all heightened risks for sexually active teenagers (Moore and Rosenthal 1993). Reports of sexually predatory behavior among groups of adolescent boys and even among young children are becoming disturbingly common. The related fear that adolescent sexuality reflects the erosion of parental authority over willful and uncontrollable young people who are increasingly outside the boundaries of family control in ways that are historically new is a powerful contributor to the sense that American families are in trouble and that traditional social roles and statuses are no longer as binding as they once were. Following an era of general liberalization in sexual attitudes and behaviors during the late 1960s and 1970s, there has been a growing concern among many Americans that sex education and birth control programs for teenagers may be ineffective, at best, or actually work to promote sexual activity, at worst (Whitehead 1994). The growing social hostility of the public toward single mothers on welfare—erroneously assumed to be predominantly teenage, black, and sexually promiscuous—also reflects a related concern about a serious social problem and the dilemmas inherent in the contemporary life stage of adolescence.

The theme of resistance to control by parents, the family, and the dominant culture is a central one in the history of adolescence. This chapter is organized in three sections around the theme of the tenuous and ambivalent relationships between adolescents and families, on the one hand, and adolescents and the larger society, on the other. It begins with a discussion of the broad trends that have defined American adolescence as a stage in the life course. As is true of childhood, adolescence has not always carried the same meaning or social implications at all times in the historical past. Looking at the emergence of "the adolescent" and "the teenager" at various points in American history will offer a foundation for the more specific discussion of adolescent sexuality.

A second section provides an overview of the changes in sexual attitudes and behavior in the United States since the critical period of the 1920s, with an emphasis on the institutions that helped shape a distinctive youth culture and modern definitions of sexuality. Adolescent girls are key to this historical account, in particular because it was their new and more public expression of sexuality that was identified as socially problematic and in need of adult regulation and control. A dual concern—both to protect girls and to control female adolescent sexuality—shaped many of the social movements and social policies in the United States in the period between 1880 and 1920.

Finally, because one of the most frequently cited consequences of less restrained adolescent sexual behavior is a modern epidemic of premarital pregnancy and early childbearing, a third section will investigate these trends historically and in modern times. To what extent is adolescent pregnancy a key indicator of the breakdown in parental authority and traditional family control? When, how, and why have the restraints on adolescent sexual behavior lessened and with what social consequences? It is, of course, not only adolescent childbearing per se that is defined as a current social problem but the greater propensity for childbearing and childrearing to occur outside of marriage. The failure of parents and of other adult authorities to make increasing numbers of young people adhere to the "proper" sequence of family events—one that begins with marriage and is later followed by sexual experience and childbearing—is seen as another primary example of the decline of family control in contemporary American society and one with particularly costly societal consequences.

The Historical Contours of American Adolescence

Historical claims that adolescence emerged at one particular point in time have been widely disputed by a variety of studies over the past two and a half decades. Although some have contended that the concept of adolescence was an invention of the nineteenth century (Demos and Demos 1969; Demos 1986), others have cited evidence of its behavioral existence much earlier in colonial America (Beales 1975; Hiner 1975) and in early modern Europe (Davis 1975; Stone 1977; Fox 1977). Ultimately, the historical study of adolescence rests not on dating the origin of the term but on uncovering the different meanings and experiences attached to it. Even similar behavior can carry very different social meanings, as in the case of youthful rebelliousness, which has been variously interpreted in different eras as the activities of brash and troublesome youth, who need stricter discipline, or of "maladjusted" youth, who need help and understanding. From this perspective, the contemporary American version of adolescence as a prolonged period of great emotional "storm and stress" has a relatively short history dating from the early years of this century. A brief overview of this history reveals the extent to which the life stage of adolescence, as well as that of childhood, has been socially constructed.

Transitional Statuses: Dependence, Semidependence, Independence

In American history, the critical eras in which youth was reevaluated and given new social meaning corresponded to two key periods of significant, unsettling economic transformation: the late eighteenth to early nineteenth century (1790–1840) and the late nineteenth to the early twentieth century (1880–1920). The economic transformations, first to an early industrial society and later to one rooted in an advanced industrial economy, meant that continuity in intergenerational experience was, at least temporarily, disrupted. During times of rapid social change, the young face a social world unlike that of their parents, and in each of the specific historical periods cited, those changed circumstances produced both new opportunities and new constraints. These periods of historical transition provide some important clues to adolescent experience in the contemporary era as well.

In a preindustrial society, such as colonial America, boys and girls tended to take gradual and continuous steps toward assuming their adult roles. From an early age, they were exposed to the unambiguous social expectations that accompanied adulthood, and they began to practice their gendered roles even at relatively young ages (Demos 1986: 96–99). In the American context, generally only the experience of religious conversion among the young created an unsettling emotional upheaval in the transition to adulthood. The hysteria that spread among a group of adolescent girls in seventeenth-century Salem, Massachusetts, for example, was from one perspective the last gasp of the witchcraft epidemic that had erupted throughout Europe and in parts of North America during the early modern period. From another perspective, however, it was a sign of a more tumultuous adolescence that was taking shape in the context of changing social structural conditions (Boyer and Nissenbaum 1974). Puberty, reached around age sixteen for boys and age fifteen for girls before the mid–nineteenth century, was more often understood as a time of increased energy than of biologically based emotional turmoil (Kett 1977: 44, 134).

In much of the historical past, differentiation by chronological age was less relevant than by broader categories that marked the passage into new statuses. American young people experienced the transition from a relatively short state of complete dependence on the family of origin to a much longer state of semidependence, stretching from approximately age ten to age twenty-one (or older), before they achieved the social and economic independence that marked adulthood (Kett 1977). Over the century and a half from the American Revolution to the Great Depression, the stage of life characterized as semidependence underwent significant changes. It was given its broadest outlines by the forces of social change dictated by the political economy and more specific shape by the conscious policy-making and institution-building attempts of adults and the active responses of young people themselves. Looking at the new ideas about youth and at the new behavior that appeared in two key periods of social transition, 1790 to 1840 and 1880 to 1920, provides an important backdrop to our understanding of and approaches to adolescence today.

Restless Youth: 1790–1840. By the beginning of the nineteenth century, the United States had a very youthful population. The median age was 16 years (in contrast to 30.8 years in 1950 and 34 years in 1994), and only 9 percent of the population was made up of people between the ages of 45 and 64 (Kett 1977: 38). A high birthrate in colonial America accounted for this youthful population, and the development of new industrial opportunities by 1800 allowed the young an unprecedented kind of geographic and social mobility. One noted characteristic of youth at the turn of the nine-teenth century was their "restlessness," particularly in the fluidity with which they moved in and out of their family homes in pursuit of seasonal work.

New opportunities for freedom coexisted uneasily with old patterns of authority, however. One of the striking differences historians have noted between the youth of this period and their peers in later eras is the extent to which the young had considerable freedom from control by regulatory institutions in their daily lives, but also the extent to which they were sub-jected to the erratic but harsh authority of adults. The early nineteenth cen-tury is replete with stories, on the one hand, of students engaging in spon-taneous rebellions against the overbearing authority of their teachers, and, on the other, of fathers' frequent and protracted interventions in the lives of their young adult sons (Kett 1977; Demos 1986: 100). Deference to pa-triarchal authority by the young was expected and often enforced, yet it was also actively resisted whenever possible. The primary historian of American adolescence has noted that the myth of compliant and tractable youth who were once held in control by tightly knit preindustrial families and communities was just that: a myth. It was one constructed in the mid–nineteenth century by reformers who painted a romanticized picture of the stability of rural society and the young in the preindustrial era in stark contrast to the troubling mobility and independence of youth that they saw emerging in an urbanizing and industrializing society. In fact, "patterns of disorderliness and violence" rather than order, stability, and control were more often characteristic of the experience of young men in the period before the 1840s (Kett 1977: 60–61). The early history of ado-lescent girls is more difficult to reconstruct, in part because girls were more closely bound to the domestic sphere and because of the subordinate status of all women in the colonial era. By the early nineteenth century, however, Tocqueville noted the extraordinary freedom of young women in America, in sharp contrast to their status as married women (1969: 592–593).

The transitional period between 1790 and 1840 was characterized by the beginning of a shift in some of the old patterns of authority and sub-ordination that had governed intergenerational relations in a preindustrial society. This shift revealed the new social and cultural space that began to open up for the young with the advent of an early industrial economy. Commercial and industrial jobs and the lure of urban life drew many young people away from agriculture and rural communities. It is not sur-prising that a society in the throes of transition would begin to define these "restless" young people as a new social problem. Particularly as gangs of lower-class and working-class young men began to be more visible in ur-ban street life, the social problem of "restless youth" took on more threat-ening and ominous tones as "dangerous youth." The prevalence of itinerant street waifs had long been a source of concern to middle-class reformers (Nasaw 1985), but these new, more dangerous youth were characterized by their embeddedness in local gangs and by a subcultural style that celebrated physical prowess and spontaneous, provocative outbursts of rowdy and potentially violent behavior. The shift in terminology by which adults referred to youth was thus a sign of the greater class differentiation that was emerging with industrialization and that resulted in vastly different economic and social opportunities available to the young.

Defining the Youth Problem in the Mid–Nineteenth Century. By the mid–nineteenth century, middle-class adults had begun to identify and respond to the "youth problem." They sought to differentiate middle-class youth from their dangerous working-class and lower-class counterparts. New attention to gender differentiation was also characteristic of this era, with Victorian concerns about precocious sexuality focused particularly on the need for protection of middle-class daughters. While class and gender divisions meant that young people experienced their youth very differently according to the availability of resources and the corresponding life chances these resources produced, the new ideological construction of adolescence in the making sought to encompass all young people as a universal category. Not coincidentally, adult spokesmen and reformers began to articulate an ideology of the developmental perils of youth at the same time as the parallel ideology of vulnerable and priceless childhood was being fashioned. The idea of the innate innocence of young children turned a new spotlight on the stage of puberty as a period in which sexual awakening threatened to taint childhood purity. The solution the adult reformers constructed was to envision and create a more regulated, age-segregated environment, initially designed for middle-class young people, during the perilous years of growing up. The public high school with its strictly age-graded environment was developed as an institution perfectly suited to the newly redefined needs of the young. For those who were considered more intractable and either directly or potentially delinquent, the institution of the reform school provided a new means of control and containment (Rothman 1971; Brenzel 1983).

The Ideology and Institutions of Adolescent Control: 1890–1920. By the late-nineteenth century, a high school education had become an important credential for access to the white-collar jobs in the emerging corporate and bureaucratic world of an advanced industrial economy. In addition to containing and regulating the young, the high school was an institution that could socialize the next generation of professionals to the values of sociability, group conformity, and controlled competition crucial to adult success in this new economic environment. By the early twentieth century, a college education was required for access to middle-class professional jobs, and the high school student body increasingly included working-class, as well as middle-class, youth. School tracking maintained class differentials, even as young people from diverse backgrounds were grouped together in the same setting.

Besides its role in channeling the young into the different layers of a stratified capitalist economy, the public high school played a significant role in redefining youth in the period between 1880 and 1920. As an institution that insulated young people from the adult world and that regulated and contained them as a distinct social group, the high school promoted a longer period of semidependence than ever before. The late nineteenth century was also the era in which a variety of youth organizations—the Boy Scouts and Girl Scouts, the YMCA and YWCA, among others—were developed by adult reformers to provide supervision during the after-school, leisured hours of middle-class youth. In schools and social organizations, the young were subjected to much less of the kind of arbitrary and harsh discipline they had experienced previously from their teachers, employers, and parents and now to a seemingly more benign but vastly expanded scope of adult regulation and control over their lives in its place. Young people who came of age at the turn of the twentieth century were thus immersed in a complex institutional matrix designed to socialize them to the demands of bureaucratic, corporate capitalism, one significant consequence of which was a greater delay in entering into adulthood. The sharpest contrast in intergenerational experiences was between this newly regulated environment for the young in place by the late nineteenth century and the casual, unstructured, and noninstitutionalized context that youth had experienced in the period before 1840.

Along with the development of institutions that kept the young in a prolonged state of semidependency, new ideas about youth were articulated by adults—the so-called architects of adolescence—in the first two decades of the twentieth century. G. Stanley Hall is widely credited as one of these key architects, who, in his multivolume book of 1904, *Adolescence: Its Psychology, and Its Relations to Anthropology, Sex, Crime, Religion, and Education*, helped to construct "the adolescent" as a new social type: vulnerable, awkward, moody, and subject to the "storm and stress" of a biologically based sexual maturation process. What Hall saw as a natural developmental process that deserved considerable adult indulgence as young people experimented with their new status, others simply saw as a period of predictable crisis. What was new was that adolescence was now thought to be a universal developmental stage for all young people on the road to adulthood. There was a widespread acceptance of the belief that adolescence was a stage of life that routinely produced the experience of personal crisis among the young, which if left unregulated could generate social crisis as well. Immature boys who were saddled with adult responsibilities too early or vulnerable girls who were sexually precocious in adolescence not only jeopardized their own futures but that of their children and all future generations.

It was not the discovery of adolescence, then, but the social invention of the adolescent ("the youth whose social definition, and indeed whose whole being, was determined by a biological process of maturation") that marked the beginning of the modern understanding of adolescence (Kett 1977: 243). The institutions and ideas that redefined adolescence in the early twentieth century have continued to shape the meanings and experiences attached to this life stage ever since. In particular, Americans in the late twentieth century have come to expect that adolescence naturally—physiologically—involves intense emotional upheaval in the process of reaching sexual maturity and that it is a life stage inherently defined by the condition of prolonged dependency.

Adolescents into Teenagers: Growing Up in the Twentieth Century

Between 1920 and 1950, the institutions that gave a more standardized shape to the stage of life known as adolescence were firmly established. Chief among them was the high school and the peer culture that was generated there. Through the twentieth century, American adolescents have followed a pattern of extended education that has effectively prolonged their state of semidependency. Using the behaviors of leaving school, entering the labor force, departing from the family of origin, getting married, and establishing a household as the markers of the transition to adulthood, Modell, Furstenberg, and Hershberg (1976) argued that the process of becoming an adult in the late twentieth century is more orderly, predictable, and condensed in terms of time than it was a century ago. Many young people found achieving economic independence a long and difficult process in the past, and it was not uncommon, for example, for the youngest daughter to remain at home to care for her aging parents. Adulthood was not a status that was routine and automatic. It was one that had to be achieved, sometimes at great personal cost.

Although the transition to adulthood has been routinized and expanded to include all young people, it is a period of time more fraught with trauma for adolescents today because it is experienced in an individualized way, as the personal decisions of each adolescent, rather than as the collective consequences of family and community demands. What constitutes the transition to adulthood may also be undergoing change. Labor force participation of the young starts early, but it is sporadic and may signal the desire for discretionary consumer income rather than real economic independence. Years of schooling are prolonged by the escalating demands for more credentials as the passports to occupations, and age at first marriage has been increasing for both young men and young women as educational opportunities expand. At the same time, "new mores [have] incorporated an enlarged range of sexual and emotional intimacy outside of marriage" (Modell and Goodman 1993: 107). Modell and Goodman argue that although the transition to adulthood is in fact shorter now than in the past, "the years of preparation for adulthood are fuller, tenser, and more overwhelming to the young people moving through them" (1993: 118–119). Against this backdrop of the psychological stresses of adolescence, the new social and cultural power of an emerging youth culture presents its most striking contrast.

If the adolescent was a social construct of the early twentieth century, the teenager emerged in the 1940s and post–World War II era to define a group that was socially and culturally distinct (Palladino 1996). Teenagers in the second half of the twentieth century have been most closely identified as a powerful consumer market, a group with particular cultural tastes and with the demographic numbers and economic buying power to support them. Still understood as emotionally vulnerable and socially inexperienced, but now as full-fledged consumers as well, they occupy a position that is ambiguously poised between economic and political marginality and cultural power in American society. The history of American adolescents and teenagers is in no small part a history of adult attempts at control and containment and of the responses by young people to evade that control. At school, the young successfully resisted a closed environment of adult moral influence and authority by developing their own peer culture with well-defined norms for social behavior. In the realm of popular culture, teenagers have been equally successful in shaping their own norms as cultural taste makers and powerful consumers.

In tracing the rise of the teenager from the 1940s through the 1970s, Palladino (1996) focused particularly on music as the cultural force through which teens emerged as a self-conscious youth culture. "Bobby soxers," defined by their taste for swing music, represented the mainstream version of this culture in the early 1940s, but one that was still largely defined by adult control over a white, middle-class market. A new emphasis on consumption, leisure, and fun characterized this emergent teenage taste culture, although it was quickly interrupted, if only temporarily, by World War II. The war helped to confer new legitimacy on the young, particularly on teenage draftees who were lauded as courageous and heroic soldiers, although those same risk-taking behavioral traits in adolescent boys had previously been defined as troublesome or even delinquent. In the postwar decades, the social power and personal freedom of the young gained new momentum. Between the 1950s and 1970s, a resurgence of teenage cultural dominance, fueled by a rapidly expanding consumer economy, was punctuated by critical moments of significant political involvement on the part of the young, particularly in the civil rights and the student-based antiwar movements. The contemporary social understanding of teenagers as both marginal to and central in American culture is rooted in the postwar era.

If swing was the music and dance most closely associated with the teenage cultural style of the 1940s, rock and roll was its equivalent with even greater consequences in the 1950s. Teenagers began to dominate the popular music market in this decade, accounting for 80 percent of its sales by 1955 (Palladino 1996: 124). Teen taste and style were not easily accessible to adults; indeed, the flagrant rejection of adult conventions and subversion of mainstream values were no small part of the appeal. One significant characteristic of teenage culture since the 1950s is that age, far more than race, ethnicity, or social class, has defined the broadest outlines of this cultural group. It is a sign of the breadth of the emerging youth culture in the 1950s that adults began to express worry about all teenagers as potential juvenile delinquents, not just working-class and lower-class youth. The adult fear that the young were slipping out of their control was not born in the postwar era, but it took root then as a relatively permanent feature of the presumed generational divide between adolescents and adults that has persisted throughout the second half of the twentieth century.

Music, style, language, and ideology were important forces in shaping an ascendant youth culture among post–World War II American adolescents.[1] Adult promoters and marketers catered to this new mass youth market, but they could not completely dictate the content of the cultural product or the direction of the trends. In 1964 there were 22 million teenagers, the fastest growing segment of the U.S. population, who composed a $12 billion consumer market (Palladino 1996: 195). The demographic power of this baby-boom cohort gave teenagers an economic credibility they had not fully had before. This economic power also coincided with attitudinal and behavioral changes among young people that reflected an erosion of respect for hierarchical authority in American society more generally and a diminished capacity for effective adult regulation of the young (Veroff, Douvan, and Kulka 1981).

By the last three decades of the twentieth century, teenagers had come into their own as a distinct social and cultural group, although their power was never permanently guaranteed. Indeed, some contemporary social critics have argued that the demographic downturn among teenagers in the United States between 1977 and 1992 fostered a sharp reversal of adult sentiments that turned teens into a "scapegoat generation" for all contemporary social problems (Males 1996). How adults understand adolescence and how the young both respond to and create their own collective identity are continually evolving processes. The arena of adolescent sexuality is one particularly volatile aspect of the history and contemporary politics of American youth, and here gender has played an especially dramatic role in shaping the contours of adolescent experience.

Modern Sexuality and the Development of Youth Culture

Contemporary adolescent sexual behavior takes its cues, of course, from the meanings attached to sexuality more generally in the larger culture. The history of sexuality in America has involved the progressive decoupling of sex from its procreative functions and the rise of a new ethic throughout the nineteenth and twentieth centuries that gave primacy to romantic love, dyadic intimacy, and erotic expression in adult interactions. While individualism became prominent in the nineteenth century as the undisputed ideology of the American political economy, the heterosexual couple, bound in marriage by the ideology of romantic love, was understood to be the social glue that could moderate in private life the intense individualism of a competitive capitalist society (Bellah et al. 1985).

Historians have focused on two key themes in their studies of sexuality in Western societies. One is the transformation in the meaning of sexuality that shifted attitudes and behavior toward greater sexual liberalism in the twentieth century. The shift that occurred between the eighteenth and twentieth centuries from the instrumental use of sexuality for procreation and an ethic of sexual control and regulation to an emphasis on using sex to achieve personal satisfaction, self-expression, and erotic pleasure is deeply rooted and, most likely, culturally irreversible. But this change has not occurred smoothly and seamlessly. The second key theme for historians of sexuality is the contested nature of sexual attitudes and behavior—a contestation that continues even as sexual liberalism has infused much of contemporary culture. Bitter divisions over the accessibility of birth control, women's roles and sexuality, the regulatory role of the state, and the emergence of a commercialized sex industry have persisted since the nineteenth century. Successive waves of sexual liberalism and sexual repression characterize the history of sexuality in the United States, and these are the same trends evident in the more specific history of adolescent sexuality as well.

Adolescents and the New Sexual Ethic

By the 1920s, historians have noted that a new sexual ethic was clearly established in American culture. Unlike the nineteenth-century Victorian sexual ethic that had stressed control, regulation, and restraint, this set of values celebrated a more open form of sexual expressiveness, a less rigid kind of gender differentiation, and a new emphasis on the heterosexual couple (D'Emilio and Freedman 1988). Although the 1920s is the decade in which these new sexual values and behavior fully flowered, they had been set in motion by many underlying structural changes in American society in the preceding decades. The massive societal transformation encompassed by the interrelated processes of industrialization, immigration, and urbanization in the nineteenth- and twentieth-century United States had a special impact on young people. It offered them unprecedented social opportunities, but it also generated new concerns about youth problems and inspired the creation of new institutions of social control.

Youth at Work: Peer Sociability.   The first industrial enterprise to develop in the early-nineteenth-century United States offers a case in point about the unintended social consequences of new economic opportunities for youth inherent in industrialization. Although the history of adolescence has often been told as a universal story applying equally to both boys and girls, the impact of industrialization on the life experiences of young women is particularly dramatic. Young women from rural New England were initially recruited as the first workers in the new textile industry of the early nineteenth century. The hope of the early industrialists was that young women would make ideal laborers—both tractable and transitory, since they would work only briefly between childhood at home and marriage. Rural girls came to factory towns, such as Lowell, Massachusetts, to live as boarders with their peers in a work setting that was designed to be safe, clean, and respectable (Dublin 1979).

The hopes that the pioneering industrialists may have had of creating an easily controllable and subordinate labor force of young women who were willing to work for a few years before marriage was dispelled with a series of strikes and labor demands in the 1830s (Dublin 1979). By the 1840s, the first wave of northern European immigration to the United States brought whole families of more impoverished and desperate workers to the textile mills in place of the Lowell girls and their like, but not before an important precedent—work opportunities outside the domestic sphere—had been set that offered new opportunities and new social and economic freedoms to young Americans. Over the next century, these work opportunities would become a significant factor in shaping the social lives of adolescents in the United States.

By the early twentieth century, the labor market for the young had expanded, although it was sharply differentiated by race, class, and gender. Opportunities for white, middle-class young men were the most promising, since educational advantages and personal networks exposed them to jobs with mobility in business and the professions. White working-class young men also often followed fathers and relatives into the skilled trades or industry, where unions promised them some measure of job stability and a living wage. Minority men of all ages were the most likely to be relegated to the ranks of unskilled labor or the unemployed, although periods of an expanding industrial economy and labor demands during crisis periods such as wartime still offered some possibilities of access to stable manual work for men. For most young men in the nineteenth- and early-twentieth-century United States, then, work was an expected and relatively continuous feature of their adolescent and adult lives. The world of work they entered as young men had been shaped by their fathers, uncles, and older brothers; it replicated and reinforced the models of authority and power that adolescent boys found in their families and neighborhoods.

For many adolescent girls, conversely, the industrial work world broke radically with the traditional experiences of their mothers. Although white, elite, and middle-class daughters had the most privileged, leisured, and sheltered existence of all groups in the United States, adolescent girls who were working class or poor, both white and nonwhite, found themselves charting new territory in the world of work. As in the case of the Lowell girls in the early nineteenth century, young women workers in the mid- to late nineteenth century and early twentieth century were often the first women in their families to be employed outside the home. Domestic service, the first avenue of employment for many immigrant girls and often the only opportunity open to minority women, did offer women a close view of middle-class "Americanized" life that their brothers did not have (Katzman 1978). Some historians have speculated that such a view may have accelerated the acculturation process for second- and third-generation immigrants, as daughters were exposed to new consumption tastes and values in their working lives that they carried with them to their own families and communities as married adults.

Domestic work was too strenuous, isolating, and subject to the immediate supervision of the employer to provide a long-term lure to most working girls. By the late nineteenth and early twentieth centuries, the factory, department store, and office presented new opportunities, available at least to white women, that were far preferable to domestic work. The percentage of women working in nonagricultural jobs doubled between 1880 and 1910, and in 1900 nearly half of all women in the labor force were young, between the ages of sixteen and twenty-four, and single (Kessler-Harris, 1982). In these new work settings, young women were immersed in a sociable world with others of their same age. Historians have noted that working-class girls were less likely than their male counterparts to be closely supervised by older adults. Work was often in a setting in which they could escape the community surveillance and control of family and neighbors as they heard about and explored the new tastes, styles, and norms associated with American adolescent life (Tentler 1979).

Such adolescent networks of communication represented an unusual social opportunity for immigrant and native-born young women alike, since most girls experienced in their domestic lives the gender restrictions associated with a traditional, patriarchal family structure. Most employed youth continued to have responsibilities to their families of origin, for parents relied on the contributions of children for the family's economic survival. Yet, access to more disposable income did provide the leverage for many young people to claim a measure of independence, even while living in the parental home. Increased economic opportunities for the young provided the opening wedge in their claims for more social independence. For daughters, in particular, gaining a measure of control over their leisure time was worth the protracted conflict it generated with parents, who correctly understood that this freedom came at the expense of their own parental authority. Thus, although work itself was rarely liberating or empowering to young women, at least in the modern meaning of offering inherent satisfactions and economic independence, it provided them with other powerful attractions, most notably the sociability of an immediate peer group and the allure of American consumer culture.

Historians have noted a particular irony in regard to this battle for social freedom. Although young women in the early twentieth century gained more autonomy over their adolescent social lives than ever before, their intense preoccupation with social and sexual freedom from parents most often led them directly into a culture of romantic love, early marriage, and quite conventional family roles for women. The adolescent peer group thus functioned in highly conservative ways for young women. In accentuating the social interests young women had in common—especially leisure activities, style, friendships, and heterosexual relationships—peer group culture deflected them from gaining either political consciousness about the conditions of work or real economic independence achieved on their own outside of marriage (Tentler 1979). Work opened a wedge for more autonomy, but for many young women in particular it was a limited autonomy restricted to the years of adolescence and focused around the related attractions of consumption and romance.

Youth at Play: The World of Urban Leisure.   In addition to the mobility provided by jobs, urban settings offered up new sites for entertainment. Working-class youth claimed the dance halls, movie theaters, clubs, amusement parks, and street corners as the leisure spaces that allowed for social mingling with their peers beyond the surveillance of parents and other adults (Nasaw 1993; Stansell 1987; Peiss 1986). Poolrooms, bowling alleys, saloons, and clubs had long provided working-class men with social spaces of their own, whereas married women experienced sociability with female kin and neighbors almost exclusively within the domestic sphere. The most dramatic shift in the use of social space occurred in the period between 1880 and 1920 by young men and women who sought out mixed-sex arenas for their after-work entertainment. The opportunity for participation in the public world of commercialized leisure was particularly alluring for young women, since those activities epitomized fun, pleasure, independence, and individualism over and above the values of social obligation, deference, and control that were the hallmarks of family life, especially in immigrant families. Young women and men together entered a "heterosocial culture" in the public world of commercialized leisure that appealed to the tastes, style, and mores closely associated with an emergent American youth culture. It was a world that was appealingly "modern": consumer oriented, focused on pleasure, and in direct opposition to the world of work (Peiss 1986). Indeed, as labor struggles to reduce working hours achieved success and new measures of protective legislation were introduced in the early twentieth century, the world of leisure time took on even greater significance. It represented everything work did not; it was the ultimate reward and justification for having to work at all.

One of the key features of this heterosocial world was its more open sexual expressiveness. Part of the appeal of the early movies at neighborhood nickelodeons, for example, which were common in urban immigrant communities in the late nineteenth century, was the opportunity for intimacy and more private courting that darkened movie theaters provided (Ewen 1985). With the rise of the Hollywood studio system in the 1920s, movies gained wider audiences and played an important role not just as sites for courtship but as social scripts that offered clues to the norms and behavior associated with consumption and romance (May 1980). The young were quick to adopt new behavioral expressions of this more sexualized sensibility. The popularity of the dance hall among the young was enhanced by the close bodily contact that dancing allowed and by the sexual suggestiveness of the movements in the popular style known as "tough dancing" (Erenberg 1984; Peiss 1986: 100–104). Early-twentieth-century amusement parks, such as those at Coney Island, were popular with young people for the spectacle and sensation of their physical settings and because the rides they offered both literally and figuratively shook up proper Victorian decorum by lifting skirts, blowing off hats, throwing strangers into each others' arms—in general, upsetting the balance of the more traditional, reserved style of gender interaction in public (Kasson 1978). Kathy Peiss has argued that young women "pioneered new manners and mores" in their uses of leisure time (1986: 7). Whether negotiating this new social world in female pairs to maintain some semblance of respectability or engaging in "flirtatious companionship" with men on whom they relied for the economic favor of "treating," adolescent girls were experimenting with the new behavior and attitudes associated with modern sexuality. They, more visibly than their brothers, were experimenting with this modern sensibility, and in so doing, they were also among the first to be censured by social critics and reformers when concerns about the pace of social change, the decline in parental authority, and the alarming precocity of adolescents began to surface in the public rhetoric.

The Constraints of Modernity: Social Controls over Sexuality

Sexual liberalization was part of the social and cultural history of the nineteenth- and twentieth-century United States, but by no means the full story. Rather than a linear development, sexual liberalization has repeatedly been followed by waves of sexual repression in U.S. history. One of the many paradoxes in the history of sexuality is that as the whole topic of sex became a more legitimate and normalized one in public discourse, the tendency to define what was normal also sharply delineated what was considered abnormal, pathological, or illicit. A thriving enclave of gay life and sexual expression was evident in New York City in the 1920s, for example, but had been forced underground and stigmatized by repressive social and political forces between the 1930s and the 1960s (Chauncey 1994; Faderman 1991). The liberalization of adolescent sexuality that was characteristic of the first two decades of the twentieth century was also not without its setbacks. There were both external sources of social control imposed on adolescent sexuality and internally imposed peer-group controls that set the parameters for the sexual experience of young women and men. Both kinds of social control need to be considered in the context of the constraints—as well as the opportunities—that defined modern sexuality for young people in the recent historical past.

External Social Constraints.   Single working girls experimented with new sexual norms and behavior but often in spite of publicly expressed concern over declining morality and many attempts both to protect and control young women as the repositories of that morality. An ideology of female passionlessness and of women's innate virtuousness rooted in their domesticity was a cornerstone of Victorian beliefs about gender and sexuality (Welter 1966; Cott 1979b). Young women coming of age in the second half of the nineteenth century were presumed to be asexual and therefore naturally better able to tamp down the stronger sexual passions attributed to men. While not all women behaved at all times in accordance with this ideology, it held quite powerful normative sway through most of the nineteenth century and served to define the parameters of acceptable behavior.

Although it might be considered healthy (if properly curbed) and inevitable in boys, evidence of sexuality in adolescent girls was considered a sign of unnatural moral perversion and extreme deviance. The boundary between "good girls" and "fallen women" had already been sharply drawn by the middle of the nineteenth century, but contestations over this line—and over the meaning of adolescent girls' sexuality—became a major battleground in the late nineteenth century. The fact that there was a "class of fallen women available for the uncontrollable passions of men" (Burnham 1993: 179) only intensified the struggle to define proper female sexuality. Gender norms were forged in a cultural context in which class, ethnicity, and race were already outlined in sharp relief.

Victorian gender ideologies proclaimed that men and women were different by nature: Men were rugged individualists, while women were pious, pure, and domestic. Women's greater virtuousness justified their role as caretakers of innocent children in the sanctity of the domestic sphere, but it also gave them a legitimate claim to carry their domestic virtues into the more corrupt, public world of men. Because women were defined as the keepers of public virtue—an especially important social role in a period of rapid social change—those who strayed from virtue were subject to unusually harsh punishment. The expression of female sexuality was understood not just as an individual aberration but as a potent social danger. Indeed, lurking just behind the ideology of female passionlessness in the nineteenth-century United States was an older belief in female sexuality as dangerous and, once unleashed, as difficult to restrain (Laqueur 1990).[2] Protection and control were the two interrelated responses to the new problem of adolescent female sexuality being articulated by the mid-nineteenth century and debated over the next century.

One solution to the problem of adolescent female sexuality was institutionalization. The first reform school in the United States for girls was established in Lancaster, Massachusetts, in 1856, with its first client sentenced there for "chronic disobedience," larceny, and potential prostitution (Brenzel 1983). Between the mid-nineteenth century and the 1920s, girls were considered delinquent for any overt expression of sexuality and were often committed to reformatories for violations of sexual morality. In these special settings they might be rehabilitated—that is, convinced by a combination of positive incentives and coercion to adopt a Victorian conception of deferential, virtuous girlhood (Alexander 1992: 284). Resistance and disobedience led to the charge of incorrigibility, in which case, it was deemed girls should be removed from the public for the protection of society. Young women who were poor and working class were the most likely to be sentenced to these reformatories, in part because weaker familial supervision and their lack of adherence to the middle-class norms of pious and virtuous womanhood were seen as rendering them more vulnerable to criminality and prostitution. The historical record suggests that women have always been punished more severely than men around charges of immoral behavior, and poor women more harshly than their wealthier counterparts (Hobson 1987). But in the late nineteenth century there was a particularly acute sense of moral crisis that developed around the waywardness (i.e., sexuality) of young women.

This sensitivity had multiple roots. Demographically, the proportion of single young women aged fifteen to twenty-four in the population was higher (at nearly 25 percent) than at any other time in U.S. history, including at the peak of the baby-boom coming-of-age in the early 1970s. These young women were geographically concentrated in cities in the Northeast and north central states, and they were increasingly visible as workers and as consumers of urban entertainment. By their numbers and their public visibility, young unmarried women began to blur the markers of gendered space (private versus public) and behavior (respectable versus deviant) that had so clearly delineated good girls from bad in an earlier era (Nathanson 1991: 127–131).

Victorian ideas about sexuality were also beginning to change in the first two decades of the twentieth century. Scholars have noted that one effect of the strident Progressive Era campaigns against prostitution and venereal disease was to give sex and sexuality new legitimacy as topics of discussion (Nathanson 1991; D'Emilio and Freedman 1988). In part this was a response to the considerable attention that had been directed toward issues of health and sexual morality among soldiers during World War I. The Commission on Training Camp Activities organized programs of active sports and social hygiene to promote an ethic of sexual abstinence for men. The educational program urged soldiers to "erase sex from their consciousness; . . . 'Sex organs do not have to be exercised or indulged in in order to develop them, or preserve virility,'" according to one training camp lecturer (Brandt 1987: 64). And yet, the effect of such advice was to heighten a consciousness about sex—both its pleasures and its dangers. The dissemination of the ideas of Sigmund Freud and Havelock Ellis in the early twentieth century is also credited with helping shift the understanding of sex as behavior with a strictly procreative function to one that included personal satisfaction and emotional expressiveness. But this spread of a more psychologically based understanding of sexuality was doubleedged: It allowed women to be seen as having a sexual nature; at the same time, it expanded the number of institutions and experts that had a stake in managing the sexuality of adolescent girls.

The girl who voluntarily chose to be sexually active, as opposed to the one who was the unwilling victim of male sexual license, was reviled in the late-nineteenth- and early-twentieth-century United States (Nathanson 1991: 106). She was considered incorrigible, irredeemable, and consequently was likely to be sentenced by the courts to a reformatory. Often working-class parents themselves initiated court proceedings against their rebellious adolescent daughters, attempting to use the legal system as a means of restraining the nontraditional kinds of autonomous social and sexual behavior of which they disapproved (Odem 1995: 157–184; Alexander 1995, 1992). Under the influence of the Freudian psychoanalytic model of behavior that had taken hold in the United States by the 1940s, sexual delinquency was redefined as the product of psychological forces rather than the victimization of young women. The most deviant girls were those who did not acknowledge their unconscious motivations in bringing about their own downfall and who were unwilling to reinterpret and modify their sexual behavior according to the prescriptive norms of the legal, social services, and medical experts. Female adolescent sexuality was reinterpreted from being a sign of moral perversion to one of psychological pathology. The shift in policy responses away from a focus on controlling male sexuality to one emphasizing the control of the young women themselves was largely completed by the 1920s. A period of intense social crisis dominated by campaigns that called for the state regulation of female sexuality marked the beginning of this transition.

In the period between 1880 and 1920, social anxiety over the changing roles and behaviors of adolescent girls, in particular, took the form of several intensive national campaigns to raise the age of consent (that is, the age at which sexual intercourse with a young woman would no longer be legally defined and prosecuted as statutory rape) from age ten to age sixteen or older and to prohibit what was widely feared to be the organized trafficking in white, teenage girls for prostitution (the so-called White Slave Traffic Act, or the Mann Act, of 1910). These campaigns were part of the larger social purity movement of the late nineteenth century—centered on criminalizing obscenity, abortion, and prostitution and on addressing other moral concerns of the era (Brodie 1994; Gordon 1976). Historians have noted the brief, intense flare-up of concern around the specifically gendered and racialized issues of age of consent and white slavery: the near hysteria with which they were originally addressed and then the suddenness with which the concern and the campaigns had disappeared by 1920 (D'Emilio and Freedman 1988; Nathanson 1991). Both campaigns were justified on the grounds of the protection of innocent (white) female victims, yet both ultimately resulted in expanding the range of state regulation or control over female sexual autonomy. The threat of prosecution, for example, redefined the meaning of sexual behavior by (now) under-age young women. Such behavior might be seen as provocatively enticing or naively misguided, but it could no longer be the choice of a sexually autonomous young woman. Teachers, lawyers, judges, social workers, physicians, and psychiatrists would henceforth be responsible for controlling female ado-

lescent sexuality—experts who represented an expanded web of adminis-
trative surveillance, power, and regulation that spread throughout all Western societies in the nineteenth and twentieth centuries (Foucault 1978).

Peer Group Constraints.   By the 1920s, schools rather than jobs had become the key sites of adolescent experience. Fass noted that high school en-
rollments increased 650 percent between 1900 and 1930, with nearly 60
percent of fourteen- to eighteen-year-olds attending high school by 1930
(1977: 124). The 1920s was the era in which school-based peer groups
were first institutionalized on a mass scale in American society. In the
1930s the Depression greatly increased the numbers of young people in
school because of the scarcity of work; by 1939, nearly 75 percent of
American youth of appropriate age were attending high school (Palladino
1996: 45). Dramatic as these numbers are, they do not tell the whole social
story of the youth culture that was fomenting in the schools. A far smaller
proportion of American youth went on to college in the first half of the
twentieth century, for example, yet the kind of peer culture these students
formed first on college campuses in the 1920s had widespread social consequences. By the decade of the 1930s, the norms, behavior, and style of
this peer-based youth culture had spread to high school students and other
adolescents in the United States.

One of the most striking aspects of school-based peer culture was the
degree of social conformity it demanded. In her study of college students in
the 1920s, Fass noted that "peer groups helped to homogenize patterns of
behavior and attitudes among increasingly diverse elements of the school
population" (1977: 126). College culture was defined by fads and fashion,
and these were widely disseminated throughout American society through
the movies, popular magazines, and the new national industry of advertising. Youth culture was built on a demographic foundation, but it took
shape in the context of an expanding consumer culture. The centrality of a
consumerist ethic was particularly pronounced in the norms about dating
and sexuality that developed among both college- and high school-based
peer groups in this era.

When young working-class women flooded into the labor market in the
early twentieth century, they found themselves in a new and highly age-
graded working environment with patterns of sociability that were focused
around heterosexual relationships, fashion, and the uses of leisure time. In
that case, the new opportunities for independence presented by the world
of work were often traded for a social world emphasizing romance, dating,
and marriage. The norms and behavior forged within youth culture from
the 1920s through the mid-1960s also emphasized the primacy of the heterosexual couple and the consumer-based institution of dating. These
norms and behavior were developed by young people themselves, quite au-

tonomously from the standards and expectations that parents, teachers, and counselors had encouraged and promoted. Among college women, as Fass noted, dating was a central activity:

> The average coed went on dates four nights a week, and the more popular had a date every night of the week. Women at Northwestern University made a pact to have a certain number of dateless nights every week in order to have time to do some studying, which suggests both how engrossing and time-consuming the social life of a student could be and how sharp the competition for popularity. All had to agree so that no one girl might get a competitive edge (1977: 200).

Through this dating system and the expectations that governed it, young people on college campuses in the 1920s helped usher in the sexual revolution in the twentieth-century United States. They recognized and legitimized a more open expression of female sexuality, although within the limits of a gendered double standard that still judged male and female sexual behavior differently. They expanded the boundaries of acceptable sexual exploration to include petting and necking on the grounds that these forms of erotic expression paved the way for more satisfying relationships within marriage. Indeed, college students in the 1920s were instrumental in helping to establish a new normative standard for emotionally expressive heterosexual relations that would become the basis of the modern companionate marriage. Yet historians have also noted that this trend of sexual liberalization operated within strict limits. Exploratory and revolutionary though their behavior was, college students set and enforced clear limits on what was permissible by scrutinizing the sexual behavior of their peers and harshly condemning those men and, especially, those women who violated the group-defined rules of conduct (Fass 1977: 260–290).

In an article written in 1937 titled "The Rating and Dating Complex," Willard Waller pointed to the rigidly peer-controlled, competitive system through which young people ranked each others' popularity and social status. A system of stratification existed on high school and college campuses in which young men and women were ranked according to various criteria of desirability, with physical beauty and popularity especially important for women and resources, family background, and occupational promise crucial for men. Young people ranked each other according to a status hierarchy of dating desirability, with the most power in the hands of those with the highest status. To be accepted and successful in this peer group culture, young men and women had to compete and to conform. Promoting and preserving one's "reputation" pressed young men into the role of aggressive sexual initiators and young women into the role of vigilant sexual managers. These roles would remain in place through the 1950s and mid-1960s, eroding only with the new normative and behavior changes introduced by the second stage of the sexual revolution in the late 1960s and beyond (May 1988; Rubin 1990; Breines 1992).

The development of youth-based peer groups on college campuses in the 1920s and in the high schools from the 1930s on thus provided the young with new opportunities to redefine sexual norms and behavior. Through their segregation in age-graded school settings and their considerable degree of freedom from the supervision of adults, young people forged the basis of a new peer-defined and self-regulated culture. This culture encouraged casual heterosexual mixing on college campuses and in the high schools. It paved the way for a new sexual ethos in American society by promoting romantic love, dyadic intimacy, and a more eroticized sexuality as the appropriate precursors to marriage. Although the peer-group sanctions of the 1920s were powerful enough to keep premarital erotic expression within bounds, it is easy to see how, once normatively established, a link drawn between sex and love could be expanded to justify premarital sexual intercourse among soon-to-be-married, engaged couples. The most reliable studies of the sexual behavior of college students in the 1930s found that one-fourth of the women and half of the men sampled had experienced sexual intercourse (by the median ages of seventeen for men and eighteen for women) and that, at the time of their marriages, 47 percent of college-educated women had had sexual intercourse, although most with limited frequency and exclusively with their future husband (Fass 1977: 275–276).

Sexuality among the young became more permissible in the first half of the twentieth century within the context of an expanded marriage system based on romantic love. Female sexuality, although more openly expressed in this era, could be called marriage-directed since the majority of college women in the 1930s saw marriage as their primary goal. A 1949 article in the *New York Times Magazine* tracing 784 graduates from the Seven Sisters colleges' class of 1934 found that the majority had married within four years of their graduation. Over the next fifteen years, most were occupied as housewives and mothers; only 12 percent were working outside the home in 1949 (Ware 1982: 67–68). Although the topic of marriage will be explored in greater depth in the next chapter, it is worth noting here that adolescents were allowed more scope in their sexual behavior only when that behavior appeared to be in tune with the general cultural norms and therefore more socially manageable. If adolescent girls could be predictably and willingly channeled into marriage, then their early expression of sexuality was no longer as socially threatening as it had seemed when it first broke out of the strictures of traditional family and community controls. In her analysis of the moral panic over adolescent sexuality that characterized the age-of-consent and white slavery campaigns of the late nineteenth and early twentieth centuries, Nathanson (1991) astutely noted that it was the "domestication of adolescent female sexuality"—that is, its reinterpretation from being dangerously unorthodox to being a first step into marriage—that soothed the intense social anxieties behind those campaigns by the 1920s. Because adolescent female sexuality could be appropriately channeled and ultimately contained—either by propelling girls into marriage or by controlling their behavior through the array of new social institutions and state regulations—public anxiety subsided for a while, at least until a new era of social change in the late twentieth century again targeted the sexuality of adolescent girls as a serious social problem.

By the 1920s, the dominant culture had wholeheartedly adopted the new social ethic that the young had so brazenly ushered in only a few decades earlier. Adults could chastise youth for their adherence to the new; they could punish them if they appeared to be too uncontrollable. But adults also usurped the attitudes and behavior of the young as their own. Fass has argued that "through a complex process of vicarious association with youth styles and vicarious self-condemnation of youth's behavior, Americans used youth at once to denounce change and to adapt to it" (1977: 234). The ambivalence about youth that many adults continue to feel—particularly in their association of the young with all of the pleasures and dangers of social change—has been a persistent theme since the nineteenth century.

Contemporary Dilemmas of Adolescent Sexuality

Young people today face many changed circumstances, but also some striking continuities in the ways adults attempt, with considerable ambivalence, to protect and control them. The concerns about adolescent sexuality today (How much, if any, is permissible and at what age? What kind of social problem or danger does such sexual expression among the young represent?) suggest that there is still considerable adult anxiety about young people as the representatives and active agents of social change in sexual norms and behaviors. The themes of romantic love, dyadic intimacy, and greater sexual permissiveness that the young helped introduce in American culture in the early twentieth century are now well entrenched and quite widespread as the dominant ethos. But rather than seeing teenagers, for example, as moving along an appropriate developmental continuum in which they are preparing to acquire the socially condoned attitudes and behavior of adulthood, many adults in the latter part of the twentieth century have identified some new social problems exclusively associated with adolescence. Since the mid-1970s, adult concerns have taken the form of widespread social anxiety about teenage pregnancy and young, single mothers on welfare.

Not surprisingly, given the history of adolescent sexuality, social alarm continues to be primarily focused on the attitudes and behavior of young women. This is the case not only because of historical precedent but for a number of sociological reasons. First, the social threat posed by unregulated female sexuality is, more precisely, a threat to the family-based social order resulting from illegitimacy. Sociologists, following Malinowski, have long recognized the socially conservative, stabilizing function of the principle of legitimacy: the social rule that children be identified not only with a particular care-taking mother but with a socially recognized father who confers all the benefits of social placement on that child (i.e., a set of kin, rank and status, and inheritance rights).[3] Therefore, female sexual experience and the potential for nonmarital conception and illegitimate childbirth that are its consequences always threaten to produce social disruption with high social costs. In times of rapid social change, that threat seems particularly tangible.

Second, social observers and policy makers from the 1970s to the late 1990s who have expressed alarm about adolescent sexuality have, in fact, been responding to dramatic demographic trends and evidence of real social changes in the sexual attitudes and behaviors of young people. During the decade of the 1960s the number of adolescents relative to adults in the U.S. population increased more dramatically than ever before. Because of their sheer numbers, then, postwar baby boomers reached adolescence in a highly visible way. As they entered the public sphere, a new industry charting and analyzing youth culture was born.[4] From the late 1960s on, young people were specifically identified as the source of many new political, social, and cultural problems. Sexual permissiveness in the culture at large and the adoption of new, visible sexual attitudes and behavior by the young headed the list of these new social problems. How the problem of adolescent sexuality was interpreted depended once again on the political lens through which young people were viewed. Liberals tended to stress the immaturity of adolescents, extending the category of vulnerable children to encompass them, and hence focused on the danger that early adoption of adult behavior posed. Conservatives focused on the rebelliousness of teenagers and the problematic way in which their behavior signaled the breakdown of familial and social controls.

The second wave of the sexual revolution that began in the late 1960s and early 1970s highlighted the sexual behavior of young women rather than young men because it was women's younger age at first sexual encounter and greater frequency of premarital sexual intercourse that constituted the basis of this revolution. In fact, the sexual revolution among young people in the 1970s and beyond can largely be summed up as young women, especially white, middle-class young women, catching up with the sexual experience of their male peers (Kantner and Zelnik 1972). From one perspective, the dissolution of a sexual double standard was cause for celebration. In the early twentieth century, Havelock Ellis and other critics of Victorian sexual norms and ideology had promoted the idea that sexuality unconstrained by societal conventions and rules would bring fulfillment and liberation. But the widespread acceptance of the belief that sexual liberalization was easy and unproblematic for young women was soon reassessed in light of the expansion of a sex industry that demonstrated a great capacity for sexual exploitation and sexual coercion (Schur 1988). Clearly, young men and young women can both be exploited and coerced by this sex industry, but the focus of social attention has continued to be on adolescent women, their nonmarital patterns of sexual behavior and reproduction, and the resulting social need for both their protection and control.

The Sexual Revolution Among Adolescents

Estimates of adolescent sexual behavior for most of the twentieth century are scarce. Not until 1971, for example, were national survey data on age of first intercourse collected (Brooks-Gunn and Furstenberg 1989: 250), and this variable—despite its limitations as a full measure of sexual behavior—remains the primary one used in most contemporary studies. An explanation of adolescent sexuality must first begin with the recognition that the age of puberty has substantially decreased over time. Primarily because of changes in health, diet, and nutrition, American girls in the 1990s first experience menstruation at about 12.5 years; in 1890 they did so at 14.8 years, whereas in colonial America those ages were closer to 15 or 16. This decrease in age at puberty is striking in itself, but coupled with an expanded interval between puberty and marriage (from approximately 5 years for women in colonial America, to 7.2 years for women in 1890, to 11.8 years for women and 12.5 years for men in 1988), it reveals just how elongated the period of adolescence has become (Alan Guttmacher Institute 1994: 7; Vinovskis 1988: 4). With a longer period of adolescence, of course, there is expanded opportunity for young people to engage in premarital sex. Whether or not they do so depends on the power of social sanctions to curb and contain that behavior. When new values promote sexuality as an avenue of emotional expressiveness, when norms about sexual experience become more permissive, and when the age at marriage begins a steady climb as it has since 1970, the social context becomes far more conducive for—even encouraging of—premarital sexual behavior.

This coalescing of social patterns is essentially the story of what happened to change the sexual behavior of young Americans over the course of the twentieth century. The Kinsey studies reported that about 14 percent of women born before 1900 and still unmarried at age twenty-five had had

premarital sexual experience, compared with 36 percent women born in
the 1900–1909 cohort—the latter, of course, young women who came of
age in the era of liberalization during the 1910s and 1920s (Kinsey et al.
1953). Much of this shift in the patterns of women's sexual behavior can
be explained as "engagement sex"—the greater social acceptance of having
limited sexual experience with a future spouse in the period preceding the
marriage. For men, premarital sexual experience was historically far more
routine and predictable than that of women. The Kinsey studies showed
that the majority of young men surveyed had had some sexual experience
before marriage, although there were differences in premarital sexual experience according to education level among men with a college or high
school education (68 percent and 85 percent, respectively) and those who
had not gone beyond the eighth grade (98 percent) (Kinsey et al. 1948).
But among women—white, middle-class women in particular—sexual experience in adolescence began to increase dramatically, especially after
midcentury.

By the mid-1950s, just over a quarter of women surveyed had had some
sexual experience by the age of eighteen. The biggest increase occurred in
the decade of the 1970s, when the sexual experience of white women aged
fifteen to nineteen jumped from approximately 30 percent in 1971 to 46
percent in 1979 (Zelnik, Kantner, and Ford 1981). By 1983, the National
Longitudinal Survey of Youth could report that 60 percent of black men
had had sexual intercourse by age sixteen (42 percent by age 15 or earlier);
60 percent of black women and 60 percent of white men had this experience by age eighteen; and 60 percent of white women joined the ranks of
the sexually initiated by age nineteen (Brooks-Gunn and Furstenberg 1989:
251). The general pattern has been one of earlier age of sexual intercourse
in adolescence and, ultimately, of a majority of young people today having
had some sexual experience as teenagers.

What has become a majority experience in terms of behavior in the late
twentieth century is not necessarily socially condoned, however, particularly if adolescent sexuality results in premarital pregnancy and childbirth.
Perhaps not surprisingly, given the historical precedent of intense social
anxiety generated around changing patterns of female sexuality in the late
nineteenth and early twentieth centuries, social concern once again flared
up, this time around a perceived epidemic of adolescent pregnancy, in the
late 1970s. This era's version of the wayward girl was the pregnant
teenager, a sexualized adolescent whose behavior had newly visible, costly
reproductive consequences. The sexual revolution among the young was
first and foremost a revolution in effectively separating sex from marriage,
and the social consequences of this separation continue to have repercussions in the debate about adolescence and the role of young people in
American society.

The Reproductive Revolution:
Trends in Premarital and Nonmarital Pregnancy

Premarital pregnancy among young women in the historical past was constrained by their late age in reaching sexual maturity and their relatively early age at marriage. But these demographic facts only set the basic parameters within which behavior could vary greatly. In colonial New England, for example, there was a low rate of premarital pregnancy in the seventeenth century, in keeping with the Puritans' emphasis on internalized self-control and the external pressures of community sanction. But by the second half of the eighteenth century, as the power of Puritan institutions and ideology waned and new social values about love and sexuality in the context of marriage began to take hold, there was a sharp increase in the rate of premarital pregnancies. This pattern did not become a permanent feature of American social life, however. By the early nineteenth century there was once again a sharp decline in the rate of premarital pregnancies in the United States, a trend which preceded by half a century a similar downturn in premarital pregnancy rates in western Europe. Historians accounting for this decline have pointed to a variety of new social constraints on premarital sexual behavior that arose in the early-nineteenth-century United States: the wave of evangelical religious revivals that swept through the Northeast; a new ideology about proper womanhood that stressed respectable women's piety, purity, and passionlessness; and the rising social power of the medical establishment that successfully redefined sexuality as behavior falling under its umbrella of control (Smith and Hindus 1975; Vinovskis 1988). All of these social forces converged in the early nineteenth century to restrain the sexual behavior of young people outside of marriage for nearly another century.

One of the most striking aspects of the historical trends in premarital pregnancy rates is that they were not always considered problematic, even when they occurred among adolescents. Paradoxically, the 1950s was the era in American history when the adolescent birthrate peaked, with the United States leading all major industrial countries (Nathanson 1991; Luker 1996). White, middle-class, single-but-pregnant girls generally faced three options in the era between the 1950s and early 1970s: They were propelled by pregnancy into an early marriage; they privately arranged with a doctor for an abortion; or they were hidden from public view in a maternity home for the duration of their pregnancy and encouraged to put their baby up for adoption after delivery. Black, single, pregnant women more often remained at home in their communities and were far less likely to put their children up for adoption, a response to illegitimacy and family formation that was considered pathological and socially irresponsible by white, middle-class social service workers and policy-making legislators.

In the 1950s, the cause of pregnancy among single white women was explained in psychological terms, while pregnancy among single black women was attributed to biology—a racial distinction that has had significant staying power in the characterization of the social problem of adolescent pregnancy (Solinger 1992). One consequence of this racialized construction of teenage pregnancy has been to accentuate the public perception of out-of-wedlock childbirth and single-motherhood as an exclusively black issue. White illegitimacy rates, even though increasing rapidly, were initially hidden from public view. The truly revolutionary shift taking place in American family patterns beginning in the 1970s and continuing through the 1990s has not only been the separation of sex from reproduction made possible by the availability of contraception (especially with the introduction of the birth control pill in 1960) and the legalization of abortion (in 1973) but also the growing tendency among women of all ages, races, and social classes to separate reproduction from marriage (Cherlin 1992; Nathanson 1991).

Social Construction of a Teenage Pregnancy Epidemic

The changes taking place in sexual and reproductive behavior that have so dramatically affected the nature of family life in the late-twentieth-century United States were not (and are not) exclusively the experience of teenagers. They are changes that characterize the experience of adults as well. But by the end of the 1970s, a decade of great social, economic, and political changes in American society, teenagers were the most visible representatives of the forces of social change and the ones most closely associated with adults' generalized anxieties about an uncertain future. Their marginality made them easier to label as a social problem than their adult counterparts, whose marital and family patterns, as I will argue in the next chapter, were also undergoing rapid and unsettling change. When the marginal status of the young was coupled with the ambivalence that Americans had long felt toward the life stage of adolescence—as a period in which the young hovered uneasily between vulnerable childhood and full-fledged, responsible adulthood—adolescents seemed to personify trouble in the American family and in the society at large. Did they need protection or control? This perennial question, which had dominated the discourse and public policy about adolescents for at least a century, resurfaced in the late 1970s as teenagers, especially teenage girls, became the concentrated focus of media, social science research, political lobbyist, and legislative attention.

By 1970, the federal government had recognized the need to respond to the dual problems of poverty and population growth by funding the "Title X Family Planning Services and Population Research Act" to help reduce unintended pregnancies among poor women. Although from the mid-nineteenth century through the early twentieth century population fears had focused on "race suicide" as a result of the declining birth rates among white, middle-class American women, by the 1960s the public concern had been reformulated as a problem of the excessive fertility of the poor (Brodie 1994; Luker 1996: 52). Poor women of all ages were seen as the source of a serious population problem, and poor African American women, who were now overrepresented among recipients in the Aid to Families with Dependent Children (AFDC) welfare program, were especially singled out as in need of contraceptive services or even more stringent forms of fertility control, such as sterilization.

Teenage mothers were not specifically identified as a group separate from other poor women until the mid-1970s when the Carter administration made the issue of adolescent pregnancy one of its top domestic legislative priorities with the "Adolescent Health, Services, and Pregnancy Prevention and Care Act of 1978" (Vinovskis 1988: 22). As a number of researchers have since pointed out, the rhetoric of an epidemic of adolescent pregnancy that accompanied the passage of this legislation was overblown and historically inaccurate, since the American adolescent birthrate had peaked some twenty years earlier. It was not the fact of rising rates of teenage pregnancy, then, as much as the new visibility of adolescent women's sexuality that gave definition to this social problem. The narrative of adolescent sexuality and of nonmarital, teenage fertility raging out of control emerged in this era because a coalition of youth advocates, physicians, and legislators found it in their interests to mobilize around this issue and because it was a narrative that made sense of a number of unsettling social changes to an anxious public (Vinovskis 1988; Nathanson 1991; Luker 1996). A complicated history of social and cultural changes in sexual attitudes and behaviors, of economic and political events with repercussions in family life, of rising rates of poverty and social divisions in a postindustrial society was thus simplified into a story in which teenagers, themselves barely out of childhood, were having babies and in so doing, heading inevitably into a life of poverty. According to this story, the sexual revolution placed all teenage girls at equal risk of teenage pregnancy and subsequent poverty, a theme that served to mute the more divisive and controversial issues of nonmarital childbearing, welfare, and race.

The way in which these issues have become intertwined and politicized will be explored in more detail in the next chapter, but here it is relevant to note that the concept of teenage pregnancy had the capacity to raise widespread alarm and to elicit a range of policy responses because it was framed as a universal problem, affecting girls of all races and socioeconomic levels. Following the story line that was developed in this era, the solution—as presented by the newly powerful lobbyists for Planned Parenthood, by physicians who defined birth control as a health issue falling exclusively within their professional sphere of competence and control, and by policy makers who were vocal advocates for youth—was to provide adolescents with access to affordable contraception (Luker 1996). Through this narrative, then, the prevention of unwanted pregnancy seemed to provide a rational and technological solution to a host of complex social problems with teenagers at their core.

Conclusion

The overly simplified story of adolescent sexuality and its reproductive consequences that is encompassed in the fears about an epidemic of teenage pregnancy did little to address the underlying structural changes in Americans' social and familial lives, which continue to generate waves of social, cultural, and political anxiety. As Luker has pointed out, young motherhood is more specifically a consequence of being poor rather than the cause of poverty (1996: 40). As Vinovskis (1988) has suggested, the narrow and ahistorical framing of the debate over adolescent pregnancy in the 1970s only temporarily disguised the issues that would resurface again in the 1980s and 1990s in an even more divisive cultural debate about the legitimacy of the sexual revolution, about the uses of contraception and abortion, and—most fundamentally—about the rights of teenagers versus the rights of their parents to know about, monitor, and regulate their sexual behavior. These issues have become more heated and controversial in recent years as the contradictory images of vulnerable teenage mothers ("babies having babies") and promiscuous, welfare-dependent, single mothers have come to dominate the political rhetoric.

As was true in the late nineteenth century, the sexuality of adolescent females became the central focus of widespread public debate in the late twentieth century, another era in which social changes were fundamentally transforming gender and family roles among all age groups across the society. The sexuality of women has always been more subject to social control than that of men because of the nature of gendered power relations and because of the societal consequences of unregulated reproduction. But the specific periods in which young women's sexuality was targeted as especially problematic and in need of social control overlapped with other profound social changes in American society. One could argue that it is not adolescent sexuality itself that is inherently problematic but what it represents and how it gets played out in the context of fluid social relationships and changing social structures. Nonmarital pregnancy is threatening because it represents "the ultimate loss of control: by a man driven by his lust, by the girl's mother who failed in her job of supervision, by the young woman who was overcome by passion (or drugs or alcohol or lack of ambition), or by the community in which early sex and childbearing were insufficiently stigmatized" (Nathanson 1991: 7).

It is this sense of loss of control that the image and behavioral reality of adolescent sexuality so powerfully evokes for adults. The promise of sexual experience was once the lure that enticed young adults into marriage. Married life provided the framework and context in which childbearing ideally took place. Now, however, young men and women are part of a culture in which sexuality can be expressed more openly and separated from reproduction. The ties that traditionally bound people to marriage have weakened, and it is precisely this threat—the capacity to evade the constraints imposed by adult responsibilities in marriage and family life—that modern adolescence epitomizes. When they appear to have the cultural and social power to challenge the conventions and change the rules rather than simply pass through a transitory life stage on the way from childhood to adulthood, adolescents seem threatening and in need of social restraint and parental control. If sexual expression is so freely available to the young, what will induce them to accept the mantle of adult responsibility so fully encompassed in the obligations of family life?

Notes

1. Simon Frith, *Sound Effects: Youth, Leisure, and the Politics of Rock 'n' Roll* (New York: Pantheon, 1981) discusses the significance of rock and roll in providing a sense of identity and coherence to youth culture. Barbara Ehrenreich, Elizabeth Hess and Gloria Jacobs, in *Remaking Love: The Feminization of Sex* (New York: Doubleday, 1986) argue that the cultural phenomenon of "Beatlemania" represented not only a social manifestation of this emergent youth culture in the early 1960s but a historically new kind of public display of adolescent female sexuality.

2. In many cultures and historical eras, women have been physically contained within private domestic spheres or veiled when in public because of the fears about the power of their sexuality to disrupt the social order (M. M. Charrad, *The Origins of Women's Rights: State and Tribe in Tunisia, Algeria, and Morocco*, forthcoming. See, especially, chapter three, "Women Allying with the Devil: Gender, Unity, and Division"). The ideology of female passionlessness that prevailed in the United States in the nineteenth century may appear to have contradicted this view of women's sexual threat, but there are at least two qualifications to this seeming contradiction. In the first place, it applied primarily to white, middle-class women; all others were presumed to be sexualized and therefore more socially dangerous (Cott 1979b). Secondly, the ideology applied to white women as long as they were relegated to the "separate sphere" of the private household. As women moved into more public roles (sometimes precisely because of their presumed moral virtuousness), the belief in essential passionlessness was more difficult to sustain.

3. The principle of legitimacy appears to be a normative—although not a behavioral—universal in all societies. This does not make it a necessary rule for a society, just a remarkably efficient and effective way to ensure the socialization and social placement of offspring and for entrenched elites to protect the existing stratification of their society. The principle of legitimacy can be violated, and it routinely is in the case of poor people who have children outside of marriage although they express a preference not to or in the case of successful revolutionaries who have a vested interest in overturning the inherited privileges and status order of the old regime. Such revolutionaries usually reinstate the principle of legitimacy once it is in their own interest to do so—another indication of the usefulness of this social rule. See articles by Malinowski, Goode, Freilich and Coser, and Coser and Coser, in Rose Coser, ed., *The Family: Its Structures and Functions, 2d ed.,* (New York: St. Martin's Press, 1974).

4. Paul Goodman, *Growing Up Absurd: Problems of Youth in the Organized System* (New York: Random, 1960); Erik H. Erikson, ed., *The Challenge of Youth* (New York: Anchor Books, 1965); Kenneth Keniston, *The Uncommitted: Alienated Youth in American Society* (New York: Dell, 1965) and *Youth and Dissent: The Rise of a New Opposition* (New York: Harcourt Brace Jovanovich, 1971) are examples of the kinds of youth culture analysis that emerged with the new demographic visibility of the baby boomers. By the 1990s, books about youth tended to focus on gangs (e.g., Luis Rodriguez's *Always Running* [1993]) or on problem kids (e.g., Donna Gaines, *Teenage Wasteland: Suburbia's Dead End Kids* [New York: HarperCollins, 1991]; Charles R. Acland, *Youth, Murder, Spectacle: The Cultural Politics of "Youth in Crisis"* [Boulder, Colo.: Westview Press, 1995]; and Henry S. Giroux, *Fugitive Cultures: Race, Violence, and Youth* [New York: Routledge, 1996]).

4

Marriage

For many people in the United States and for most of its history, love, marriage, childbearing, and childrearing have defined the package of growing up and assuming the status of adulthood. Getting a job, leaving home, achieving financial independence—all of these traditional markers of youth entering adulthood—have, at least since the Great Depression, been shaped by the state of the economy and other social and political forces. Becoming an adult by these measures, from the vantage point of the late twentieth century, seems largely outside of individual control. But falling in love and its logical corollary—getting married—seem to Americans to be the most individualistic choices they ever make in their lives. These choices matter to Americans. The United States is among the most prone-to-marry societies in the world.

But all is not well with the institution of American marriage. In recent decades, young people have been postponing marriage, possibly putting it off altogether. More women are having children outside of marriage, ignoring the traditionally sanctioned sequence of love and marriage followed by childbearing. Overt challenges to the culturally dominant model of the heterosexual couple are far more visible and accepted than ever before. Among those who do marry, the divorce rate has reached epidemic proportions, widely cited in the popular press as one out of two marriages ending in divorce.[1] The United States has achieved the dubious distinction of having one of the highest divorce rates of all industrialized societies in the world. A strong commitment to marriage and the family—the one choice to enter full adulthood that is seemingly within our control—appears to have eroded. To many, the institution of marriage is in jeopardy, which seems particularly disturbing because it is the one arena in which we seem to have only ourselves and our eroding sense of long-term commitment to intimate relationships to blame. A "marriage crisis," the result of an apparent retreat from and declining commitment to marriage by Amer-

93

ican adults, is taken as yet another sign of eroding family values in the United States at the end of the twentieth century.

The perception of crisis, on the one hand, and marital patterns of American adults, on the other, are not always easy to match up. A snapshot of the current situation in the United States shows that marriage is still the majority experience for men and women of all racial-ethnic groups, even though there are significant variations. In 1996, for example, approximately 83 percent of white women and 76 percent of white men aged eighteen or older had ever been married (that is, were currently married, widowed, or divorced). Seventy-six percent of Hispanic women and 64 percent of Hispanic men, as well as 63 percent of black women and 58 percent of black men, were in this category of the ever-married (U.S. Bureau of the Census 1997: 55). Looking at marital status by age is even more telling about how normative the experience of marriage in the United States is. In 1996, although only a small minority of women and men aged eighteen to nineteen were ever married (8 percent and 2 percent, respectively), some 29 percent of American women and 18 percent of men acquired this status by the ages of twenty to twenty-four. Between the ages of twenty-five and twenty-nine, a majority of American women (56 percent) and 44 percent of American men had been married at least once. Before reaching age thirty-five, 69 percent of women and 62 percent of men in the United States have been married, and, over the rest of the adult life span, nearly 95 percent of Americans have had this experience (U.S. Bureau of the Census 1997: 56).

Given these numbers, it is not surprising that many assume marriage to be the natural state of things, a status that defines becoming an adult. But the fact that marriage continues to be a majority experience for Americans for some portion of their adult lives does not address the questions of why marriage rates vary by group, what marriage means to those who experience it, or why marriages dissolve at such a high rate. These questions are addressed in this chapter in an attempt to understand why most Americans choose marriage, how they get married, and what they both expect and experience in that institution. But to investigate modern marriage is also to open questions about its alternatives. What does it mean that there are more alternatives to marriage than ever before? To what extent does the growing acceptance of many of these alternatives have a corrosive effect on the institution of marriage itself, challenging its dominance as an adult life stage and undermining couples' commitment to a permanent relationship in the face of new choices?

Why Marry? Traditional and Modern Perspectives

Most Americans would be puzzled by the sociologist's question "why do people marry?" since it seems obvious that they do so as a natural response to falling in love. And since love is personally experienced as a set of physiological emotions, the answer seems rooted more in biology and psychology than in the sociologist's realm of culture and society. But such an individually based explanation of love and marriage does not account for its broader sociological importance. The institution of marriage is found in some form in all human societies because it is an effective way to ensure societal continuity through reproduction and socialization, as well as societal extension through the kinds of alliances that are produced when families are joined. If societies are to persist, they need both intergenerational continuity (that is, to perpetuate themselves over time through reproduction) and intragenerational extension (that is, to establish interconnected alliances among families in a particular period). Such concern about family continuity and extension was always prevalent among European royalty, for example, for whom keeping the family dynasty going with adequate numbers of legitimate male heirs and building political and economic alliances through strategic marriages of sons and daughters was common practice. Family building was thus a prime means of consolidating and maintaining power among those with access to important resources, and most of the norms, customs, prohibitions, and taboos governing family life, such as the control over sexuality and reproduction, can be understood as strategic attempts to control the family patterns of descent, succession, and inheritance.

The same dynamic, though less rigorously and self-consciously pursued, characterizes families at all social levels. Marriage matters because it has consequences for the members of extended families, not just for the couple themselves. Sociologists therefore make the claim that marriage is not primarily an individual act but a social one. All societies have some vested interest in promoting it, since marriage has been the most systematically effective means of promoting societal longevity. Socially recognized marriage, across cultures, is the only sanctioned context for having children, and in most cases the marital bond helps solidify a family unit in which children will be cared for and raised to become socially productive adults. So it is not surprising that most societies will provide a variety of incentives, inducements, and forms of coercion to get young people bound together in marriage and thereby establish new family units. Rarely is marriage left entirely to chance. From child betrothal to bride abduction to the arranged marriages of young adults by members of their extended families in traditional societies, and from explicit guidance to implicit pressures in modern ones, there are multiple ways of ensuring that marriage will happen in systematic and regulated ways.

In most traditional societies in which the family is the only social institution available to provide the social support services individuals need, marriage is a necessity because it forms the nuclear family unit that will be the core of the social order. Gender is one socially sanctioned category through which the division of labor is established in most societies, and marriage serves to institutionalize the provision of services by both men and women living together within households. A division of labor by gender within marriage has defined the "traditional" American family according to both custom and law, with men responsible for economic provision and women for household maintenance and childcare. Marriage was also the primary way that young people gained any measure of autonomy as adults; to remain unmarried in traditional societies was to be relegated to a perpetually dependent status in the household of one's parents or older siblings. The function of marriage under such social and economic conditions has been called "instrumental" because marriage operated as a pragmatic necessity for both men and women. Although marriage is important in societies with extended family systems—those that are organized around wider kin relations beyond parents and children—it becomes an even greater necessity in societies like the United States that have always considered the core family unit to be the heterosexual couple and their dependent offspring. To be without a spouse in a society based on nuclear families (parents and children) and in which there existed few other social institutions that provided supportive services was to be truly vulnerable. This was the case in early America, a society in which marriage and family carried a particular meaning and relationship to the community that we have lost today.

Marriage in Preindustrial Society

Marriage in colonial America was never part of a formal arranged-marriage system, although it involved parents and other adult authorities in the community far more extensively than most young couples in the United States today would likely either encourage or welcome. The marriage system of the seventeenth and early eighteenth centuries might best be described as one that was open to choice but highly regulated. For the most distinctive characteristic about marriages in colonial America was that they were contracted in a community context, and the families that resulted from them were neither private nor autonomous. Marriage required parental consent, for example, or masters' consent in the case of servants and apprentices. Courts were not reticent about punishing those who married or published banns without such prior consent, and after marriage, parents, neighbors, and authorities all continued to intervene and wield influence over the newlyweds (Wall 1990). Marriage addressed the instrumental needs of individuals for economic provision and of communities for the social regulation of people within family units. It was understood as both a pragmatic necessity and an important step in the process of achieving adulthood and acquiring an independent household. It was fundamentally a social act, however, rather than a personal and private one. To get married was to enter into a wider community-based web of social relations and to accept a set of social values and obligations that included intensive community scrutiny and the subjugation of individual interests to larger, collective goals.

Despite the high level of oversight over their marriage choices (from a late-twentieth-century perspective), many of the young people in colonial America wished for even more parental involvement than they apparently received, for they understood their decisions about marital partners to be momentous ones. Young men in seventeenth- and early-eighteenth-century New England were likely to speak of marriage as their "debt to society," whereas young women worried more specifically about their personal choice of marriage partner, with a bad choice potentially subjecting them to economic and emotional hardships from which there would be little opportunity to escape (Norton 1980: 40–46). Both understood marriage as something more than just one life choice among many. It was the most fundamentally important and momentous choice in adult life one would make—the tie that created the family unit and brought young adults fully into the circle of community life.

Marriage in colonial America was generally a lifetime choice. It required parental and community approval to contract and the sanction of powerful authorities to dissolve. Divorce was relatively rare and was granted only in those unusual cases where preserving the marriage produced more conflict and community disruption than ending it or, in the case of spousal desertion, where abandoned wives and children would require the community's financial assistance if remarriage could not occur. In most cases, the authorities simply refused divorce petitions. Wall (1990) cites the case of a seventeenth-century Salem wife who claimed that her husband's "base, brutish, and Inhumane carriage [made it] Impossible . . . to live with such a Tyrant." The court ordered her first to return home, and then, a year later, following another plea for a divorce decree based on his abusive behavior, they levied a fine against the husband. A New York woman who claimed in her divorce petition that "she would prefer to be dead or imprisoned for life rather than live with [her husband]" was forcibly returned to him and then encouraged to accept a reconciliation mediated by outside authorities (Wall 1990: 81–82). As these examples suggest, marriage established a social obligation that was not readily abandoned. Authorities were loathe to dissolve marriages because they believed this would pose a threat to morality, social order, and the system of economic provision that was rooted in the family. When marriages ended, they generally did so because of the death of one of the spouses, particularly in Virginia and Maryland where mortality conditions were especially harsh. Remarriage was often swift for both men and women, signaling not so much the lack of emotional commitment in the former marriage as the instrumental necessity of having a spouse.

Age at first marriage is another indicator of how necessary or useful marriage is in a particular era. In the seventeenth and eighteenth centuries young men married in their mid-to-late twenties, requiring some measure of economic independence before they could assume family support. Young women in colonial America married around age 20, at younger ages than their European counterparts, suggesting that the demographic demand for wives in a colonial society was great. This pattern of early age at first marriage for women was most evident in the Chesapeake region, where the gender imbalance was greatest and wives were most in demand.

An instrumental approach to marriage did not preclude love and attachment between spouses. The Puritans saw marriage as a covenant and love between spouses as a sign of that shared agreement. Yet there was still a necessity behind marriage in this traditionally based, preindustrial society, and the social obligation that came with marital status always took precedence over the affective ties between spouses or between parents and children. For one thing, marriage and the family structure it created helped preserve the hierarchical nature of the Puritan community. A man was the head of his family and responsible for social order within it, just as the Puritan male elders were the recognized heads of the church and commonwealth. For another, the gendered division of labor that was characteristic of a domestic or household economy made spouses economically useful to one another. Men's jobs of planting, harvesting, hunting, and fishing were seasonal and cyclical. Women's housework, on the other hand, involved the repetitive tasks of cleaning, washing, ironing, cooking, baking, sewing, and knitting, and was often experienced as drudgery by colonial wives. Spinning and weaving were so closely associated with their understanding of women's roles that eighteenth-century white colonists were shocked to find Native American women spending their time cultivating crops instead. Visitors and missionaries attempted to inculcate a more appropriate notion of femininity among Native American women by introducing them to the proper women's work of cloth production (Norton 1980: 18–20, 1996: 5–6).

So established were these gendered expectations of the duties of men and women in marriage that claims that a spouse did not fulfill his or her given role were readily cited in divorce petitions. Through the first half of the eighteenth century, divorce petitioners in Massachusetts cited such reasons as a spouse's unbecoming conduct, family neglect, wastefulness, or inadequate economic provision in making their cases to the courts. In fifty-eight petitions submitted between 1736 and 1765, there were no claims of the loss of love or affection as the reasons for the breakup of a marriage (Cott 1979a). Love may have been expected and valued when it appeared between spouses, but it was neither considered the best reason for getting married nor perceived as a defining characteristic of the marital relationship.

The Shift in the Meaning and Uses of Marriage

After the mid–eighteenth century, this community-based marriage system began to change. The great transformation in process in this period was a redefinition of the nature and meaning of marriage: from a previously instrumental relationship, defined as "duty and usefulness," to one based primarily on love, intimacy, and emotional attachment. Divorce petitioners from Massachusetts between 1766 and 1786 began to cite alienated affections, the loss of nuptial happiness, and the rupture of romantic and emotional bonds in the marital relationship in their claims for divorce (Cott 1979a: 123–124). Marriage shifted from being a public institution, scrutinized and regulated by the larger community, to being a private relationship, based on affection. Thomas Paine's article, "Reflections on Unhappy Marriage," written in 1774 after he had separated from his wife in England because of irreconcilable differences, made the case for marriages based solely on love and compatibility. Colonial Americans in the revolutionary era began to draw parallels between individual freedom represented in the voluntary marriage contract and political freedom from an intolerable union with Great Britain. As domestic tyranny and international tyranny were equated, a new language of marital choice and domestic happiness entered the popular vocabulary (Fliegelman 1982).

Following the American Revolution, the structural basis for this change was the transformation of society that accompanied industrialization. As the household economy was increasingly supplanted by a market economy and as new institutions from schools to hospitals, asylums, and welfare agencies began to develop outside the family and subsume some of its previous functions, the uses and meanings of marriage and the family also underwent change. Men and women were less inclined to marry because it was their duty or because they each needed the services that only a spouse could provide and more because they looked for the kind of companionship and emotional attachment that was now expected in a spouse. A host of other social changes, from the decline of a cohesive religious establishment to rapid population growth and migration, also helped bring about these changes in Americans' private lives. The power of the community to oversee and regulate all aspects of personal life was one casualty of these social changes. After the mid–eighteenth century, Americans were less likely to accept the legitimacy of community intervention in their lives. The most dramatic change in the institution of marriage in American history has been this internal transformation in its meanings and uses.

The structure of American marriage—with its continued emphasis on the adult couple as the core of a nuclear family system—has retained its shape over the past three centuries, but the reasons that people choose marriage and the hopes and expectations that they bring to this institution have been radically transformed. This transformation was realized, first, for the middle class for whom the new uses and meanings of marriage as a highly personalized relationship based on love rather than social obligation fit the new emphasis on individualism that was the ideological complement of industrial capitalism. But the ideal of companionate marriage focused around the dyadic relationship was a powerful and pervasive one that spread from its middle-class origins to other class levels throughout the nineteenth and into the twentieth centuries.

Today, romantic love, dyadic intimacy, and the committed emotional support between spouses characterize the ideal of all marriages, from the upper class to the working class. Even European royal marriages—those that were most obviously determined by dynastic calculations in the past—are today subjected to the same standard of intimacy and emotional fulfillment as the marriages of commoners.[2] At the other end of the social class spectrum, working class couples are also now fully enmeshed in a culture of romantic love, reinforced by the popular culture industries of talk-show television, Hollywood movies, pop songs, and national advertising images. Only those ideologically opposed to marriage, those excluded by law from attaining marital status, and the very poor seem to exist outside of this love-marriage nexus. In the latter case, where the resources for family life are the most limited, the commitment to marriage appears to have eroded quite substantially. But for most Americans the equation of love and marriage, and its corollary notion that lack of love leads directly and inevitably to divorce, is a "social fact" that is widely accepted at all social class levels. As the institution of marriage slipped from its mooring of community oversight and control, the choice about whether or not to marry, what to expect from marriage, and—if those expectations were not met—of whether or not to divorce became far more open-ended and individualistic than ever before. Family obligation and community control seemed to have no place in the highly privatized realm of marriage that was emerging by the early nineteenth century.

Love and Marriage:
Couples in an Era of Individualism

Love as the basis for marriage was not a social invention of the nineteenth century, but it did take root then as part of the new ideology of individualism that was coming to define an ascendant middle class. Intense self-reflection was a quality that had always marked American Protestantism, especially New England Puritanism in the seventeenth and early eighteenth centuries. Whereas the emphasis on the individual's private, internal life was prevalent even in a society that was hierarchical and communal in its social structure, full-fledged individualism was suspect in this era and always subordinated to the demands of the community. The religious revivals of the eighteenth century gave new legitimacy to examining the emotional life of individual women and men, and a set of other political, economic, and social changes through the second half of the eighteenth century laid the groundwork for a new self-consciousness about and social acceptance of individualism by the early nineteenth century. Lawrence Stone has referred to this as "affective individualism," a cultural trend toward greater personal autonomy and respect for privacy that encouraged the development of warmer emotional ties between husband and wife and between parents and children (Stone 1977: 221–269).

As much as this ethos seems a given social reality to Americans in the late twentieth century, it is important to be reminded that it was neither easily nor unambiguously accepted as a way of life. Widespread communal alternatives to traditional marriage and the nuclear family and to the rationalized world of industrial capitalism continued to flourish throughout the nineteenth century. The Shakers, the Oneida community, and the Mormons, all with highly different approaches, were intent on creating communal social organizations in which the energies, commitments, and attachments of their members were directed to the larger community and not focused exclusively on the couple or the nuclear family relationship (Kephart 1987; Kanter 1972). "Selfish love" or "too-exclusive love" between husband and wife was understood as a serious threat that could lead to dyadic withdrawal, and the communities developed a wide range of ideological commitments and behavioral strategies—from celibacy to polygamy to "open marriage"—to counteract that threat. Privatism and individualism were tendencies they watched out for with vigilance, recognizing the power of these beliefs to remove people from collective life into the intensity of an exclusive relationship.

Even members of the bourgeois business class, for whom independent entrepreneurialism was an achievable reality in the economic realm, were alarmed by the prospects that too much individualism could undermine the bonds of social life. A long-standing concern of social philosophers and theorists had been the question: How is social order possible? or, What is the social glue that will bind people together into a cohesive social whole? In the early-nineteenth-century United States this question stood out in particularly sharp relief as the political ethic of equality, the economic ethic of independent entrepreneurialism, and the social ethic of individualism provided the threads that began to be interwoven as the foundation of the new social order.

One response to the problem of intense individualism in the United States in the early nineteenth century was a new cultural construction of gender roles in which the idealized masculine traits of independence, toughness, and rugged individualism were balanced by the idealized feminine traits of nurturance, sociability, and other-directedness. The early nineteenth century was an era in which both the gender roles and the socioeconomic roles of men and women were given new definition. The private and protected world of the home, dominated by the repetitive, cyclical demands of domesticity and caretaking, was seen as the appropriate sphere for middle-class women, and their nature—defined as virtuous, pious, pure, and domestic—was interpreted as well suited to these tasks. Men were understood as more naturally suited to the harsh world of competitive capitalism, their inherent individualism more sharply defined than that of women. Thus, the world of the nineteenth-century United States was neatly divided into two spheres, public and private, with men and women defined as having opposite, but mutually complementary, natures attuned to the role demands of those different social spaces. This bifurcation of men/women, culture/nature, and public/private offered one obvious solution to the problem of maintaining social bonds in an era of individualism: the institution of heterosexual marriage (Rubin 1975, 1984). For, through marriage, two incomplete personality halves, opposite by nature, could be united to make a whole. Men's competitive individualism could be tempered by women's orientation to familism.[3] Love would act as the adhesive—the social glue—that would bind people together, at least into the small social worlds of interconnected nuclear families, which would help to mitigate the fragmenting potential of individualism.

Romantic love flourished as a cultural ethic among middle-class Americans in the nineteenth century. Although the gender role prescriptions of this era stated that men and women were diametrically opposed in their natures and sensibilities, in fact much evidence suggests that men, in particular, were expected to maintain strict codes of personal reserve and self-control in public but to show considerable emotional expressiveness in private (Rothman 1984; Lystra 1989). In courtship and within the protected realm of marriage, middle-class men routinely revealed the emotional side of their selves that was rendered invisible in public. "O happy hours when I may once more encircle within these arms the dearest object of my love," wrote one suitor to his fiancée in 1842, "—when I shall again feel the pressure of that 'aching head' which will delight to recline upon my bosom, when I may again press to my heart which palpitates with the purest affection the loved one who has so long shared its undivided devotion" (Rothman 1984: 122). And if men could readily express the sentiments of romantic love, women were no less capable of expressions of sexual passion, despite a prevailing ideology that claimed women's essential passionlessness (Cott 1979b). "Cheek and soul and brain are aflame at the thought of you," wrote a young woman to her suitor in 1867; "every fiber of my being trembles with passionate, weakening thrills" (Rothman 1984: 134). These examples illustrate the rich worlds of emotional intimacy and self-revelation on the part of both men and women that are contained in the private courtship letters of nineteenth-century Victorians, even though the prevailing gender ideologies promoted very different scripts in the public world.

The expression of romantic love between couples encouraged a new emphasis on emotional feeling within the individual and on mutuality and companionship within marriage. Even though power differentials between men and women were reinforced by men's economic advantage in the public world, it is important to recognize that, in private life, new expectations about self-expression, intimacy, and achieving emotional fulfillment through the dyadic relationship gave women a particularly strong role in defining the new goals of marriage. Nineteenth-century social critics recognized women's covert power when they spoke of the "subtle, yet loving, manipulation" with which married women should ensure that their husbands remained closely bound to the social system of the family in their role as economic providers. The shift in the family's center of gravity, from the patriarchal father of the seventeenth and eighteenth centuries to the "moral mother" of the nineteenth century, gave a new legitimacy to women, not only to their role as child rearers but also to the role they assumed in controlling male "passions" in general and, more specifically, in controlling their husbands within marriage (Bloch 1978).

Romantic love, therefore, served a number of important functions in the nineteenth-century United States. It set new standards of emotional experience and behavior for both men and women that reinforced the ethic of individualism emerging in American society. Yet it also moderated the too-intense individualism of men, which was seen as appropriate to the economic world of industrial capitalism but not to private life, by placing new emphasis and importance on the intimate, dyadic relationship that could be achieved within marriage. Nineteenth-century, middle-class Americans began to define love as the sacred bond that led to the most intimate relationship, marriage—no longer simply as an instrumental or pragmatic step in the adult life course. They drew on religious sentiments and traditions to develop, in the words of one historian of this era, "a new theology of romantic love, . . . [which] contributed to the displacement of God by the lover as the central symbol of ultimate significance" (Lystra 1989: 8). Clearly, love could act as a powerful social adhesive in a culture moving toward individualism. The appeals of revealing one's "true self" in an intimate relationship, of having a more expansive range of emotional expression in private than was allowed in public, and of finding a kind of companionship that was not available elsewhere in the social world were powerful inducements to enter into the world of courtship and marriage in young adulthood. How individuals negotiated their way from a romantic relationship to the marital state—and how they did so in such a patterned and systematic way without the mechanism of overtly arranged marriages characteristic of traditional societies—is a key sociological question. Love was, and continues to be, an effective social glue in getting people into marriage, but it operates in the context of a courtship market with its own structure and dynamic that, in the twentieth century in particular, has shaped the social experience of young adults in American society.

The Courtship Market and the Dating System

Who marries whom and how? Love appears to operate as a highly individualistic and idiosyncratic force: irrational, unpredictable, and randomly selective. The cultural aphorisms we hear about love—"love is blind," "all's fair in love and war," or even the medical analogy "love is like the measles; we all have to go through it"—reinforce the idea that love operates spontaneously outside the rules of everyday life. Love seems to be a mystical or sacred force—to many people something not to be scrutinized too closely, particularly not with the calculating rationality of the social scientist. But the aura that surrounds love disguises its routines, predictability, and structures. Currently some 90 percent of Americans marry at least once in their lives, most claiming love as their motivation. And, most strikingly, among marriage partners there will be a great degree of similarity: by class, by race, by religion, and by geographic area. Another cultural aphorism suggests that "like marries like," and this indeed has been the pattern throughout American history, which suggests that structural forces are strongly at work in shaping the most private attitudes and behavior.

Whereas some societies have institutionalized child betrothal, familial arrangement, or strict chaperonage systems to regulate the sexual behavior and marital choices of young women in particular, the potential marriage pool for young Americans has always been shaped more indirectly by powerful but less visible institutional controls. Where people live, where they work, and where they socialize are largely determined by the boundaries of social class and race in American society. Since one is most likely to meet a potential marriage partner in these settings, the general "appropriateness," or similarity, of that potential spouse is, in many cases, already predetermined by the structural arrangements that maintain class solidarity and racial and ethnic divisions within neighborhoods, at work, and in social settings. Ensuring that "like marries like" matters most where there are substantial resources of wealth, status, and power at stake. It is therefore not surprising that the upper class has managed to have the greatest control over the courtship market through the kinds of institutional barriers it has erected and maintained. Upper-class residential enclaves, private schools, country clubs, and debutante balls traditionally acted as the boundaries within which the social life of the young was carried out, as well as the filters that screened out inappropriate marriage partners (DiMaggio 1982; Farrell 1993). Within this circumscribed elite social world, young people could be trusted to choose their own marriage partners since their choices would almost always be deemed appropriate according to social class, or family background, criteria.

Falling in love, then, was defined by the relatively invisible barriers of social class. The economic and social worlds of the middle class and working class were also bounded by distinct social spaces and taste cultures, even though ultimately more permeable than that of the elite. In all of them, a marriage based on love appeared to be exclusively a personal choice, determined by the individual qualities of the other person and the particularity of shared tastes. In American society the relative openness of the marriage system operated through a courtship market that was strongly class specific. Only in modern colleges and universities, as merit has come increasingly to replace family background as the basis for admission, are young people from different class or racial backgrounds likely to meet as potential marriage partners. Here, training for the professions and the opportunity that education creates for mobility into the upper-middle class has tended to blur, if not erase, the significance of family background differences.

Whereas shaping the marriage market through institutional control remained the prerogative of upper-class parents into the twentieth century, the courtship practices of middle-class and working-class Americans took a progressively greater turn away from family controls. Nineteenth-century courtship had been centered in the home, subject to family and community controls. The institution of "calling" located courtship in the family home of a young woman. But, by the early twentieth century, under the influence of the emerging youth culture, courtship shifted to the public world of commercialized leisure. As it did so, dating—a new stage in the courtship system that was not always a direct step toward marriage—became the new behavioral standard.

In her historical account of American courtship conventions, Beth Bailey (1989) argued that the dating system, which developed in the period between 1890 and 1925 and held sway through the first half of the twentieth century, moved courtship into the public world with several long-term consequences. As the world of public leisure replaced the private home as the site of courtship, parental power lessened and the economic power of men—with "men's money [becoming] the basis of the dating system"—altered the balance of power between the courting couple. The severe limits on women's economic power had been institutionalized by the definition of separate spheres in the nineteenth century. But even as young women began to enter the labor force and public social world in the early twentieth century, their limited job options, constricted mobility, and low wages continued to thwart their chances for economic independence.

These economic constraints were carried over to social life as dating came to be defined by a new consumption standard—that of spending money, and an "expensive date" increasingly became the measure of the intrinsic value of a relationship and the extrinsic social status that it was accorded. The economic-status exchange institutionalized in the system of dating in which men traded economic resources for women's attractiveness, popularity, and status honor reinforced gender inequality and served to commodify the relationship. As Bailey has pointed out, the dating system brought love relationships more fully into the realm of peer culture, with its newly defined standard of social and economic competition: "You had to rate in order to date, to date in order to rate. By successfully maintaining this cycle, you became popular. To stay popular, you competed" (Bailey 1989: 30). In its earliest form, the idea of romantic love had contained within it the appealing utopian promise of escape from society. But by the early twentieth century, the utopian promise of the couple's dyadic withdrawal into an internal intimate world was subverted by the rise of a dating system in which love, romance, courtship, and marriage were redefined according to the terms of consumer culture (Illouz 1997). Far from being an occasion to escape society, dating pulled couples ever more forcefully into a market economy, with escalating consumption standards regulated by powerful peer pressures.

The Companionate Marriage Ideal and Its Discontents

One of the many paradoxes of the modern era is that the roles of men and women were loosened from the strictures of community control and dramatically reshaped by the spread of the ethic of affective individualism, but this reshaping often came with unintended and unpredictable consequences. Over the course of American history, women, in particular, have gained new freedom, first as a consequence of the decline of patriarchal families and communities by the middle of the eighteenth century, and then by the redefinition of their role as the idealized "moral mother" in the nineteenth century (Bloch 1978; Kerber 1980). To identify women as more virtuous than men and as best-suited to the task of socializing the next generation was to concede to them an important measure of power. Yet the limitation of this power, confined as it was to the domestic sphere, was evident by the late nineteenth century. By then, middle-class women had experienced half a century of the ideology of domesticity, with its emphasis on their innate virtuousness providing the basis for their collective identity.

This ethic pushed many beyond the boundaries of the domestic sphere as middle-class women began to join campaigns for temperance, antivice, and urban reform. In the late nineteenth and early twentieth centuries, the ideal of women as mothers—to their children, husbands, families, communities, and the nation—provided the impetus for many women to engage in social activism in the public world. Thus, one paradox of this era was that the ideology of domesticity, which had initially defined women's roles as best-suited to the private sphere of the home, ultimately provided the justification for their emergence as activists in a variety of public causes. Another paradox was that the cultural ideal of the "moral mother," coupled with new opportunities for women in education and the professions, resulted in producing, by the late nineteenth and early twentieth centuries, the largest proportion of never-married career women in American history, as college-educated women flocked to the professions of teaching, nursing, and social work and pursued these careers in place of marriage and motherhood.

By the 1920s, following the passage of the Nineteenth Amendment to the U.S. Constitution giving women the right to vote and thus ostensibly according them the status of equal citizens, there was another paradoxical twist in the cultural current. The idealized mother was replaced in this era by the ideal of the wife-companion—a more individualistic ideology of proper womanhood that shifted the focus from women as a group with a shared identity in motherhood to an emphasis on their role as a wife and on the romantic, eroticized, dyadic relationship of the heterosexual couple (Rothman 1978). Companionate marriage, which emphasized the mutuality of the heterosexual relationship, was the new cultural ideal, and all roads increasingly converged on it. Education for women, for example, became less controversial when it could be justified as a means of producing better wives and mothers. College sororities flourished in the 1920s, in part because they were organized around the dating system and thus helped lubricate the mechanisms of the courtship market that would lead college-educated women into marriage. Work was defined as most appropriate for the young single woman, a temporary life stage before she achieved her true role as a full-time housewife and mother. This middle-class life trajectory did not apply more broadly to working class or poor women, but it carried great ideological weight anyway as a generalized cultural ideal. It had serious consequences for all women, most especially those whose life circumstances did not allow them to achieve it. Women's solidarity, which had been bolstered in this era by an ideology blind to race and class differences but stressing women's essential commonality, was increasingly replaced by women's competitiveness with each other, as they vied for popularity and success in the dating and marriage markets.

The epitome of the cultural ideal of companionate marriage was reached in the 1950s. Put on hold during the Depression and World War II, a revitalized belief in the essential privacy and domesticity of middle-class family life swept like a cultural wave over the United States in the postwar era. Economic affluence produced by a burgeoning consumer economy and generous veteran benefits supported the single-breadwinner/full-time homemaker family ideal for the middle class. Working-class and poor families, by contrast, could only look longingly at that privileged family structure in which a single male income could support a whole family of dependents. The political climate of the 1950s also encouraged the turn to a privatized, domestic family structure with its emphasis on companionate marriage.

The external threats of the Cold War and the nuclear age produced an inward turn toward the relative safety, security, and control that family life represented. Elaine Tyler May (1988) has argued that the Cold War policies of containment and brinkmanship applied to family life as well as to the political realm. The desire for control over the private sphere of the home, the one seemingly manageable area of life, as against the enormity of what was uncontrollable and unknown, focused attention on family life and domesticity in the 1950s. Although consumerism and technology loomed ominously as powerful forces in the postwar world, the home seemed the appropriate place to harness and contain them. Marriage also appeared to be the institution that could best control the looming threat of nonmarital sexuality, made evident to Americans with the widely heralded publication of the Kinsey studies in 1948 and 1953. Homosexuality was equated with communism—a threat that had to be harshly suppressed if it was not to lead to the destruction of the American way of life. Premarital sexuality was also a threat, but within limits (those set primarily by women) it could be justified as a means of preparing young people for a more fulfilling, eroticized marriage.

The decade of the 1950s resonates for many Americans as the era of stable family life. In the current debate over family values, it has served as the benchmark against which contemporary marriage and family life are most often judged. But the 1950s were unusual in many ways, and to use this era as a baseline measure leads to a distorted understanding of family trends. In at least three distinct ways the cohort of young adults who came of age in the immediate postwar era were unlike those who preceded them and those who followed: They married at younger ages than ever before; they had more children, earlier, and at closer birth intervals; and they experienced a lower divorce rate during the early and middle years of their marriages.

Analysts offer two possible explanations for the resurgence of familism reflected in the "early marriage–long marriage" pattern of the 1950s cohort. One explanation focuses on the values about the importance of family learned by these children of the Depression and the war years who entered adulthood in the 1950s. Having experienced economic hardship but also family resilience in their youth, these young adults brought to their own marriages a commitment to strong family life in the face of a harsh and insecure world. Another explanation focuses on the demographic and economic realities of the small birth cohort of the 1930s who became adults in an era of economic expansion. Faced with the favorable labor market conditions of the postwar era—that is, with an expanding economy and a relative lack of economic competition because of the small size of their cohort—those young adults coming of age in the 1950s found it possible to construct a viable middle-class family life based on the economic support of a sole breadwinner-husband and the social support of a full-time homemaker-wife (Cherlin 1992). The companionate marriage ideal stressed complementarity and mutuality in the relationship between spouses but not necessarily equality, which readily fit the gendered division of labor that was coming to characterize this family type.

The cultural ascendancy of the middle-class, breadwinner-homemaker family model was helped by the introduction of television as a staple of household consumption in the 1950s. The primary fare of early network television was the family sitcom, a formulaic genre of sentimental realism in the form of a domestic narrative and in the space of a thirty-minute time slot, wedged between the commercials that paid for the program's air time. But just as Hollywood's depiction of romance and modern marriage in the films of the 1920s and 1930s had provided a model for behavior against which Americans measured their own experience and new expectations (May 1980; Wexman 1993), so television's family sitcoms of the 1950s provided an increasingly diverse population of Americans with an extremely narrow vision of what "ideal" family life (i.e., white, middle-class, heterosexual, and suburban) looked like (Spigel 1992). Whether replayed in syndication or newly created as program "retreads" according to the same formulaic version even though they may have included a new and more diverse cast of characters, these television-produced images of family life have had remarkable staying power over several subsequent generations. It is noteworthy that the one televised attempt to look at a real American family, the 1973 PBS-sponsored documentary, "An American Family," on the Loud Family of Santa Barbara, California, recorded family conflict, a parental divorce, and a gay son's coming out—a far cry from the idealized sitcom version of family life.[4]

Against the backdrop of the television family of the 1950s, many Americans experienced a different reality. Breines (1992) pointed to many of the era's contradictory and ambiguous messages for young women in her sociological memoir, *Young, White, and Miserable: Growing Up Female in the Fifties*. She wrote,

> When I think of my adolescence, I remember with dread the importance as-
> signed to clothes and boys and popularity, undoubtedly a signal that I was not
> a wholehearted participant in teen culture. I was a successful participant,
> however, an interesting doublemindedness that was characteristic, I believe, of
> many girls' lives. I read the movie magazines and saw the movies and listened
> to the music with pleasure. I pasted Rock Hudson's picture on my wall and
> joined movie star fan clubs" (1992: 84–85).

For many young women, "secrets, lies, evasions, and role-playing" were the only ways to cope with the restrictions imposed by the era's sexual norms and gender expectations. For others, the price was much higher. Breines's chapter on Anne Parsons, the daughter of the most prominent sociologist of the era and an anthropologist in her own right, is an espe-cially poignant example of the way cultural norms can have a devastating psychological impact on individual lives. Parsons found the gap between love and work unbridgeable, and her profound sense of being alone, iso-lated, and marginal as a single, professional woman in the 1950s resulted in her suicide in 1964. Many older women as well as younger (Friedan 1963), and men as well as women (Ehrenreich 1983), found the immedi-ate postwar era a constricting one in terms of gender roles and marriage norms. The tension between an idealized family life and the personal re-strictions that many experienced in the 1950s and early 1960s was an un-derlying source of structured strain that began, quietly at first and then with more momentum, to challenge the notion of a singular path to adult-hood.

By the late 1960s and early 1970s, the rise of a demographically strong youth culture, the first effects of this era's sexual revolution, and challenges to marriage from the feminist and gay rights movements combined to un-seat the hegemony of the dating system, which had been the foundation of the courtship market since the late nineteenth century. The result was not the turning away from romance, dating, courtship, and marriage. These have remained important experiences framing the life stage of young adult-hood for the majority of Americans. But as educational opportunities ex-panded for baby boomers and subsequent generations of young people since the 1970s, the age at marriage has shifted back to its historical norm from the all-time low point it had reached in the 1950s. In addition to later age at marriage, there are a variety of alternatives to the heterosexual cou-ple relationship, including singleness, gay and lesbian relationships, and nonmarital family formation, that are increasingly widespread and socially acceptable. The dominant characteristics of the contemporary dating system are its lack of systematic regularity, its apparent casualness, and its invisibility to the young, many of whom now show a preference for socializing in mixed-gender peer groups rather than as couples.

Nevertheless, romantic love remains a powerful cultural ideal, its images and themes the staple of television and movie plots, popular song lyrics, and romance fiction. The courtship market is still at work, more commercial and visible than ever before with computer dating services, personal ads, and best-selling "how to" books now a standard part of the relationship package.[5] Perhaps the key change since the 1950s is that the institution of marriage is no longer without its challengers and critics. The dominant mode is now one of ambivalence about marriage rather than the unquestioning acceptance of its legitimacy as a natural and automatic step in the transition to adulthood. The paradox is that Americans continue to marry in large numbers, but they do so against a cultural backdrop that validates and enshrines romantic love as a cultural ideal even as it questions marriage as the only—or the best—way to achieve it.

The State of the Marital Union: Contemporary American Marriages

On March 12, 1998, the *Boston Globe* reprinted an Ann Landers column that had first run in December 1970, titled "Sparks have died down, but she should be grateful." The writer requested it with the preface, "I guess people's problems never change; . . . someone very close to me needs to see [this column]," and Ann responded "It's good to know that something I wrote 27 years ago has stood the test of time."

> **Dear Ann:** I am a married woman in my early 30s who is puzzled and searching for answers that might not exist. Every now and then . . . , I get word that friends . . . who have been married for 25 years or longer are getting a divorce. I . . . fear that one day that "older couple" might be us.
>
> "Timmy" and I have always gotten along well. We have four terrific kids. . . . But there must be more to life than PTA, housework, cooking, cleaning, laundry, and sex with your husband. I ache to feel that special electricity when my eyes meet those of a handsome man across a crowded room. It never happens. I yearn for a lover who will make my heart pound a mile a minute. Timmy used to, but the thrill is gone. Things are quiet, calm, and . . . dull as dishwater.
>
> We have a lot to be thankful for—good health, attractive, well-behaved kids, and a promising financial future. Why isn't this enough? Is something wrong with me? Am I chasing the impossible dream? I will be watching and waiting for your answer. Please don't fail me.

• • •

Put away your storybooks, little girl. You've got some growing up to do. Yes, there is more to life than PTA, housework, cooking, cleaning, laundry, and sex with your husband. There's illness, infidelity, and emotional breakdowns that make it impossible for some women to do the cooking, cleaning, and laundry.

As for sex with your husband, don't knock it, honey. There are plenty of husbands who aren't interested and an equal number who are getting sex someplace else. There is also alcoholism, in-law trouble, out-of-control children, unemployment, and money worries. Read the papers. Look around.

No marriage can maintain the . . . honeymoon level of excitement forever. And it's a good thing. We would all collapse from exhaustion. Time diminishes the raging fires to a soft glow—present, but no longer ferocious and demanding. Count your blessings. Too many people fail to appreciate what they have until they have lost it. Don't let this happen to you.

Not all of Ann Landers's advice, even by her own admission, makes claim to withstanding the test of time quite this unambiguously, so the view of marriage presented here posits a strong continuity of cultural values. The message about marriage seems to be: Romantic love and sexual passion, both of which may work well in getting couples married in the first place, do not (and should not) last over time. Marriage is about stability, loyalty, security, and adulthood—the opposite of the tempestuousness, excitement, and volatility experienced as youthful romantic love. Grow up. Look around at the lurking dangers. Count your blessings. And lower your inflated expectations. A "dull-as-dishwater" quality is to be expected in long-term marriage, but the tradeoff is respectability, committed attachment, and security.

Despite its emphatic certainty, Ann Landers's advice about the nature of marriage has not acquired the status of conventional wisdom over the past twenty-seven years. Indeed, one of the persistent themes about modern marriage since the early twentieth century has been its inherent instability. Subject to the kinds of high expectations that were produced by the romantic love ideology, modern marriage, no longer based on a notion of adult responsibility, obligation, and self-sacrifice, seemed to many observers in the twentieth century to have lost its bearings (Swidler 1980). One of the first analysts to approach the study of modern marriage and the family from the perspective of the new discipline of sociology was Ernest R. Groves, who cited birth control as the source of the "marriage crisis" of the 1920s. Birth control, he argued, elevated companionate marriage—defined as "the union of a husband and wife who from the beginning were determined not to have children"—to new cultural dominance, and made pleasure-seeking, rather than self-denial and social obligation, the new goals of the marital relationship (Groves 1928: 32–38, 45–53).

As a social scientist, Groves did not seek to repudiate this new model of marriage; rather, he attempted to make sense of it as a social phenomenon, and he advocated a number of practical solutions to the perceived crisis, including college courses that would prepare young people for marriage, parenthood, and family responsibilities. He was one of the first sociologists to articulate the concept of the "happy marriage" as a new cultural ideal: "The fact that there are so few motives for marrying at all except this desire to join in the fellowship of love . . . makes modern matrimony as it now exists . . . predominantly an expression of the profound need of men and women to find their highest happiness in the close character-developing experiences of marriage and the family" (Groves and Ogburn 1928: 29). "Failure to achieve happiness in marriage is frequent enough to attract especial attention," Groves noted in the preface to *The Marriage Crisis*. "The extreme collapse of matrimonial experience as recorded in the divorce statistics is compelling evidence of the quantity of unhappiness now found among the married" (1928: vii). Over the next seven decades, as perceptions of a crisis in marriage have grown far beyond those first identified by Groves, other researchers have attempted to define the characteristics of successful, long-term, and happy marriages: those that could withstand the intensity of the high expectations and external pressures that have helped produce what one writer has called the contemporary American "divorce culture."

Happy Marriages, Long-Term Marriages

For the team of researchers who set out in the mid-1970s to investigate what had happened to the community of Middletown (i.e., Muncie, Indiana) in the fifty years since Robert and Helen Lynd had conducted their studies there (1929; 1937), nothing so dramatically illustrated the resiliency of the American family to adapt to social change as the responses they received to the surveys on marital happiness. The Lynds had painted a dark picture of marital dissatisfaction, alienation, and general lack of communication between the spouses in the majority of the working- and business-class families that they observed in the mid-1920s and again in the Depression years of the mid-1930s. In the 1970s, by contrast, the authors of the Middletown III Project discovered a decidedly more upbeat perspective on marriage among their interviewees. Fifty-seven percent of the married respondents described themselves as "very satisfied" with their marital relationships, 38 percent were "satisfied," and less than 5 percent felt "neutral" or "dissatisfied" (Caplow et al. 1982: 126) Working-class

couples were generally as satisfied with their marriages as their business-
class counterparts. And the majority described their own marriages as
"better than most," contrasting their experience to images of divorce-
prone, unhappy marriages that they were sure characterized everyone else
(Caplow et al. 1982: 128). The authors concluded that marriages in Middletown had improved in the fifty years since the Lynds's studies, with a
new emphasis on open communication between spouses, more leisure time
spent together, and a higher degree of marital companionship.

Other survey research supports the conclusions of the Middletown authors about the advantages of marriage. In the most comprehensive, scien-
tifically reliable survey to date about Americans' sexual attitudes and behaviors, Laumann et al. (1994) found that married people had the most
frequent sex of any other group in the study and were the ones most likely
to report being physically pleased and emotionally satisfied (1994:
112–113, 124–125). In contrast with the image of sexually freewheeling
singles, the authors noted that "in real life, the unheralded, seldom discussed world of married sex is actually the one that satisfies people the
most" (1994: 131).

Such upbeat reports on the state of American marriage, however, have
not quelled the widespread doubts about this social institution. Studying
long-term marriages continues to intrigue social scientists, despite Tolstoy's
famous dictum that "all happy families are alike; each unhappy family is
unhappy in its own way." As Cuber and Harroff (1966) argued in their
study of marriages among upper-middle-class professionals, longevity of
the marriage is not always synonymous with happiness. In their sample of
437 men and women between the ages of thirty-five and fifty-five who had
been married for ten years or more, the authors distinguished five types of
marital relationships falling into the two broad categories of "utilitarian
marriage" and "intrinsic marriage." The majority fit the utilitarian definition, in which the marriage endured but marital happiness was often minimal or absent. Among utilitarian marriages, for example, they identified
the "conflict-habituated," in which conflict served as the basis of the couple's sustained interaction over time; the "passive-congenial," in which
consistently low expectations had characterized the marriage from the beginning; and the "devitalized," in which the couple had adapted to lowered
expectations over the course of their married life. Intrinsic marriages, constituting a small proportion of all sampled, included the "vital" and the
"total" types, with a high degree of intensive companionship, intimate attachment, empathy, and identification between the spouses. As one husband in such a marriage described it, "I haven't the slightest interest in doing anything that I can't share with her or that she can't participate in with
me. . . . I just don't have or want to have any separate existence that
amounts to anything" (Cuber and Harroff 1966: 134). The emphasis in in-

trinsic marriages is on togetherness, mutuality, and partnership: the husband and wife who, for thirty years and at considerable inconvenience, had carved out time for lunch at home together, or those who managed to weave all aspects of their work lives and leisure time together as the basis of a shared experience (Cuber and Harroff 1966: 58–59).

More recently, Wallerstein and Blakeslee (1995) sought out fifty couples who had been married at least nine years, had one or more children, and were in marriages in which both spouses expressed happiness with the marital relationship. These authors, too, found a variety of types of marriages that fit these criteria. Some 15 percent of the happily married couples in the study were in "romantic" marriages: those that had retained sexual passion, along with a high degree of companionship, intimacy, and attachment over the twenty-year or longer duration of the marriage. Another 20 percent were in "rescue" marriages in which one or both partners had overcome traumatic or tragic family backgrounds to establish a long-term, happy relationship in adulthood with a spouse and children. Two other types of happy marriage posed a more direct contrast with each other. In "traditional" marriages, husbands and wives adopted different roles and responsibilities—provider-protector and nurturer-caretaker—in their commitment to the family and home. All of the couples who had married in the 1950s and early 1960s fit this category, as did about 25 percent of the couples who had married in the 1970s and 1980s. In "companionate" marriage, by contrast, Wallerstein and Blakeslee found couples who strove for equality in all aspects of their marriage, family, home, and work lives. This category was more commonly found among younger couples in the study, particularly those who had a deep ideological commitment to egalitarian gender roles.

Despite the positive finding that there are multiple categories of long-term, successful marriages that work, Wallerstein prefaced the book with the story that her initial call for subjects for this study of happy marriages had elicited widespread amusement from a group of professional women (Wallerstein and Blakeslee 1995: 3). Joseph Epstein, in a study of divorce (1974), also noted anecdotally a similar prevailing sentiment about long-term marriages: Rather than being culturally lauded, they were often met with incredulity, as though those who stayed married were, in fact, lacking in imagination. The long-term, happy marriage seems an anachronism to many today, a vestige of a distant "golden age" of the past rather than a contemporary reality.

All of these studies of ongoing marriage—and, indeed, a veritable industry of self-help literature—suggest that modern marriage requires *work*. Far from providing a refuge from the world of work, as the nineteenth-century construction of separate spheres had it, and far from being a relationship that simply comes naturally, marriage is now seen as a relationship that replicates many of the qualities to be found in the work world. Like a business, marriage is an instrumental partnership, a relationship that requires constant attention to detail and nuance, and one that needs to be worked *on*. Marital work is perceived in the self-help literature and the therapeutic tradition as a specific problem with a specific solution: more and better communication, for example (Tannen 1990), or more leisure time for the couple to focus on the relationship. Most proposed solutions to the marriage crisis involve personal change or intervention at the individual, interpersonal level. But the sociological perspective differs. Sociologists suggest that it is the very way in which marriage has come to be defined and understood—as the fulfillment of dyadic intimacy and an intensively exclusive attachment—that is problematic and self-limiting. From this perspective, marriage contains within it the structured strains that make long-term marriages difficult to sustain and happy marriages subject to constantly escalating demands and expectations.

Structured Strains: The Fault Lines of Modern Marriage

Just as intact communities standing along an earthquake fault can be ruptured and destroyed by invisible forces at work below the surface, so modern marriages are always at risk of disruption and dissolution, not primarily because of a mismatch of personalities but because of the social forces at work that render them fragile. One of these forces is routinization, the process by which the high intensity of romantic love wears off through the combined forces of time and energies diverted to the competing demands of children and other family responsibilities, work, and community obligations. The self-help literature has been particularly aware of and concerned about the problem of routinization, particularly in terms of its effect on the marital sexual relationship. From Marabel Morgan's *The Total Woman* (1975), which provided married women with tips and strategies for keeping their husband's sexual interest alive, to the contemporary best seller *Men Are from Mars, Women Are from Venus: A Practical Guide for Improving Communication and Getting What You Want in Your Relationships* (Gray 1992), advice about how to identify and overcome the eroding forces of routinization has been a persistent theme of this genre. Although rational appeals to couples that they should allow romantic love to be transformed into more stable and responsible companionate love are a staple of this advice literature, in fact the spontaneous appearance of romantic love and the lure of nonmarital sexuality always present a potential threat to a seemingly stable companionate relationship.

Existing survey data on the extent of adultery in the United States suggest, somewhat surprisingly, that it is a relatively rare phenomenon in contemporary American marriages. Laumann et al. (1994) found that only 18 percent of their random sample of men born between 1933 and 1942 had had two or more sex partners during their marriages; all other cohorts of men and all cohorts of women in the study reported substantially lower rates, ranging from 6 percent to 14 percent for men and 1 percent to 5 percent for women (209–210). Other studies (Hunt 1969; Richardson 1985; Lawson 1988; Heyn 1992), however, give more insight into how and why ongoing marriages are always vulnerable. In extramarital affairs, people seek to experience "romantic courtship, playfulness, the intensity of new sexual experience, the excitement of mutual disclosures and unveiling" (Hunt 1969: 179). In a culture that celebrates the high emotional intensity of romantic love and sexual passion, the familiar, the known, and the routine inevitably suffer by contrast.

Another source of structured strain in contemporary American marriage is the particular intensity that is invested in the dyadic relationship. Unlike the marriage systems in many other cultures and parts of the world that subsume and minimize the dyadic relationship, American marriage places all of its expectations for intimacy, attachment, emotional support, and personal fulfillment on the couple's relationship. The burden of these expectations is unduly heavy, particularly in a highly mobile society in which other kinds of social ties—between friends, neighbors, and acquaintances—are relatively weak. An intense dyadic relationship has the paradoxical consequence of making the marriage tie more fragile. Jealousies, disappointments, petty irritations, and all unmet expectations work like corrosive agents on the dyadic relationship, making it highly vulnerable to disruption. Without other moderating forces to dispel such intensity or strong social sanctions, such as the obligations imposed by extended family that work to keep the marriage intact, the high expectations built into modern American marriages are almost bound to be dashed. The good or successful marriage studied by social scientists and promoted in the self-help literature is the one in which the couple adopts strategies to counteract both the effects of routinization and intensification of the couple relationship. But these efforts are often the exception rather than the rule. In many cases, structured strains weigh too heavily to be recognized as the consequences of social and cultural forces rather than as individual problems with psychological or interpersonal roots.

Finally, another structured strain built into contemporary marriage is the historical construction of heterosexual gender relationships. Despite the theory of opposite but complementary personality halves that are merged into a complete whole through the institution of marriage, patterned gender divisions routinely produce tensions and challenges in a conventional marriage. As early as the 1830s, Tocqueville had noted the discrepancy between the freedom accorded to young single women in the United States and the constraints imposed on American women after marriage. "In

America," Tocqueville reported, "a woman loses her independence forever in the bonds of matrimony. While there is less constraint on girls there than anywhere else, a wife submits to stricter obligations. For the former, her father's house is a home of freedom and pleasure; for the latter, her husband's is almost a cloister" (1969: 592). Jessie Bernard (1972) coined the phrase "his and her marriages" to make the point that men's and women's different social positions and situations resulted in very different experiences and outcomes for each. Whereas married men were far better off on multiple measures of physical and mental health than their never-married counterparts, married women were worse off than both married men and never-married women of their same age. Bernard explained this discrepancy as a function of the constraints and isolation of the housewife role and of the toll it took on married women. Those data have since been challenged by scholars who argue that marriage provides benefits for both men and women, although they concede that since 1972 marriage itself has changed in ways that may be more satisfying to women (Waite 1995). Although there may be more convergence in the roles of American men and women than in the past, there are still some significant differences. Other analysts have since added to the list of gender tensions structured into heterosexual relationships the patterned gender differences produced in the socialization process (Chodorow 1978, Gilligan 1982), the burdensome cultural expectation that women do the "emotion work" within marriage (Hochschild 1983, Cancian 1987), and the unequal division of labor that persists at home, even as married women have joined men in the labor force (Hochschild 1989).

Anxiety about the state of American marriage today might best be summed up by a current controversy over the way that marriage is represented in twenty college textbooks published between 1994 and 1996. In a report called "Closed Hearts, Closed Minds: The Textbook Story of Marriage," sociologist Norval Glenn (1997a) argued that the texts overemphasize the problems of marriage and teach students and future professionals that "marriage is a dirty word." The evidence that marriage confers positive benefits on adults and on children is minimized or ignored. In summary, Glenn has argued that current marriage and family textbooks "are a national embarrassment. They are both a cause and a result of a society in which marriage as an institution is growing steadily weaker."

Responses to this report were elicited from sociologists in a symposium sponsored by the American Sociological Association (1998a, 1998b). The debate hinges primarily on whether or not family change is interpreted as an inevitable adaptation to changing circumstances or a preventable threat to adult and child well-being. In all cases, however, critics from both sides of this debate concur that American marriage is an institution in jeopardy. The proportion of Americans ever married and the survey results on marital happiness notwithstanding, marriage looks to be in trouble, a victim of its own high expectations and the fluidity with which Americans now move into the status of the "formerly married."

Divorce and Remarriage

At a recent party to celebrate the sixtieth birthday of a three-times married man in Cambridge, Massachusetts, the new young wife of the host introduced herself cheerfully, and without a hint of irony, as "the future ex-wife." This anecdote highlights what Barbara Dafoe Whitehead (1996) and others have come to call the "divorce culture" prevailing in American society in the last decades of the twentieth century. From this perspective, divorce has quite recently come to be seen as an individual right, even an opportunity for personal change and psychological growth, rather than a radical and traumatic severing of the ties of a family unit. In the context of this prevailing culture, its critics argue, divorce is understood as a positive social good, even if personally traumatic: It involves choice and often liberation from an undesirable relationship; it opens up new possibilities rather than promoting constraints. But this emphasis on individual choice rather than family responsibility in the American propensity to divorce is precisely what alarms many contemporary observers. A divorce culture relentlessly demands that marriage live up to the high expectations placed on it. It erodes both stigma and sanctions against divorce and thereby makes leaving marriage too easy. It ultimately pits the needs and desires of adults against other family "stakeholders," specifically children, to the detriment of the latter (Whitehead 1996).

Critics of the divorce culture do not generally argue that divorce should be abolished, only that greater attention be given to the older values of family responsibility, obligation, and adult self-sacrifice. The divorce culture, they believe, is not inevitable, but a set of values that can be recognized and then modified or reversed. As one such policy response, the Louisiana legislature recently passed a measure called "covenant marriage"—a more stringent contract that engaged couples could choose over the standard marriage and no-fault divorce package, which would allow the marriage to be dissolved only after a mutually agreed upon two-year separation or after proven fault in the cases of adultery, abandonment, or abuse. The long-range effects of this law have yet to be seen, but it is based on the questionable assumption that engaged couples will be able or want to distinguish between different levels of commitment to marriage at the very time when the romantic love ethic is at its highest peak in the dyadic relationship. As a policy designed to help lower the divorce rate, the covenant marriage contract will have to face the challenge of some formidable cultural norms.

The argument that divorce can have positive personal and social effects is a relatively new one that began to appear in the popular press in the 1970s, the period in which the divorce rate reached its highest level in American society. The far more standard response to the prevalence of divorce, both historically and in the present, has been to see it as a profound crisis. Social commentators at the end of the nineteenth century decried the lapse in morality, the entrance of women into the labor force, and the impact of urban life as the probable causes of divorce. At the end of the twentieth century many of the same concerns are still being voiced. From one perspective, of course, the high rate of American marriage itself helps explain the high rate of divorce, since the more people that marry, the larger the pool potentially at risk of divorce. The shifting meaning of marriage, then, is the backdrop against which statistics on divorce must be read. Of all the "causes" of divorce, the high rate of marriage is the most significant and, in many ways, the most intractable. Even those who seek to lower the divorce rate might not be willing to trade the high expectations placed on love and intimacy in marriage as the price that must be paid.

The Historical Roots of the Rise in Divorce.   In a study of divorce in Los Angeles, California, from the 1880s to the 1920s, Elaine Tyler May (1980) found a striking shift in the nature of the complaints that dissatisfied spouses made in their petitions to the courts. In the 1880s, traditional Victorian expectations about gender roles in marriage still prevailed, and a husband who did not provide adequately for his family, who forced his wife to work outside the home, who did not exhibit appropriate sexual restraint at home, or who allowed his involvement in public vices to taint the tranquillity of the domestic sphere was a clear candidate for divorce. Similarly, a wife who did not adhere to the ideals of proper Victorian womanhood—exhibiting virtuousness, modesty, domesticity, subordination to her husband, and an overriding devotion to motherhood—was also vulnerable in the divorce courts. By the 1920s, in contrast, expectations of marital happiness and personal satisfaction were increasingly reflected in the divorce petitions of both men and women, yet these new demands coexisted uneasily with the older belief that marriage should entail sacrifice rather than fun and should provide security rather than self-fulfillment. The tensions that American couples experienced in the early twentieth century around the changing nature of work, the opportunities and demands of urban life, and the spread of new social and cultural mores, all of which had unsettling effects on the meaning of marriage, spurred the divorce rate to new heights. May reports that "between 1867 and 1929, the population of the United States grew 300 percent, the number of marriages increased 400 percent, and the divorce rate rose 2,000 percent" (May 1980: 2). As it would turn out, such a rise was only the beginning.

Divorce in the United States began rising in the middle of the nineteenth century and has been on a steady upward trend during the twentieth century, with temporary jumps in the rate after the Civil War and World War I, a dip during the Depression as the economic downturn made divorce an unaffordable choice, and a sharp increase after World War II. The pattern from the 1950s to the 1990s has followed the same general upward trajectory. While divorce rates declined during the 1950s from the high point reached after World War II, they surged in the 1960s and 1970s, then declined slightly and leveled off, although at a very high level, in the late 1980s (Goode 1993; Cherlin 1992). A comparative-historical look at the experience of different marriage cohorts helps put these trends in perspective. For the cohort that married in 1870, the likelihood of divorce was only 7 percent, while for the cohort that married in 1950, it ranged from 17 to 27 percent. Researchers now predict that, if current rates continue, between 44 and 64 percent of recent marriages will end in divorce within thirty years, a potential tripling of the divorce rate from that which prevailed at midcentury (Preston and McDonald 1979; Martin and Bumpass 1989).

Changing divorce rates alone never tell the whole story. Even though divorce has become more common as a social experience, the personal toll it takes is bound to be emotionally devastating. "The divorced are the fraternity of those who have gone through an emotional ravaging," noted Joseph Epstein in his memoir-study, *Divorced in America*, "that, short of starvation, imprisonment, disease, and death itself, is probably equal to most that the world has to offer. . . . [T]o go through a divorce is still—no matter how smooth the procedure, no matter how "civilized" the conduct of the parties involved, no matter how much money is available to cushion the fall—to go through a very special private hell" (1974: 19). The loss of an intimate dyadic relationship in a culture that values love and attachment highly is a psychological blow that exacerbates the social disruptions in the aftermath of divorce. Although many contemporary critics claim that divorce is too easy and that people resort to it too readily, the pain and trauma that affect those who experience divorce are much more visible today for all to see. Choosing such an emotional ravaging rather than its alternative of remaining in and coping with a less-than-ideal marriage suggests the level of desperation many must feel in their private lives. As more Americans experience divorce themselves or feel its effects at close emotional range, the fragility of marriage is noted and underscored. The long-range impact of a persistently high rate of divorce in the United States may be to erode the norm of marital permanence and therefore to weaken the foundation of marriage even further.

Cohabitation. While divorce rates were increasing, other significant changes were taking place in the living patterns of American adults. Cohabitation, or living together outside of marriage, has greatly increased among young, never-married adults and among divorced adults since 1970. Historically, cohabitation was a pattern more characteristic of the poor, for whom marriage was often an unattainable luxury. In the late 1990s, it encompassed a broader spectrum of the adult population, at all education and income levels. Most couples who cohabit in the United States do so for a relatively short period of time, with half of all relationships resulting in marriage or a break-up within the first eighteen months, and 90 percent reaching these conclusions within five years. Rather than an alternative to marriage, then, the American pattern of cohabitation has been experienced as a temporary stage that preceded (or followed) marriage. But the western European, especially French, model of cohabitation, which is both longer-lived and less likely to lead to marriage, may be a harbinger of American cohabitation in the future (Cherlin 1992). The meanings and uses of cohabitation can be as elusive and shifting as the meanings of marriage itself and just as unlikely to remain stable. The current data show that the marriages of cohabitors have a higher rate of dissolution than those of noncohabitors, which suggests that the former may have a different set of expectations about the nature of the marital relationship—a higher degree of individualism, perhaps, or a less permanent sense of commitment—which may work subtly to undermine the longevity of the marriage when it occurs.

Remarriage.   Remarriage has also undergone change. Before the 1930s, most remarriages were the result of the death of a spouse rather than of divorce. Between the 1930s and the 1940s, the high rate of remarriage after divorce suggested that Americans may have been giving up on a particular husband or wife but not on the institution of marriage itself. Remarriage has been described as the prime example of "hope winning out over experience," of commitment to romantic love and of the willingness to try marriage again. But the rate of Americans remarrying after divorce has declined since the 1970s. Most of the divorced first enter cohabiting relationships rather than a new marriage. Many eventually remarry—but more men do so than women, especially after age thirty, and far more whites than blacks. Marriage, divorce, and remarriage patterns among African Americans will be considered in detail below, since what has been seen as an aberrant pattern may, in fact, be a precursor of future trends in all American families. Overall, remarriages have tended to have a higher dissolution rate than first marriages, a finding which is not surprising given the many difficulties involved in negotiating complex step-family relationships. In describing remarriage as "an incomplete institution," Cherlin (1978) noted the lack of norms governing all the relationships associated with remarriage, both internal and external. If recent social changes have had a profoundly unsettling effect on all marriages, then remarriage is an even more fragile institution.

Based on these trends in marriage, divorce, cohabitation, and remarriage, several conclusions can be drawn about the state of American marriage. Marriage has become more fragile as an institution than it was in the past, and it is a less central part of the adult life course than formerly. American men and women since the 1970s have married later than their parents did but closer in marriage age to their grandparents and great-grandparents. Faced with more educational and career opportunities than their mothers or grandmothers had, young women in particular face a greater range of nonfamily life options than ever before. Their response has been to delay marriage, to delay childbearing, to enter cohabiting relationships more readily, and, once married, to continue working even with young children at home. Today's marriages are more apt to break up than American marriages in the past, in part, no doubt, because of the structured strains that affect all contemporary relationships, but also because the greater economic resources and social opportunities that are now open to women reduce their dependence on the support of a husband. The changes in both attitudes and behavior about the family have been dramatic and far-reaching. A recent issue of the *New York Times Magazine* on the dilemmas of motherhood cited the changing responses of adults to the following survey question: "Do you agree or disagree that it is much better for everyone involved if the man is the achiever outside the home and the woman takes care of the home and family?" In 1977, 66 percent of American adults agreed. By 1996, only 38 percent did so (Cherlin, 1998). Marriage and family roles—and the social expectations that are embedded in them—are in a state of flux. It is not surprising that the institution of marriage, once a key indicator of having achieved adulthood, now seems precarious. As in other periods marked by rapid social change, Americans seem poised, awkwardly and with considerable ambivalence, between old and new expectations of what marriage means and how it will define their adult lives.

Challenges to Marriage: Current Practices and Future Trends

The question of what life choices individuals will make in constructing adulthood is never a neutral one, of course. Modern societies no longer depend on families exclusively to promote the social order, since the bureaucracies that impinge on every aspect of political, economic, and social life provide quite an effective measure of social control over individuals. But the family has been, and remains, an effective institution for redistributing economic resources and for ensuring the socialization of children. In this way, marriage has retained a social, as well as personal, significance. Challenges to the dominance of marriage as a stepping stone to adulthood are therefore likely to be met with considerable social anxiety, including expressions of hostility at the prospect of social change. At least three such challenges are currently visible in subgroup patterns in the United States: the growing number of adults who never marry or have children; the increasing propensity for women to bear children outside of marriage, which is most pronounced in the family patterns of African Americans; and the demand by many gay and lesbian couples that the institution of heterosexual marriage be legally redefined to become more inclusive.

Singleness and Childlessness.   In the 1920s, when Groves and other social scientists identified companionate marriage as the consequence of birth control, thereby effectively making reproduction a choice within marriage, social critics worried that the most fundamental rationale for marriage had been undermined. Marriage has traditionally served as a license for reproduction. Once birth control could effectively separate sexuality from its reproductive consequences, many worried about what would tie men, in particular, to the institution of marriage. For this reason, feminists in the early twentieth century were initially opposed to birth control since they feared that removing the reproductive consequences from sex would unleash the essential licentiousness of men and give them few incentives to marry (Gordon 1982). The possibility of remaining childless by choice is a distinctly modern phenomenon, and it highlights more clearly than any other marital arrangement the distinction between the dyadic relationship of husband and wife and their parental role as fathers and mothers. Until the twentieth century these roles had overlapped, since marriage for most Americans had been synonymous with childbearing and childrearing. Modern marriage, by contrast, is weighted on the side of the spousal relationship. Declining birthrates and adult longevity have meant that parenthood occupies a much smaller part of the life cycle than previously. The fragility of the spousal relationship, however, has led some to argue that it is the mother-child bond that should be made primary in the eyes of the law (Fineman 1995). Still, as many choose childlessness, both within marriage and by remaining single, new ideas about what constitutes appropriate adult life stages are being forged.

Historically, remaining childless within marriage was a problematic status. A childless woman was to be pitied if she was not able to bear children and often publicly vilified or scorned if she voluntarily chose that status. We are, in the words of historian Elaine Tyler May, "a nation obsessed with reproduction . . . , preoccupied with [our] own and each other's procreative habits" (1995: 1). Childbearing has never been an exclusively private decision made by individuals, couples, or families. Indeed, the variable rates of population growth among different social classes and racial-ethnic groups in the United States have fueled many social and political contro-versies. Fearing "race suicide" among the native-born, white middle class, whose birth rate had been declining since the early nineteenth century, President Theodore Roosevelt gave voice to the growing eugenics move-ment in 1905 when he condemned "the viciousness, coldness, and shallow-heartedness of any woman who avoided her [reproductive] duty" (Gordon 1976: 142). Mother's Day, established in 1914 by a joint resolution of Congress in a unanimous vote, was another symbolic attempt to counter-act the declining birthrates among native-born white women in the early twentieth century and to sanctify motherhood as central to women's iden-tity. The class and racial politics of this ideology were clear when working class and poor women, both white and nonwhite, were vilified and pun-ished, through policies such as sterilization programs, for producing too many children.

In the late twentieth century, motherhood is an even more contested sta-tus. Some women have actively decided to remain "childfree," whereas others confront the threat of infertility with an overwhelming array of new reproductive and adoption options. A growing number of Americans re-main single well into their adult lives, foregoing both marriage and child-bearing either by design or by unintended consequence. Remaining single or getting married without having children are now viable options in adult lives as they have never been before. In 1996, 25 percent of all households in the United States were made up of people living alone, and among the 70 percent of family households, well over half were made up of a married couple only (U.S. Bureau of the Census 1997: 60). This represents a snap-shot of American society at one point in time and not a picture of how many of those living alone will eventually cohabit or marry or how many couples may eventually have children. Yet the snapshot also reveals that, for many Americans, remaining single or getting married without children is a more common life stage than ever before.

Nonmarital Childbearing: The African American Experience.   The flight from marriage but not from childbearing is also the pattern of a growing number of Americans. Many African American women in particular have made this choice, and I present it here not as an example of black family patterns that are pathological or aberrant, as has often been the argument, but as one response that may be a harbinger of future trends among all other American families. Researchers have long noted the ways in which the marriage and family patterns of black and white Americans have dif-fered. Two characteristics stand out as distinctive features of African American family structure: a higher proportion of single-parent families and a greater number of extended family households that include other kin (Ruggles 1994a).

These patterned differences between black and white family structures have deep historical roots, evident in the census records of 1880 and persisting into the twentieth century. Analysts have produced a variety of explanations to account for the distinctive features of African American families: They are a vestige of African cultural patterns, particularly matriarchal family structure; they are a consequence of slavery; and they are a response to more recent social structural conditions, such as the dislocation caused by the rural-to-urban migration of blacks from the South to the North during the first four decades of the twentieth century, the impact of high rates of black unemployment and underemployment, and the effects of overt prejudice and discrimination. As a response to the argument that slavery weakened the black family, a number of historians in the 1970s and 1980s focused on the resiliency of black families, even in the face of horrendous conditions and severe constraints. They argued that most slave children grew up in two-parent households, and that, in the half century between 1880 and 1930, the typical household of Southern rural and urban blacks included two parents and their children, as did the households of migrant blacks to the North in the early twentieth century (Gutman 1976; Pleck 1979). But despite this evidence about the experience of the majority of blacks in the United States, single parenthood and living in extended families have been persistent features of a significant minority of African American families at least since the turn of the century (Gordon and McLanahan 1991; Morgan, McDaniel, Miller, and Preston 1993; Ruggles 1994a). These distinct characteristics of black family life may have supported and reinforced each other; the capacity of a single parent to support a child, for example, is undoubtedly aided by a network of supportive kin. In the second half of the twentieth century, however, the underlying framework supporting this construction of African American family life began to weaken. Since 1960, single parenthood among African Americans has rapidly increased while the number of extended family households has substantially declined.

In the decade of the 1950s and since, marriage and family patterns among blacks began to change in dramatic ways that were particularly distinct from white patterns. Although they had previously married at younger ages than whites, now black men and women began to marry at later ages, and a growing number never married at all. It is estimated that only 75 percent of the cohort of black women born in the 1950s will ever marry, compared to 91 percent of white women in this cohort (Cherlin 1992: 94–95). Marriage, when it does occur, tends to be a more brittle institution among blacks. More marriages among blacks end in divorce, and fewer of those who get divorced experience remarriage. The "flight from marriage," which has characterized greater numbers of all Americans since the late 1960s, is more pronounced among African Americans than any other group in the United States. Based on the marriage and divorce rates prevailing in 1975–1980, researchers have estimated that a white woman will now spend less than half of her lifetime—43 percent—in a first marriage or remarriage. For black women the comparable figure is 22 percent, leading one analyst of family patterns to note that "marriage has become just a temporary life stage for blacks; . . . a long stable marriage is [now] the exception rather than the rule" (Cherlin 1992: 95).

If there has been a flight from marriage among blacks, there has not been a comparable flight from or postponement of childbearing. White women have been postponing both marriage and childbearing; black women have foregone marriage but have continued to have children at relatively young ages. The traditional expectation that marriage is the necessary license for childbearing has been overturned as a behavioral reality among recent cohorts of African Americans. Black children are therefore far more likely to be born to a young, unmarried mother than are white children. In 1994, 70 percent of all black births in the United States were to unmarried mothers, compared to 25 percent of all white births (U.S. Bureau of the Census 1997: 79). One result is that fewer and fewer black children now grow up in two-parent families (with either their own parent or a stepparent), and eight times as many black children as white live with a never-married, single parent. As discussed in a previous chapter, children growing up in any type of single-parent family, whether caused by the divorce or nonmarital status of their mother, face many disadvantages, primarily in the form of lack of access to social and economic resources, compared to children growing up in two-parent families. Poverty among single-parent families— and among all children—is clearly a significant social problem. But because many young, unmarried women were already poor before they gave birth, their single-parent status cannot be claimed as a cause of poverty, even though there is substantial evidence to suggest that this family structure makes it harder to escape from that economic state. The nonmarital family often continues to be sustained by a network of supportive kin (especially grandmothers), friends and acquaintances, and government aid. Yet these sources of support are not available to all single mothers and their children, and the networks themselves are often neither an adequate means of economic and social support nor a secure safety net.

The different routes through which women reach the state of single-parenthood have not been fully studied or comparatively analyzed. The growing phenomenon of the nonmarital family may carry a very different meaning for women, for example, than one that results from divorce, in that the former represents more choice in constructing an alternative family arrangement. To skip marriage altogether but to choose childbearing suggests a very different conception of adulthood than has traditionally been the case. It represents a choice of an adult stage of life that highlights the mother-child tie and perhaps the pull of an extended kin network over the dyadic relationship of the adult couple. That this trend has been on the rise in an era when gender roles are being questioned, when heterosexual relationships have been subject to more visible structured strains, and when marriage appears to more Americans as a problematic institution is no coincidence. Although nonmarital childbearing may be understood at one level as a particular family response of African Americans, rooted in both cultural and social structural conditions that have historical and contemporary roots, it is also a more general pattern emerging among all Americans. Nonmarital childbearing carries little stigma anymore, and, despite the considerable vulnerabilities that this status imposes on women and their children, it has appeal in appearing to sidestep some of the most problematic issues surrounding modern marital relationships. The nonmarital family promises to provide young women with the reward of enduring parental love while avoiding the complications of fragile adult relationships and ephemeral romantic love. In overturning the traditional package and sequence of love-marriage-childbearing, it also offers a new model of how to achieve adulthood by an alternative route.

The Case for Gay Marriage.   Nowhere in contemporary culture is the debate about the meaning of marriage being played out more overtly than in the gay community, where the controversy in the 1990s over legalizing same-sex marriage has generated internal tensions, provoked external hostilities, and, in general, brought the simmering ambivalence about the meaning of modern American marriage to full boil. When the Gay Rights Movement began in the early 1970s, the institution of heterosexual marriage was a prime target. "Smash monogamy" was a popular political catchword of the day, and sexual freedom from the constraints of heterosexuality and the key institution that enshrined it, marriage, was at the top of the gay rights political agenda. "Marriage is a great institution . . . if you like living in institutions" read the tee-shirt motto. Marriage was suspect because it was fundamentally based on a heterosexual norm and because it supported and reproduced the ideal of opposite and mutually exclusive gender roles and the practice of unequal power relations. Most gay and lesbian activists initially sought to shift the direction of mainstream culture rather than to join it, and marriage was a key target, since it represented the epitome of mainstream American conceptions of adulthood.

By the 1980s and 1990s, however, different positions on the marriage issue surfaced within the gay community, with a more radical camp continuing to oppose it as a heterosexist institution and those with a more assimilationist perspective making the argument that the benefits conferred by legal marriage—inheritance rights, custody claims, tax benefits, and shared insurance policies and pension plans, among others—constituted important resources to which gays and lesbians wanted equal access (Nava and Dawidoff 1994; Nardi 1996). The issue of same-sex marriage came into full focus in 1991 when three homosexual couples sued the state of Hawaii over the denial of their applications for marriage licenses. Two years later, in 1993, the Hawaii State Supreme Court ruled in *Baehr v. Lewin* that the state had to show a compelling reason why the couples should be denied marriage licenses, in violation of the state constitution's equal rights amendment forbidding discrimination based on sex. In response, a conservative U.S. Congress overwhelmingly passed the 1996 Defense of Marriage Act (H.R. 3396), reserving federal rights and benefits for male-female couples only and permitting states not to recognize same-sex marriages performed in other states. In case there was any ambiguity, the act specified:

> In determining the meaning of any Act of Congress, or of any ruling, regulation, or interpretation of the various administrative bureaus and agencies of the United States, the word "marriage" means only a legal union between one man and one woman as husband and wife, and the word "spouse" refers only to a person of the opposite sex who is a husband or a wife (Baird and Rosenbaum 1997: 18).

A recent poll reporting that 70 percent of Americans support most forms of gay rights but oppose same-sex marriage highlights the ambivalence that this controversy generates among the general public. "I think I know what the gays and lesbians want—what I have. A normal life," noted a man married for fifty years who was interviewed by the *Los Angeles Times* (July 10, 1996, A15). "I feel for them. But I just can't reach the feeling that [gay marriage] is normal. I'm just not ready for it, I guess." Many would agree. At the heart of the ambivalence or the outright opposition to same-sex marriage is the question "what is marriage for?" Although conservatives continue to argue that procreation is fundamental to marriage, it is clear that a widespread shift in the meaning of marriage as an adult life stage, not necessarily including children, has long been in the making. The emphasis in modern marriage on love, attachment, intimacy, and personal fulfillment would seem to weigh in favor of any committed relationship, homosexual or heterosexual. That was, in part, why the editors of the conservative British magazine *The Economist* argued "Let Them Wed" (January 6, 1996):

> It is true that the single most important reason society cares about marriage is for the sake of children. But society's stake in stable, long-term partnerships hardly ends there. Marriage remains an economic bulwark. Single people (especially women) are economically vulnerable, and much more likely to fall

into the arms of the welfare state. Furthermore, they call sooner upon public support when they need care—and, indeed, are likelier to fall ill (married people, the numbers show, are not only happier but considerably healthier). Not least important, marriage is a great social stabilizer of men. Homosexuals need emotional and economic stability no less than heterosexuals—and society surely benefits when they have it. . . . If marriage is to fulfill its aspirations, it must be defined by the commitment of one to another for richer for poorer, in sickness and in health—not by the people it excludes (Sullivan 1997: 181–185).

Recognizing the uneasy alliance between the liberal and the conservative sources of support for same-sex marriage, still others argue for changing the terms of the debate itself. Kath Weston (1991) has called for an extended concept of kinship, which would go beyond the legally recognized family ties of blood, marriage, or adoption. Her concept of the "chosen family" would allow an individual "to pick any one person as a partner—domestic or otherwise—and designate that person as the recipient of insurance or other employment benefits, even when that choice entails crossing household boundaries" (1991: 209). In radically redefining the family itself, in keeping with the changes toward dyadic intimacy and emotional support that have been evolving as the new basis of modern marriage for over a century, Weston and others hope to bypass the potential that a recognition of same-sex marriage would simply extend the same set of power relations embedded in the heterosexual institution to gay couples.

As this debate continues, many political progressives as well as conservatives understand the profound significance of a legal recognition of same-sex marriage, arguing, "it would certainly amount to the single greatest victory in all of gay civil rights, the watershed event in which homosexuality and the loving and committed relationships it spawns finally began to take their place as recognized and fully legitimate" (Rotello 1996). Changing the very definition of the family to be more inclusive of socially chosen ties would have even more far-reaching consequences. The final paradox for this era of family change might well be this embrace of marriage by those who have been among its most serious critics, a reaffirmation by gays and lesbians of the importance of the institution just at the moment when ambivalence about marriage among heterosexuals has reached new heights.

Conclusion

Arguments for and against marriage are not unique to the contemporary era. At the turn of the twentieth century, some feminists denounced marriage as sexual slavery for women, just as Ernest R. Groves and other social scientists in the same period were beginning to define the companion-ate marriage as the route to happiness. In 1967, at the height of the sec-ond-stage feminist critique of marriage as an oppressive institution, the U.S. Supreme Court struck down Virginia's miscegenation law in the *Loving v. Virginia* case, in which a black woman and white man had been con-victed of criminal charges for marrying. In his ruling, Justice Warren noted:

> The freedom to marry has long been recognized as one of the vital personal rights essential to the orderly pursuit of happiness by free men. . . . Marriage is one of the basic civil rights of man, fundamental to our very existence and survival. . . . Under our Constitution, the freedom to marry, or not to marry, a person of another race resides with the individual and cannot be infringed by the State.

Today, the debate about marriage is posed in terms of morality, religious tradition, historical precedent, and civil rights. Although it is not a new de-bate, it is one of the strands of the contemporary family values rhetoric that has the capacity to generate the most impassioned response.

Why do Americans marry? Because marriage confers the status of the most special dyadic relationship in an era of considerable sexual freedom; because it appears to many to be an appropriate step at a certain stage of life; because there is pressure from family and friends to do so; because of the desire to have children; because it provides a means of escaping from other life circumstances; because it offers access to an established sexual re-lationship; and because it promises economic security, emotional security, and companionship. These and many other reasons have traditionally worked quite effectively to get Americans to marry at least once, and often multiple times, over the course of their adult lives. Marriage may be a step that is undertaken with careful consideration or one that simply results from drifting in that direction. In her extensive interviews with fifty women around the United States about their expectations for and experiences in marriage, Charlotte Mayerson (1996) found a distinction between the "sleepwalkers," who as girls had daydreamed about romance and drifted into marriage, and the "calculators," who had specific expectations about the kind of husband, marriage, and adult life they wanted and made plans for achieving those goals. Mayerson was surprised to find that few of her female interviewees of any age had daydreamed about future careers but almost all had assumed that growing up meant getting married. Even in an era of new opportunities, many women and men continue to experience what one poet has called "the centrifuge of marriage." There is a powerful pull toward it, even in a culture that increasingly questions whether mar-riage is the only legitimate stage of adulthood. Marriage, although more ambiguously than in the past, still represents a significant coming-of-age ritual. It holds out the promise of permanence, even though contracted in a "sea of possibilities" and in an era defined by its impermanence. It elevates an intensely individual relationship to a social act and confers on it a sense of sacredness. The high hopes and elevated expectations placed on it make marriage emotionally more important but structurally more fragile as an institution. It continues to have an allure for many, but its tarnished side is also more visible. As Americans spend less of their lives in marriage than ever before, it may be easier to romanticize marital status but much harder to make the kinds of personal accommodations necessary to live under its strictures. The meanings attached to adulthood have been undergoing change for more than a century, but the changes associated with marriage continue to provoke social concern and anxiety. It is hard to imagine it being otherwise, since marriage remains one of the most powerful symbols Americans can cling to as a milestone in an increasingly fluid and unpredictable life course.

Notes

1. Divorce statistics are notoriously incomplete and difficult to interpret. The National Office of Vital Statistics established Marriage Registration Areas in 1957 and Divorce Registration Areas in 1958 to record national data, yet not all states participate. Divorce is also measured in various (and variously useful) ways when it is recorded: as the ratio of divorces to marriages in any particular year; as a rate (e.g., the number of divorces per 1,000 married people); or comparatively, as the proportion of divorces in different marriage or birth cohorts. The popular press commonly reports that half of all marriages currently end in divorce, although this figure is considered too high by some analysts. Norval Glenn argues that the 50 percent rate is valid, however, since it is based on

> sophisticated projections made by demographers using life-table techniques similar to, but more complicated than, those used to compute life expectancies. Such projections are not necessarily accurate predictions, but they are good summary indications of how unstable marriages were during specific periods of time. These sophisticated projections show that between 40 and 65 percent of recent marriages in the United States will end in divorce or permanent separation. An accurate statement is that about half of all marriages entered into in recent years in this country will end in divorce or separation if recent marital dissolution rates continue. It is already apparent that at least half of all marriages in some recent marriage cohorts will end before a spouse dies. Data from the General Social Surveys indicate that 39 percent of all first marriages (which are more stable than remarriages) entered into during the 1970s had already ended in divorce or separation before their 15th anniversary (Glenn 1997a: 5).

2. The shift in marital roles and expectations that has so strikingly marked a generational divide in the contemporary British royal family is a case in point. The ex-

traordinary public interest in the idealized romance, ensuing marital troubles, and subsequent divorce of Prince Charles and Princess Diana, for example, was fueled not by the uniqueness of their marital relationship but by its very familiarity to a wide audience. Romantic love is now considered the only legitimate basis for marriage and the basis on which it is expected to be sustained. Without love, even royal couples see divorce as the expected (and increasingly accepted) outcome.

3. One of the reasons that feminism as an ideology and a social movement has created such a strong backlash is because it fundamentally challenges the idea that women are by nature less individualistic and innately more attuned to family needs and demands than are men. An ideology of "woman as person"—that is, that women should be seen as individuals, just as men are—has always been threatening, invoking as it does the question of "Who will care for the children and family?" (if women relinquish this role in pursuit of their own ends). See Rothman (1978: 221–290).

4. An article in the *New York Times* (March 20, 1997, B1) noted that "An American Family" had "seemed like an advertisement for the American Dream" and that, in 1973, "[the Louds's] gradual disintegration became a national psychodrama." The journalist, William Grimes, credits this documentary with having had a significant impact on American culture:

> "An American Family," so shocking in its time, helped change the way Americans watch television and react to the camera. The Louds played a major role in opening the floodgates to documentaries and then talk shows in which ordinary people look straight into the camera and reveal their private lives.

At least as powerful as this twelve-hour series, then, were the numerous family sitcoms that, in a fictional format, attempted to portray a realistic version of family life. Television often came to represent a more authentic way of life than many experienced. This contradiction is revealed in the words of a black woman growing up in the 1950s:

> Why didn't my mother have freshly baked cookies ready when I came home from school? Why didn't we live in a house with a backyard and a front yard instead of an ole apartment? I remember looking at my mother as she cleaned the house in her raggedy housecoat with her hair in curlers. "How disgusting," I would think. Why didn't she clean the house in high heels and shirtwaist dresses like they did on television? (Breines 1992: 80)

5. The new visibility of the inner workings of the courtship market, with its emphasis on the single-minded, rational calculation necessary to achieve the end goal of marriage, is nowhere more evident than on the nonfiction bestseller lists. See, especially, Ellen Fein and Sherrie Schneider, *The Rules: Time-Tested Secrets for Capturing the Heart of Mr. Right* (New York: Warner Books, 1995), which counsels women to lower their strident professional voices and play hard-to-get if they want to capture a husband. Similarly, Thomas W. McKnight and Robert A. Phillips offer advice in *More Love Tactics: How to Win That Special Someone* (Garden City Park, N.Y.: Avery Publishing Group, 1993). The June 2, 1986, cover of *Newsweek*, with its steeply downward-sloping graph representing a woman's probability of marrying after age thirty (a forty-year-old woman was "more likely to be killed by

a terrorist" than to find a husband, the *Newsweek* author reported, summarizing an academic study by Harvard and Yale sociologists Neil Bennett, David Bloom, and Patricia Craig) apparently struck a nerve that the advice-literature industry was quick to respond to. See Andrew J. Cherlin, "The Strange Career of the 'Harvard-Yale Study'," *Public Opinion Quarterly* 54 (Spring 1990): 117–124; and Susan Faludi, *Backlash: The Undeclared War Against American Women.* (New York: Crown Publishers, 1991), 9–19. It is increasingly clear that the courtship market is not just for the young anymore. It is an expansive consumer-oriented market that now also includes older adults after a divorce or the death of a spouse.

5

Aging

Dear Ann Landers: I am in my mid-40s, never-married, and have lived on my own and supported myself since I became an adult. Several years ago, my aging parents and I moved into adjacent housing so I would live near enough to help care for them as their health declined. I had reservations about this but felt I needed to be there for them. My four siblings live out of town so I can't depend on them for day-to-day help.

It has become an unbearable situation. I have no privacy. My mother looks out her window to make sure my car is in the driveway. She waits up until I come home, becomes upset if I stay out later than usual, and wants to know where I am at all times. She asks for the phone numbers of my friends so she can call and check on me.

My parents think I should spend all my days off with them, and they resent any time I spend with my friends. I feel like a caged bird. I love my parents but I need to have some space to live my own life. NO NAME, NO CITY

• • •

If it is at all possible, I suggest that you move. If this option is not feasible, you must explain to your parents, as you did to me, that their phoning friends to check on you is embarrassing and must stop. Be forthright and firm about it, and please don't let that demon "unearned guilt" deter you from getting your well-deserved independence (*The Boston Globe*, February 13, 1998: D12).

Concern about aging parents—who will care for them? where will they live?, how to balance the competing values of family privacy and family responsibility?—is increasingly heard among American adults at midlife. Contemporary adults are often labeled "the sandwich generation" because their pattern of deferred childbearing has resulted in having both young children and aging parents in need of care at the same time. On the one hand, middle-aged adults feel squeezed between two generations of family obligation and, on the other, pulled in different directions by the demands of family and work. Even when there are not young children clamoring for attention and care, aging parents can become a drain on one's privacy and independence. As Ann Landers's advice offered in the example cited above makes clear, individualism and independence in adulthood rank above family obligation on the contemporary American scale of values. The implicit message—one that would undoubtedly strike most Americans as reasonable rather than heartless—is that no one should feel guilt or remorse in refusing the onerous demands of aging parents. One would be justified in moving away, in reclaiming one's own life, if possible. But "if possible" begs many questions. The topic of aging and American families raises issues about the neediness of the elderly as the population of the United States grays: Just what are tolerable intergenerational constraints on one's "well-deserved" mobility and independence? To what extent should adult children be expected to assume the private responsibility of care for their aging parents? Most broadly, where do today's longer-living elderly fit in the context of the American family? Have they become more isolated as the bonds of family life have stretched and, perhaps, weakened?

The problems associated with aging are not new ones, of course, but they are coming into new focus in the context of a dramatic demographic revolution in life expectancy and longevity, of changes in family structure and the contested family values such change has generated, and of the shifting understandings of what it means to be old. That Americans are highly age conscious is no surprise to anyone living in this era, although age consciousness in American society is relatively new (Chudacoff 1989). The current linguistic impasse over what to call old people is indicative of the dilemma with which Americans currently regard aging; they are variously known as older Americans, the elderly, retirees, and senior citizens. Yet none of these labels helps clarify who should be considered old. Chronological age is an objective measure but not a reliable guide for categorizing the employment status, health, or mobility of this group. The American Association of Retired Persons (AARP), the second largest social organization in the United States after the Catholic Church, designated age fifty as the beginning point for senior status, but Social Security payments can begin at age sixty-two and mandatory retirement at any age has been legally overturned. Sports stars are notoriously old in their mid-thirties, whereas for others even "middle age" has come to be defined culturally rather than as the chronological midway point on the life expectancy charts. Baby boomers, with their characteristic demographic capacity to set cultural trends, are now beginning to turn fifty in droves, but so far have shown a greater propensity for nostalgically reliving their adolescence and young adulthood from the 1960s and 1970s than for claiming middle-aged maturity. Researchers now refer to the "old-old" as those over the age of seventy-five, to differentiate them from the "old" who are ten years younger.

U.S. cultural anxiety about aging is reflected in the all-too-predictable punch line of humorous birthday cards and in advertising jingles that promote vigor and vitality while targeting a narrowly defined demographic market (". . . because you're over fifty, and you're still swinging!"). Aging is something Americans of the late twentieth century mark but do not celebrate. Americans live in an era when getting old carries only a pejorative meaning. The largely unspoken problems of aging—debility and social and physical dependency—have special implications for family life. How do Americans best address the needs not just of a general population of elderly but of their own aging parents?

The Graying of the U.S. Population

Demographers point out that most of the gains in life expectancy throughout world history have been made in the twentieth century. In fact, "the changes have been so dramatic that it is currently estimated that of all the human beings who have ever lived to be 65 years or older, half are currently living" (Rowe and Kahn 1998: 3). For most of American history, life expectancy at birth was between thirty and forty years, a rate that still characterizes many developing nations today. Even by 1900, for example, life expectancy at birth for white men in the United States stood at forty-seven years, for white women forty-nine years, for black and other minority men thirty-three years, and for black and other minority women thirty-four years. In every decade of the twentieth century life expectancy improved steadily, although not at the same rate for each of these groups, so that by midcentury the relative rates were sixty-seven years (white men), seventy-two years (white women), fifty-nine years (minority men), and sixty-three years (minority women) (U.S. Bureau of the Census 1975: 55). In 1995, life expectancy at birth was seventy-three (white men), eighty (white women), sixty-five (black men), and seventy-four (black women), and projections for 2010 increase the life expectancy by an additional two years (U.S. Bureau of the Census 1997: 88). These numbers reflect a remarkable revolution in longevity and suggest why aging is an issue of such widespread interest. It is a historically unprecedented phenomenon with enormous social consequences.

One way to grasp the significance of this demographic revolution is to look at the characteristics of the new cohort of elderly Americans. Those over the age of seventy-five are currently the fastest growing segment of the U.S. population. Women make up the majority of older Americans aged sixty-five and over, and because of their longer life expectancy, they also compose an ever-greater proportion of the elderly population at each successive age level. Because women are less likely to remarry at older ages than are men, 52 percent of women over the age of seventy-five are living alone, compared to 21 percent of men that age (Dorgan 1996: 180). Between 2010, when the first of the baby boomers will begin to cross the threshold age of sixty-five, and 2030, when the end of this cohort catches up, the proportion of elderly in the United States will grow at an even faster rate, with new levels of demand for housing, health care, and other specialized services.

A more meaningful way to assess the impact and meaning of the demographic trend in aging is through a comparative perspective of different age cohorts. Who is old in a society has relevance in the context of who is young, who is middle-aged, and what those various life stages mean. Historically, the United States has had a very young population. From 1790, when the first federal census was recorded, to 1810, the median age of Americans was sixteen. By 1850 the median age had risen to nineteen, by 1870 to twenty, by 1920 to twenty-five, and by 1950 to thirty (Fischer 1977: 102–104). Only between 1950 and 1970, with the demographic bulge of the baby boom, did the median age in the United States decline. In 1970 it began to rise steadily again, and in 1998 stood at thirty-four. By 2025 the median age of the U.S. population is projected to be thirty-eight (U.S. Bureau of the Census 1997: 14).

In the seventeenth and eighteenth centuries, approximately 2 to 3 percent of the population were older people over the age of sixty-five; today some 13 percent fall into that category in the United States. For the first time in U.S. history, Americans over the age of sixty-five outnumber teenagers (Manheimer 1994: 3). Projections of U.S. residents for the years 2000 through 2025 show a significant shift in the age structure of the population: Children under the age of fourteen will drop below 20 percent of the total population, and adults in their prime working years, from twenty-five to sixty-four years of age, will drop from 52 percent to 48 percent. Adults over the age of sixty-five, however, will increase from 13 percent to 20 percent of the population in this twenty-five-year period (U.S. Bureau of the Census 1997: 25). An even smaller "sandwich generation," wedged between the dependent young and the elderly, will face increased financial and social pressures in the first fifty years of the new century.

In family terms, the new longevity of the U.S. population means that grandparents are now more likely to live to see their grandchildren grow to adulthood than in the past. In early America, because childbearing generally occurred over twenty years of a woman's adult life, a couple might have their youngest child at the same time as becoming grandparents for the first time. But most would not live to see their youngest child or their grandchildren grow up. As recently as 1960, only 16 percent of women at the age of fifty had a surviving parent. The projection is for this family structure to become increasingly prevalent (Dorgan 1996). In fact, women now "spend more years as the adult child of a parent older than age sixty-five than they do with children younger than age eighteen" (Maddox 1995: 362). As birthrates drop around the world,[1] the typical family of the future is more likely to consist of multiple generations of adults than of adults and young children.

Outline of an Old Age History in America

Demographic shifts, however dramatic, never tell the whole story of what it means to experience any life stage. Old age, as is true of other life stages, has a history—in this case, one that has only just begun to be retrieved from the historical record. Although many points about this history are currently disputed and much is still unknown, a general outline of an old-age history, even though predominantly of white Americans, can now be sketched.

Old Age in Early America

Historians widely agree that there was no golden age in the past when all elderly Americans had unquestioned power, status, and privilege. The aged poor were always marginalized—often despised and outcast. Elderly women were rendered socially and economically vulnerable by the death of a spouse, and black slaves continued to be worked or even sold in old age so as to reduce a planter's number of dependents. But through the seventeenth and eighteenth centuries, elderly white men with property in colonial New England did hold a social and economic position that was not diminished until the nineteenth century. David Fischer (1977), among the first of American historians to study old age, has argued that the elderly were respected and venerated in early America, particularly among the Puritans who understood the achievement of advanced age as a sign of being among God's elect. The hierarchical seating arrangements in New England meetinghouses were first arranged according to age, "graybeards" were evident in political life and continued to dominate the circles of power, and aging fathers were able to keep economic control over their land, often at the expense of their adult sons, as one important measure of their patriarchal power in the family.

Fischer cites the case of the Holt family of Andover, Massachusetts, as a typical example of the kind of economic power a landholding patriarch could wield in the seventeenth century. Nicholas Holt (1603–1686) worked his land with the help of his five sons but did not relinquish property—and therefore economic independence—to any of them until he was seventy-seven years old. By then, his eldest son was forty and had been married for twelve years. All five Holt sons achieved financial independence only at the time of their father's death. In the next generation, the same pattern continued. Henry Holt, the second son of Nicholas, had eight sons of his own. None of them received land until their father was seventy-three years old, in 1717, at which time four of them had been married between seven and seventeen years. The seventh son, William, was deeded the original homestead at the age of thirty but was required to take care of his parents for the rest of their lives, with precise provisions for that care fully spelled out in the agreement. Failure to supply any of the specified goods—from candles to hard cider—would, by the terms of the inheritance contract, result in the forfeiture of the property (Fischer 1977: 53–54).

As this case suggests, elderly property owners had considerable economic and family power in early America. They were loathe to relinquish it too soon, and a son's only recourse was to bide his time into middle age or to strike out on his own, usually through northern or westward migration, a pattern that increased in the eighteenth century as local land became less available and inheritance shares diminished in size.[2] The American historical record shows less evidence of hostility between fathers and sons than was characteristic of Europe, where an eighteenth-century Austrian folk song with the refrain "Father, when ya gonna gimme me the farm?/When ya gonna gimme the house?/When ya gonna retire to your room out of the way/And dig up your potatoes all day?" (Berkner 1973: 39) reveals these tensions rather starkly. But it is likely that the extensive economic power held by the propertied elderly in colonial America also caused some tension between the generations and created the basis for more emotional distance between fathers and sons than we might expect today.

What may be even harder for twentieth-century Americans to grasp today than the dynamics of economic power rooted in an agrarian, household economy are the different attitudes toward aging that prevailed in early America. Perhaps the most telling difference is revealed in two large censuses taken in the late eighteenth century in which respondents showed a tendency to report older ages than they actually were (Fischer 1977: 82). Today, of course, that tendency has been reversed, with the age bias distinctly shifted in the direction of youth. It is hard to imagine a situation, other than underage youth claiming to be at the legal age for assuming adult privileges, in which Americans would claim to be older than their actual age. Yet in the seventeenth and eighteenth centuries, status claims were clearly based on age rather than youth. Men's fashion was designed to promote looking older and women's to flatter the bodies of older matrons rather than highlight youthful ones. Attitudes about the elderly are cultural constructs, so they are never stable and unchanging. But there are many in-dications that the veneration of old age, at least through the late eighteenth century, was well established as an ideal, if not always as a practice.

Just when this began to change is the subject of historical debate. Fischer (1977) claims that there was an abrupt revolution in attitudes toward ag-ing between 1770 and 1820, part of a widespread upheaval of established political and social hierarchies, indicated by the proliferation of new terms of contempt for the elderly and a new glorification of youth. According to this analysis, the veneration of old age was radically overturned and re-placed with dismissal, ridicule, and abhorrence—in short, a cult of youth based on "gerontophobia." Other scholars have challenged this interpreta-tion and date the shift later, particularly after the Civil War (Achenbaum 1978; Haber 1983). Still others argue that the decline in status of the el-derly was a slow and steady process over the course of the nineteenth cen-tury rather than a sharp, revolutionary break (Gratton 1986).

In attempting to discredit a "modernization model" of old-age history—one that claims that the elderly lost power and status as a direct conse-quence of industrialization, urbanization, and of a demographic transition from conditions of high fertility–high mortality to low fertility–low mor-tality—some historians have stressed that the shift from the veneration of the elderly to the glorification of youth was primarily a shift in attitudes rather than the result of social structural change.[3] Attitudes about the el-derly are an important dimension of any historical account of old age, and many ideologies that took shape in the nineteenth century have continued to have real consequences for social groups and family life in the twentieth. It seems likely, however, that both social structural and cultural changes in the nineteenth-century United States interacted in complex ways to rede-fine old age as the social position of the elderly was being realigned relative to other social groups and family members. A number of these processes were at work in the late nineteenth century, and they contributed to a change for the worse in the lives of elderly Americans.

Reevaluating the Elderly: Structural and Attitudinal Change in the Nineteenth-Century United States

Economic change certainly had an impact on the elderly in the United States over the course of the nineteenth and twentieth centuries. Patriar-chal power based on control over land was undermined by the rise of an industrial economy, although this change occurred at very different rates depending on the geographic region. The elderly continued to be dispro-portionately employed in agriculture, both because agricultural labor was a traditional occupation of older workers and because most farmers needed to work well into old age for economic subsistence. Nevertheless, the overall labor force activity of the elderly did decline slowly over the course of the nineteenth century and through the early twentieth (Gratton 1986). The dramatic exodus of older Americans from the labor force beginning in the 1930s was a result not only of changing opportunities in the labor market but of new understandings of the elderly and old age that had emerged by this period.

While economic change was slowly transforming the structural base on which the livelihood and security of older Americans rested, other social and cultural forces associated with the growth of an urban, industrial, bureaucratic society were also beginning to reshape ideas about old age and the elderly (Haber 1983). The groups most responsible for articulating these new ideas were professionals in the fields of government, business, academia, social welfare, and medicine. By the second half of the nineteenth century and into the first quarter of the twentieth, a group of experts from a variety of different fields and perspectives had begun to direct their attention to a host of new social problems related to urban, industrial society that they hoped, through scientific study, to understand and eradicate. Disease and poverty topped the list of social problems in need of cure. Changing family relations also attracted the attention of professionals. The family still seemed to many analysts a crucible of society, a place where social relations could be strengthened or reformed for the good of the larger society. As we have seen, the newly assessed needs of vulnerable children and the special problems of uncontrollable adolescents gave rise to new programs, policies, and institutional responses in this era. Modern marriage and the shifting meaning of the family in society were subjected to the intense scrutiny of new experts. And so, by the late nineteenth century, it was not surprising that older Americans—increasingly being displaced from their former economic, social, and familial roles—would become the newest object of scientific and professional scrutiny.

One reason for the new attention to the elderly by the second half of the nineteenth century was that they had become more visible among the ranks of the poor. Almshouses, which had traditionally provided charity to the "worthy" needy of all ages in the past, were increasingly filled with the elderly poor. In Massachusetts, 26 percent of almshouse residents in 1864 were old people; by 1904, that proportion had risen to 48 percent (Haber 1983: 83). Fears about being relegated to the poorhouse were not unfounded. Sociologists and economists began to see not only a correlation between age and poverty but a causal relationship. It looked to social observers as though poverty was an inevitable outcome of old age, a result of the inability of the old to adapt to or keep up with the economic changes produced by industrialization. Orphans, widows, deserted wives, the sick, the temporarily unemployed—these were groups in need whom reformers believed they could help and, with proper instruction, redeem; hence many of the young and middle-aged poor were considered to be good candidates for other kinds of welfare measures than the almshouse, particularly outdoor relief. The old, on the other hand, were defined as a hopeless cause, rendered superfluous by an industrializing and urbanizing society (Quadagno 1986: 137). There was little that could be done for them except to provide shelter and a minimum of support as they entered the last stage of life. It was to be expected that this stage would be characterized by decrepitude and decay. The old came to be seen as objects of pity and no longer as worthy of veneration as they once had been. Their traditional experience, once accorded respect as the basis of wisdom, now seemed to have little value in a rapidly changing modern world.

A new emphasis on chronological age was another reason that the elderly began to stand out as a special group in this period. The rise of the insurance industry in the United States in the nineteenth century had produced a new interest in determining the length of the life span through statistical measurement. Age became a new way to classify people efficiently—not on the basis of individual traits, abilities, or needs, but as a category of people about whom scientific predictions could reliably be made. As age became a new means of categorizing the elderly as a group, the association of old age with disease and disability came to seem normal for everyone, not just the unfortunate few. The role of the medical establishment in helping to create this particular new understanding of old age is an especially important component in this story of the cultural shift in attitudes toward the old. While other experts were defining the old as inevitably poor and needy, doctors began to reinterpret the elderly as inevitably associated with disease, decay, weakness, and dependency. And increasingly it was doctors to whom the old were encouraged to turn for advice.

Among all the new experts emerging in the second half of the nineteenth century, physicians had been especially active in seeking new ways to consolidate and augment their professional status. They were highly successful in extending their sphere of influence over many areas of family life: wresting control over contraception from a wide variety of health practitioners, over childbirth from midwives, and over mother and infant health care from nurses and community clinics (D'Emilio and Freedman 1988). And they also turned their attention to the elderly, in particular by defining aging as an illness without a cure. At first this attitude meant that there was relatively little interest in the old, since their key illness, old age, did not lend itself to scientific research and new remedies. But as the aged came to be seen as a group apart, even their diseases were reinterpreted as something altogether different—not pneumonia, but "senile pneumonia," for example. The field of geriatric medicine was born in this era, and doctors began to assume an ever-larger role in addressing the needs of the elderly.

Even when healthy, an old person was defined as a potential patient—someone whose body would eventually succumb to the inevitable pathologies of old age. According to one doctor in 1888, "after 60, failure to recognize the changed condition and a continuance in the business habits of an earlier life . . . are often no better than suicide." In 1904, another cautioned, "the [elderly] patient must lead an absolutely quiet and uneventful life [and] curtail his business responsibilities" (Haber and Gratton 1994: 160). Withdrawal from active life was the prescription doctors gave to all elderly persons, regardless of their relative health or infirmity.

Professional social workers and government and business leaders also added their perspectives to this coalescing view of the elderly. Social workers proposed that older Americans needed to retreat from the world so that they could live out their lives "peacefully," separate from others in the society. Old age homes were designed originally for elderly women in the early nineteenth century, but by 1865 the first old-age home for men was established in Philadelphia (Haber 1983: 100). Although an improvement over the almshouse as a place of last resort, the old-age home nevertheless effectively segregated older Americans from others in the population. This idea of separation was reinforced in the world of work by government and business leaders who developed the idea of mandatory retirement for employees over the age of sixty-five or seventy in the military, government civil service, and large industries. Mandatory retirement was a rationalized, bureaucratic response that accompanied the development of corporate capitalism in the late nineteenth century. Business leaders supported it as a way to reduce unemployment and to bring in younger, more efficient, and more tractable workers. Labor leaders saw it as a strategy for transferring work across generations under conditions of a labor surplus (Graebner 1980: 13).

There would no longer be means tests to measure the ability or needs of individual workers; age was used as the new classification system, standardized for all workers. The assumption on which the program of mandatory retirement rested was that workers over the age of sixty-five or seventy were less efficient and productive than newer, younger workers. Removing the former from the labor market through mandatory retirement would decrease competition and promote the kind of flexibility that analysts believed a modern industrial economy required.

The impact of these programs was immediate in the first three decades of the twentieth century: In 1910 only forty-nine companies had private pension plans and only 2 percent of the elderly lived in old-age homes. By 1930, the number of companies offering pensions to their older employees had increased tenfold and some 69,000 Americans now resided in institutions exclusively housing the elderly (Haber 1983: 129). This shift was still small, however, in contrast to the segregation of elderly Americans from the general population that would occur after 1940. By then, the introduction of the Social Security Act, the most successful piece of legislation in Roosevelt's New Deal program, combined with the demographic revolution in life expectancy to produce a new stage in U.S. old-age history.

Old Age in the Twentieth Century:
The Revolutionary Impact of Social Security

In 1900, two-thirds of men over the age of sixty-five were employed. By 1970, just under a quarter were still in the labor force, and by 1995 that proportion had dropped even further, to 12 percent (Achenbaum 1978: 95; U.S. Bureau of the Census 1997: 48). This dramatic shift in the labor force participation of older men can be explained not only by the introduction of private pension plans and mandatory retirement regulations but by the passage of the Social Security Act in 1935, the first federally sponsored, old-age pension program to be adopted in the United States.

The United States was late among industrialized countries in establishing a national welfare program for the elderly. There was clearly an economic need to do so by the beginning of the twentieth century. A report of the New York Commission on Old Age Security, for example, estimated that between 38 and 75 percent of elderly individuals and between 10 and 48 percent of elderly couples fell below the income level necessary for basic survival (Quadagno 1988: 51). Bills for public pensions were repeatedly introduced in Congress between 1900 and 1935, yet a combination of countervailing forces prevented any from becoming national programs. Some analysts of the American welfare system have argued that military pensions established for Civil War veterans and their dependents, which by the early twentieth century had expanded into such a broad patronage program and bureaucracy that it usurped one-third of the federal budget, served to undermine public support for additional state-sponsored social welfare programs. Others have suggested that pension programs for the elderly were highly contested because they became identified with different class interests or regional and racial divisions in the United States (Quadagno 1988). Veterans' pensions and mothers' pensions epitomized the type of aid that prevailed in the United States in the nineteenth and early twentieth centuries. Both groups of recipients were considered morally worthy, unlike other groups, such as workers or the poor. This designation of worthiness remained the case until age became the new basis for classifying pension recipients (Skocpol 1992).

Many forces worked to constrain the development of economic support programs for the elderly, but the consequence was the same: Through the first three decades of the twentieth century, only a small minority of American workers had the security of a private or state-supported pension plan for their old age, and many of those plans went bankrupt or were disbanded altogether in the Depression. After 1929, it became increasingly clear to most Americans that the elderly could not rely on savings, family support, underfunded state programs, or private pension plans for adequate provision in old age. The economic catastrophe of the Great Depression created a ground swell of popular and political support for the creation of a national social security program, one that, in the words of President Franklin Delano Roosevelt in 1934, would "provide security against several of the great disturbing factors in life—especially those which relate to unemployment and old age" (Achenbaum 1978: 131).

The Social Security Act of 1935 was carefully crafted as policy to cover many competing interests and goals. Politicians were concerned with removing older workers from the labor force to cope with the high unemployment rates in the 1930s. Business interests came to support the program as a way to provide for greater overall economic stability and to ease the threat of labor unrest. Labor unions, though wary of enhancing the power of the state, had found it impossible to support their members through their own private pension plans. Still other advocates believed that the government had a social responsibility to help maintain a basic level of income for its citizens. Social Security was therefore designed both as an assistance program to those in need and as a system of social insurance for all Americans over the age of sixty-five.

Title I of the Social Security Act originally provided matching funds to the states to establish programs of financial assistance to older people in need, building on the way traditional poor relief had always been given through locally determined eligibility requirements and means tests (Quadagno 1986). In some states, for example, needy elderly persons who had family members capable of providing support were not eligible for assistance. The benefits varied greatly from state to state, since there were no uniform standards imposed by the federal government in this part of the program. Among the ten titles covered in the original Social Security Act, Title IV— Aid to Dependent Children—was a similarly constructed grant program. By the early 1970s, ADC (renamed Aid to Families with Dependent Children, or AFDC) had become the primary part of the program known to Americans as "welfare." In 1935, however, poor children, poor old people, and the blind were all still encompassed in the definition of the "worthy" needy. As the numbers and racial composition of each group needing assistance changed in the second half of the twentieth century, such determinations of worthiness were also reassessed. By that time, the neediest elderly were far outnumbered by other older Americans receiving benefits from the insurance part of the Social Security program, which quickly came to be understood as an earned entitlement rather than a welfare payment.

Title II of the Social Security Act, by contrast to Title I or IV, was set up as a tax-based, mandatory insurance program, in which contributions made by employees and employers provided the funds for benefits to all workers beginning at age sixty-five. The idea of establishing a reserve fund for future use was revised to a "pay-as-you-go" program, an intergenerational transfer in which the tax revenues of the employed provided the funds to cover social security payments to the current cohort of the elderly. The new understanding of this kind of program was highlighted by the chair of the Senate Finance Committee during initial deliberations about the act when he claimed "Social Security is not a handout; it is not charity; it is not relief. It is an earned right based upon the contributions and earnings of the individual. As an earned right, the individual is eligible to receive his benefit in dignity and self-respect" (Achenbaum 1986a: 164). Old Age, Survivors, and Disability Insurance (OASDI), as Title II came to be called, quickly emerged as the centerpiece of the social security program for older Americans.

In 1939, amendments to the original act were passed that greatly expanded the number of potential beneficiaries, adding spouses at age sixty-five, widows and dependent children, and the dependent parents of workers who had died. When the first insurance benefits began to be paid in 1940, only about 20 percent of older Americans were eligible to receive them. Over the next thirty years, as eligibility continued to be expanded to a broader group of Americans and as benefits were supplemented with higher payments, some 93 percent of all older Americans were eventually covered by the program. By the 1970s, Social Security was the basic means of economic support for people over age sixty-five (Achenbaum 1978: 144). Although it now pays out more in benefits than most workers have contributed in taxes during their working years, it is still understood as an entitlement program—one that is returning to workers their own earnings—rather than a government-sponsored welfare program. It is not an overstatement to say that the economic and political consequences of the Social Security program have transformed both the social structural position of and attitudes toward the elderly in American society. The reversal in fortune for many elderly Americans, although by no means all, has been recent, dramatic, and far-reaching in the second half of the twentieth century. Social Security is the key source of change in the history of the elderly in the United States, and it is central to the drama that is still being played out in economic, political, social, and family circles.

The Economic and Political Transformation in the
Lives of Older Americans

A primary justification for establishing the Social Security program for the elderly had been to eliminate the widespread dependency that seemed an inevitable part of growing old. The federally appointed Social Security

Board in 1937 had determined that only 34.7 percent of Americans over the age of sixty-five could support themselves through their own earnings, savings, or private pension plans. Another 19.8 percent received public or private assistance. It was therefore the remaining 45.5 percent of elderly Americans who were of critical importance, for they were defined by the board as dependent or potentially dependent on others for support (Achenbaum 1978: 140). As social security expanded to include agricultural and domestic workers, military personnel, the self-employed, and government workers in the 1950s and 1960s, a wider economic impact began to be felt. In 1959, 35.2 percent of Americans over the age of sixty-five were below the poverty line. By 1970 that proportion dropped to 24.6 percent, and following changes to Social Security authorized in 1972 that automatically adjusted benefits to current rates of inflation, it dropped again to 15.7 percent (Achenbaum 1978: 150). It has been estimated that, without Social Security, 56 percent of the elderly would have been in poverty in 1978 (Preston 1984: 436). In 1995, the proportion of elderly Americans in poverty was 10.5 percent, less than the 14 percent in poverty among the population as a whole (U.S. Bureau of the Census 1997: 476).

Not all of the elderly have escaped being poor, of course. Older Americans living below the poverty line tend to be disproportionately minorities and women, indication that many of the racial-ethnic and gender inequities structured into the political economy are reproduced at every stage of life. But the dramatic improvement of economic status in old age for the majority of older Americans in the second half of the twentieth century is striking evidence of the overall success of the Social Security program. As was true in its origin, Social Security continues to have support because it satisfies many disparate goals. It simultaneously offers financial security to the elderly, removes the burden of support from other family members, and provides the kind of large-scale economic stability that politicians, business leaders, and labor groups find it in their interests to support. Yet, the expansion of Social Security into a full-fledged entitlement program in the 1950s and 1960s took root in a specific era of American prosperity, as incomes were rising and the labor force was expanding. In one sense it was an extensive welfare program for the elderly that was put in place in the postwar era without any highly visible costs to younger Americans. Since the 1970s, however, the economic and demographic foundation on which the program was based has changed, and political tensions—many of them intergenerational—are more evident. The system of Social Security that had so dramatically changed the old-age experience for the postwar generation of older Americans is in financial jeopardy and threatens to withhold the same level of economic security from their children, grandchildren, or future generations. The politics of the family lie just below the surface of the Social Security crisis, which in the 1990s has loomed large in the rhetoric of economists, politicians, and social policy makers. Where the elderly are positioned politically is giving shape to the next stage of old-age history in the United States.

The Politics of Old Age

As the economic lot of older Americans has improved, so has the political clout of this group. Yet the original basis for political power was the result of specific policies instituted by the government rather than the consequence of a grassroots effort by the elderly or their advocates. Many groups, for example, were specifically targeted in the War on Poverty programs of the early 1960s, including blacks, rural Appalachian whites, unemployed heads of household, and children. The elderly were not targeted, yet they ultimately benefited more than any other constituency because of the introduction of the Medicare and Medicaid programs in 1965. Medicare was designed as a hospital insurance plan for Social Security beneficiaries with a voluntary supplemental insurance plan covering the costs of physicians' services, and Medicaid was intended to finance medical services for all recipients of public welfare and others who could not afford health care costs. When President Johnson signed these programs into law in 1965, he stressed the legacy of this legislation: "In 1935 when . . . Franklin Delano Roosevelt signed the Social Security Act, he said it was, and I quote him, 'a cornerstone in a structure which is being built but . . . is by no means complete.' . . . Those who share this day will also be remembered for making the most important addition to that structure" (Achenbaum 1986b: 52).

In a society in which government-subsidized health coverage is provided to no other group except members of Congress, the elderly stand out as a special constituency. Because the beneficiaries of Social Security and Medicare were determined by age rather than need, older Americans now receive a substantial share of government subsidies, more than 40 percent of the total federal budget in 1980 (Achenbaum 1986a: 182). For many older Americans, this subsidy is not based on need but is simply the consequence of age classification. What was intended to be a safety net for the neediest among the old now resembles "a well-padded hammock for middle- and upper-class retirees. . . . One third of Medicare benefits, nearly two fifths of Social Security benefits, and more than two thirds of federal pension benefits go to households with incomes above the U.S. median" (Peterson 1996: 70–72). The expansion of an institutional framework—with the passage of the Older Americans Act of 1965, the establishment of such government agencies as the National Institute of Aging, the growth of commissions and conferences on aging, and the proliferation of associations and caucuses of the elderly—now ensures that senior citizens are an effective and powerful lobby acting in their own behalf. Without an economy growing at postwar rates, however, entitlement programs to the elderly have new meaning in the realm of distribution politics. Two other constituencies are increasingly pulled into competition with the elderly over the distribution of resources: adult children of the elderly, many of them part of the baby boom cohort for whom the long-range financial viability of the Social Security system is in question, and young children, who face many current pressing needs of their own. In both cases, there are new sources of tension that are currently being played out in the social arena and in family dynamics.

Adult Children of the Elderly and the Crisis in Social Security

Within one generation, the economic foundation on which a new level of old-age security was built has begun to show signs of weakening, in part because of the demographic shift that has been occurring in American society and the structure of the Social Security program as a "pay-as-you-go" system. In 1960, there were 5.1 employed taxpayers supporting each social security recipient. In 1996, there were 3.3, and it is estimated that by 2040, when the large cohort of baby boomers will have become fully eligible for benefits, there may be only 1.6 to 2.0 such workers to support each recipient in the system (Peterson 1996: 57). Government expenses for Social Security are expected to rise precipitously, particularly in terms of health care coverage for the rapidly expanding group of older (especially old-old) Americans. The potential for intergenerational tensions may be exacerbated by racial-ethnic and class tensions as well, since a growing proportion of the future employees, who will be working to support a large group of elderly white, middle class retirees, are nonwhite and less affluent.

As current fixes for the economic problems of Social Security are being debated in the political arena—whether to raise the age of eligibility or whether to establish means testing, for example—new social and cultural questions about intergenerational relations are raised as a consequence. The question of who should take care of the elderly, once so clearly defined as a family obligation, now has new meaning for the "sandwich generation." Government support for their elderly parents has relieved (and will continue to relieve) many adult children of what would otherwise have been an overwhelming, private financial burden. The kind of family tension rooted in prolonged relations of dependency is less likely to affect parents and children today than at any time in the past. And yet, the sense that one age group benefits at the expense of another is always fertile ground for social tension. The current bumper sticker that proclaims "I'm spending my children's inheritance" has an ironic double entendre: At stake is not just a private family inheritance but the social inheritance of a national insurance program to which all adult cohorts now feel they have earned entitlement.

Children Versus the Elderly:
The Intergenerational Distribution of Resources

If their adult children have cause for ambivalent feelings about the new political power of elderly Americans of this generation, another age cohort is even more directly affected. Children, the only constituency in the United States unable to mount an effective lobbying campaign in its own behalf, have lost resources as a group as the elderly have gained them. Demographically, as we have seen, the proportion of children in the population has been declining steadily since the early nineteenth century with the sole exception of the postwar baby boom surge, whereas the proportion of the elderly has increased dramatically in the second half of the twentieth century. Along with this demographic shift, conditions have deteriorated for children as they have improved for older Americans. Apparently, the current cohorts of grandparents and great-grandparents in the United States are in competition for societal resources with their grandchildren, a competition that the elderly are, at present, clearly winning.

The growing number of children in poverty and the sharp cutbacks in programs aimed at children since the late 1970s are evidence of the deteriorating conditions for American children. In 1984, the total federal expenditure on programs for children was only one-sixth of expenditure on the elderly; spending per child was only 9 percent of per capita spending on those over age sixty-five (Preston 1984: 440). In contrast to the rising federal expenditures on health care (Medicare and Medicaid), which disproportionately benefit the elderly, the resources committed to public schools, benefiting children, have been diminishing. By most standards—including test scores, hours of school-assigned homework, years spent in school, and functional illiteracy rates—the educational performance of American children has deteriorated along with declining school resource levels over the past thirty years. One critic has argued, "If we are going to rely on just 1.6 to 2.0 workers to support every retiree, . . . we should want today's children to become the best educated, most skilled, and most productive citizens imaginable" (Peterson 1996: 74). The trends in the allocation of federal resources have been markedly in the other direction, however—away from children who do not vote, who are not politically mobilized, and who, although they may have committed adults as their spokespersons, have no direct voice of their own. Although the state has subsumed more responsibility for the care of older Americans, private families remain the primary means of support for children (Preston 1984: 443). To the extent that family life has become more fragile, then, children are at a distinct disadvantage. One of the highest social costs of having created an entitlement program solely on the basis of old age may be the unintended consequence of its impact on the well-being of American children.

The Chronological Frontier: Family and Community Life Among the Elderly

The political and economic transformation in the lives of the elderly in the second half of the twentieth century has a family and a community dimension that is not fully captured in the broad sweep of social and demographic history of this cohort. Changes in household structure, communities, and intergenerational family relations have been dramatic and without precedent. This generation of elderly Americans has been described as living on a "chronological frontier" (FitzGerald 1986: 205)—carving out new forms of social organization and redrawing the traditional boundaries of family life in the process. Whereas the other life stages of childhood, adolescence, and adult married life have been undergoing change for a century or more, the experience of growing old is being shaped now by the post–World War II cohorts of older Americans, who range in age from their fifties to their nineties. They are the pioneers of a new life stage that is still very much in the process of evolving, and, as is the case on other frontiers, there are many others who will soon be following in their footsteps into this new territory.

Households and Communities

One of the most dramatic changes in the lives of older Americans is in where they live. In 1900, only about 8 percent of persons over age sixty lived outside the family: with nonkin, as a boarder in a lodging house, or in an institutional setting. The vast majority—70 percent—headed households of their own that included both unmarried and married children or other kin. These older couples typically lived with unmarried children, often the youngest child, whose role was defined as the caretaker of the aging parents. The remaining 22 percent lived in the households of relatives (Smith 1986; Haber and Gratton 1994: 27–28). A widowed woman who was no longer able to maintain her own household would likely move into the home of her married children. An elderly person who had never married would live with siblings or other kin. Until the middle of the twentieth century, this pattern of co-residence was so standard as to be unremarkable. Although Americans have always believed strongly in the independence and autonomy of the married couple, for most of American history this norm has by necessity competed with the co-residence of elderly parents. Over the past forty years, however, older Americans have shifted from living with their children and other relatives in family households to living alone and in communities with unrelated others. One historian has called this change "a silent revolution . . . in intergenerational arrangements" (Smith 1986: 107), and it reflects not only the greater economic independence of the elderly but the high value placed on residential autonomy.

During the nineteenth century, household structure was largely determined by residence on a farm (38 percent of those sixty years of age and older in 1900), in a village (25 percent), or in a city (37 percent) (Haber and Gratton 1994: 20–47). Only more affluent white families on farms and in cities could afford to support large extended households; most elderly Americans lived instead with a single adult child or couple. The African American elderly were exceptions; their extended households were a response to the sharecropping system in the South that demanded a large family labor force. Elderly Americans who lived in villages in the nineteenth century were the most notable, however, in their capacity to establish their own independent households. Many were Civil War veterans whose pensions allowed them to achieve a form of household autonomy in retirement that would not become widespread among other elderly Americans until the second half of the twentieth century. These living patterns are an important clue to the preference for independent living that was chosen when conditions permitted. Co-residence, rather than a sign of family togetherness that has been lost, was more often an accommodation that produced tension within households. A woman who took her elderly mother into her household in the 1930s noted, "Harmony is gone. Rest has vanished. . . . The intrusion is probably a common cause of divorce, and most certainly of marital unhappiness and problems in children" (Haber and Gratton 1994: 39–40).

By 1996, among Americans aged sixty-five and older, 73 percent of men and 40 percent of women were living on their own in households with a spouse present. Another 17 percent of men and 41 percent of women lived alone. Only 9 percent of men and 19 percent of women in this age group lived with other relatives or nonrelatives (U.S. Bureau of the Census 1997: 48). Family households have become much more age-segregated as a consequence, now typically comprising young married couples at one end of the life cycle and older married couples at the other, with fewer households for shorter periods of time made up of parents and young children.

The significance of this revolution in residence patterns is particularly striking in the lives of women. Although a married woman's life was once centered for most of her adult years around childbearing and childrearing, today a much higher proportion of her life is spent as part of a married couple without children present and residing alone. Hareven has argued that the co-residence patterns of the past meant that the experience of widowhood did not always create a sharp discontinuity in family life for older women. Many moved into the homes of their married children, where the opportunities for sustained family interaction were preserved (Hareven 1986). From this perspective, the unprecedented rise in the number of older women who now live alone is evidence of the impact of the "empty nest" stage, and it signals the new potential for loneliness and solitude in place of family embeddedness. But from another perspective, the proportion of older women now living alone reflects their preference for independence rather than a breakdown of family ties. There is still considerable evidence of intergenerational exchange between the elderly and their adult children; in the late twentieth century, however, particularly because of Social Security benefits, more elderly women have been able to achieve the ideal of residential autonomy that was economically and culturally elusive in the past. "Intimacy at a distance" has become the achievable living situation Americans prefer in their old age (Haber and Gratton 1994: 22).

Communities, in addition to households, have been radically restructured by the new life stage being defined by older Americans. Although many elderly parents continue to live near their adult children and to be integrated into many aspects of their families' lives, others have helped forge entirely new ways of living. In 1956, the federal government began to subsidize housing for the elderly, mostly in the form of age-segregated apartment complexes (FitzGerald 1986: 210). One of the most dramatic innovations of the late twentieth century is the "retirement community," a self-contained, age-segregated town or city in the Sunbelt where retired Americans have self-consciously defined a lifestyle built around leisure in a community of their peers. Age restrictions in such communities specify that every household must have at least one member over the age of fifty and that there are no households that contain children under the age of eighteen (Findlay 1992: 160–213). In her study of one such community—Sun City Center, Florida—in the early 1980s, Frances FitzGerald noted the order and control that characterized the physical construction of this small town:

The curving white streets—with names like La Jolla Avenue and Pebble Beach Boulevard—lead only back upon themselves, and, since the land is so flat, they give no vistas on the outside world. Turning through the points of the compass, the visitor comes to another lake, another golf course, another series of white houses. The houses are not identical—the developer always gives buyers several models to choose from—but they are all variations on the same theme: white ranch house. Then, too, the whole town looks as if it had been landscaped by the same landscape gardener. Every house has a Bermuda-grass lawn, a tree surrounded by white gravel, and a shrubbery border set off by white stones. . . . No toys litter the pathways. The streets and the sidewalks are so clean they look scrubbed (FitzGerald 1986: 225).

The social construction of life in this community and others like it reveals a desire to preserve order and control. In the traditional manner of utopian communities, people in Sun City focus on the present without reference to the past. One resident told FitzGerald that "no one gives a hang here what you did or where you came from. . . . It's what you are now that matters" (1986: 219), although such a statement belied the more covert forms of status consciousness that characterized Sun City, as well as the kind of conformity of style and social homogeneity on which this community was built. Recognizing the special medical and caretaking needs of a population made up of the elderly, some retirement communities offer a range of types of residences, from private homes for independent retirees to nursing care centers for the most dependent. They are communities that have, for many elderly, become surrogate or substitute families, providing a variety of services and attending to the needs of an aging population in a way that used to be the sole responsibility of kin.

Age-segregated communities are not the only residential alternatives that this generation of elderly Americans has helped construct. Various experimental communities have formed around the country that stress interdependence—from age-integrated cohousing projects to suburban houses and city apartment complexes where elderly residents live together and share meals, communal activities, and opportunities for social interaction (*New York Times*, December 18, 1997, B10). Yet, since the late 1940s, the private, single-family, detached home has epitomized the American dream. Most of the housing stock in the United States has been built since 1940, and the vast majority of these units are single-family homes—ever-greater in size despite the smaller numbers of Americans per household (Hayden 1984: 12). The lack of options in housing and flexibility in living situations presents special problems in a society with a rapidly aging population. The desire for family-like living environments in which the elderly can maintain their independence and foster social connections is a challenge for planners, architects, politicians, and community activists. What is clear in this time of transition in living arrangements is that the choice of residence provides something more than simple shelter. The quality of embeddedness—for better or for worse—in a web of social interactions and obligations that characterized living in family units for most elderly Americans in the past is no longer a routine aspect of the process of growing old. How to construct the households and communities that will allow for the kind of autonomy and independence Americans value while ensuring sociability, care, and a meaningful existence for the elderly will continue to be a challenge in the next decades as more people enter this life stage.

Intergenerational Family Relations:
The Contours of Grandparenthood

Whether parents and children are living together or apart, cross-generational relations in American families must always be negotiated. Dependency—in either direction, and especially as it shifts over time from the dependence of children on parents to that of elderly parents on their children—inevitably weaves some predictable tensions into family life. Demos argued that, among seventeenth-century New Englanders, "the position of the elderly was sociologically advantageous but psychologically disadvantageous. Their control of important resources seemed to command honor and respect, but not affection or sympathetic understanding" (1978: 282). In contrast to the strains between parents and children that were rooted in need and obligation, the relationships between grandparents and grandchildren in the past were close and affectionate. Grandparents named their grandchildren as beneficiaries in their wills in colonial America, and they often became the guardians if the children were orphaned. The tendency of these custodial grandparents to show "too great indulgence" was cited in a tract on childrearing, one indication that the nature of the bond between grandparents and grandchildren differed from that of parents and children (Demos 1978: 258–259).

Although the quality of intergenerational relationships is difficult to reconstruct in the past, the number of such bonds offers another avenue for interpretation and speculation. Demos cites two cases of large families from seventeenth-century New Hampshire in which, at the time of the grandparents' deaths at seventy-five and eighty years of age, each family contained about fifty grandchildren and, in one, nearly twenty great-grandchildren (1978: 267). New England had a high fertility rate and a low mortality rate, and these were two families with exceptionally robust patriarchs. But many grandchildren in colonial New England, at least for some part of their youth, had the opportunity to know their grandparents. In seventeenth-century Plymouth County, 68 percent of twenty-year-olds lived to age sixty or older, as did 72 percent in Ipswich, Massachusetts (Haber and Gratton 1994: 26). Although the tensions and strains that characterized the relationships between landholding parents and their children did not necessarily extend to the grandchildren, it seems unlikely, given the sizes of these families, that there was much room for individual attention in the grandparent-grandchild relationship.

Through the early twentieth century, becoming a grandparent was a status that was generally achieved in middle age. It was not unusual for a couple to become grandparents in their forties and fifties, while they still had young children of their own to raise. In 1900, half of all fifty-year-old women had children under the age of eighteen; by 1980 only a quarter did so (Cherlin and Furstenberg 1986: 28). One consequence of these demographic patterns is that, throughout most of U.S. history, grandparenthood was not defined as a distinctly separate role for adults but was more often in competition with the daily demands and obligations of parenthood. As fertility rates dropped and as life expectancy rose, two new characteristics of being a grandparent emerged: More people began to be grandparents for longer periods of their life, beyond their midlife years and into old age. And the role of the grandparent became increasingly separate from that of the parent (Cherlin and Furstenberg 1986).

Today, then, Americans are less likely to be in the process of raising their own children when they become grandparents than they were in the past. They are more likely to have retired from the work force, with a considerable amount of leisure time facing them. They are likely to be more affluent and able to live independently from their families. They will have far fewer grandchildren in terms of absolute numbers but greater opportunity to construct a more intense and focused relationship with those few that they do have. They will face several stages in their career as grandparents: first, as grandparents to young children; then, to teenagers; finally, as the grandparents of adults. Although each of these stages will call for different modes of interaction, the ideal grandparent-grandchild relationship will continue to be defined by the norms of love, affection, playful companionship, and noninterference. Grandparenthood, ideally, will carry fewer responsibilities than parenthood; it will be the icing on the cake of familial social relationships, captured well in the contemporary saying, "Your children are your principal; your grandchildren are your interest" (Cherlin and Furstenberg 1986: 35–51).

Not all grandparents can achieve this idealized relationship with their grandchildren, of course. Many cross-generational ties are instrumental ones by necessity, in which the grandparents are forced to assume parental responsibilities. Grandmothers play an important role in providing assistance and childcare in low-income black families, often acting as supervisors and disciplinarians of the children, as well as caretakers. Even in middle-class, two-parent black families, grandparents have tended to be more involved in providing childcare, financial support, and discipline than have their white counterparts (Cherlin and Furstenberg 1986: 131). A 1998 New York Times article cited the incidence of health-related stress problems among the growing numbers of grandparents who were custodians to some 4 million children in the United States, many of whom had been abused, neglected, or abandoned by their parents. Many of these custodial grandparents reported feeling a sense of guilt for not being able to provide children with a more ideal family environment; a sense of incompetence in coping with school work, technology, and other complexities of the modern world; and a profound sense of isolation (July 28, 1998, B8). In these concerns, custodial grandparents share with many parents a fear of loss of control over the social world contemporary children inhabit. It is not surprising that many grandparents who are unexpectedly thrust into this instrumental role find their family obligations disorienting and stressful. An increasing number of first-time parents do as well.

As divorce has become a more common feature of American family life, its impact is felt among members of the extended family, not just parents and children. In some cases, divorce can bring grandparents into closer contact with their grandchildren, especially if the divorced daughter is the custodial parent. But a noncustodial divorced son may find his own relationship with his children constrained and that of the paternal grandparents diminished as well. One telling response to the high divorce rates in the late 1970s and early 1980s was the "grandparents' rights" legislation that many states passed to give grandparents the legal standing to request visitation rights with their grandchildren (Cherlin and Furstenberg 1986: 3).

The New Frontier of Family Life

The chronological frontier being shaped in the late twentieth century by the postwar cohorts of older Americans involves a variety of pioneering efforts. With a history that spans the twentieth century, the elderly have experienced profound social, political, and economic changes in the United States. The cultural distance they have traveled, moreover, is even greater than a list of these social structural changes might suggest. For this generation, adulthood was shaped in important ways by the ideologies and images of American family life in the 1950s. The set of expectations, values, and behavior that developed in that decade was, as I have argued previously, a socially constructed version of "traditional" American family values. The decade of the 1950s was an era in which a particular set of norms about family life took shape against the backdrop of economic prosperity and political insecurity. The importance of the family as the filter through which those social transformations were experienced should not be underestimated. Family norms shaped in the 1950s had an impact that resonated throughout the culture and over the next several decades. Although the adulthood of many elderly Americans was forged in that era, this group has shown remarkable flexibility in redefining their family commitments as they have entered the next life stage of old age. In embracing autonomy in their households and communities and an uneasy balance of autonomy and connection in their family relationships, they have been pioneers on the new frontier of family life at the turn of the new century.

In their relationships with their adult children, the elderly have articulated a norm of "friendly equality" to characterize their preference for independence and their adult children's preference for family noninterference by the older generation (Cherlin and Furstenberg 1986: 40). According to one resident of Sun City, "Our children treat us as friends. . . . They see what full lives we have, and they say we're models for them" (FitzGerald 1986: 242). FitzGerald noted that relations between the generations were respectful and affectionate but not entwined—an apt description of the complicated balance of closeness and distance many have attempted to create. Describing his relationship with his aging parents, James Atlas noted the guilt and anxiety that often characterize cross-generational interactions: How to care for aging parents at a distance? How to become your parents' parent in times of important decisions? How, indeed, to negotiate the stages of one's own life given the longevity of the old-old? Atlas cites the case of a friend, age seventy, whose ninety-one-year-old mother "calls twice a day, asking me why I don't call her up, and my children [who call] twice a day, asking me for money." Even more often, however, there is anxiety about how to bridge the distance between generations of adults in the family and how to prevent the oldest members of the family from feeling cut off, lonely, and socially adrift.

Just as this generation of elderly Americans has been trying to construct new relationships with their adult children in the 1980s and 1990s, they have also been pioneers in the latest shift in American attitudes toward young children. In their study of the new grandparent role, Cherlin and Furstenberg found that older Americans were fully aware of the changed nature of their interaction with the younger generation, in contrast to their earlier relationships with their own grandparents. One contemporary grandmother, interviewed at a senior citizen's center, was particularly articulate about the contrast with previous generations:

My grandmother was a matriarch. There's no comparison whatsoever between the grandmothers of the previous days and now. Our grandmother was the queen of the family; we looked up to her. She wasn't mean—she was good, she was kind—but she was the boss of a family. I am not a boss. . . .
The grandmother [was] the queen of the family. You must never criticize her, even when she [was] wrong. I never dared open my mouth. . . . I couldn't be a companion. The only thing I didn't like is there was no companionship. There was love, an awful lot of love and respect, whereas with my grandchildren, it is companionship. I'm their pal. He's 'Dan' and I'm 'Ruth.' Half of the time they don't say 'Grandma,' they say 'Ruth' to me. I don't get angry. I wouldn't dare have thought of calling my grandmother by her name. . . . To be a grandmother and a grandfather of the present day cannot compare to be-

ing grandparents of other days. I think these days are much happier" (Cherlin and Furstenberg 1986: 7–8).

This quotation contains much of the ambivalence reflected in contemporary relationships between the old and the young. Such relationships are built on affectionate companionship rather than respectful distance. They have the potential to be loving, joyful, and satisfying. Yet, in the erosion of authority and status within the family that the elderly have experienced as the trade-off for affectionate companionship, something more elusive is lost as well. Companionship without mutuality tends to have a hollow core. It becomes a difficult relationship to sustain, except in the most superficial manner. Cherlin and Furstenberg found that there were many styles of interaction in the grandparent-grandchild relationship: from remote (29 percent of those studied) to companionate (55 percent) to involved (16 percent) (1986: 77). That almost twice as many relationships are remote as are involved may suggest something about the difficulties built into the modern grandparent role. Sustaining the companionate relationship as the grandchildren move into adolescence and adulthood is one of the family challenges older Americans will continue to face in the future.

In the cultural context of the 1990s, children are still talked about as priceless and treasured, even though they have been losing access to valued societal resources and even though the actual relationships many adults have with them are often more attenuated than in the past. In her interviews in Sun City, FitzGerald found that some retirees said they "missed seeing children around," which they meant quite literally. They wanted to see them, but from a distance. Few wanted to have them around all the time. In the words of one resident, "I love children dearly, but I don't crave to fall over tricycles on my lawn or see young couples mooning over each other" (FitzGerald 1986: 234–236). In these attitudes, the elderly are no different than others in American society who value their own autonomy, independence, and a lighter load of family obligations. Indeed, as they struggle to find the proper balance of commitment to the family versus commitment to the self and to peers, the elderly appear to be charting new territory. The family roles they carve out at the end of their lives may be very different from the ones they experienced at earlier stages, but these roles are likely to be an important model for other family ties in the future.

Conclusion

Older Americans have developed economic, political, and demographic clout over the past fifty years. Although old age itself is not new, a life stage that is defined by the capacity for independence is. The paradox is that the same generation of Americans who were shaped by the postwar experience of the 1950s, the most intensely familistic era in the twentieth century, are now the pioneers of a new mode of family relations. "Intimacy at a distance" is the term that has been used to characterize the residential preferences of elderly Americans in the second half of the twentieth century, but it might also be used to define the new kind of relations that are being forged within many families in the United States. Intimacy and distance, connection and autonomy, affectionate companionship and involvement— these are the competing pulls that the elderly are trying to keep in balance in their family relationships. More than any other group or age cohort, the elderly have been pioneers in shifting the discussion of their needs and interests from the realm of the private family into the public sphere. Historians Haber and Gratton have noted that "the road to security [for the elderly] turned away from family and work, and toward the state" (1994: 185). In this area, as in others, elderly Americans may be leading the way in unsettling old certainties—particularly ones that claim the essential privacy and independence of the American family. In the lives of the contemporary elderly, "private and public" and "autonomous and interdependent" are taking on new meanings.

Notes

1. Currently, the birthrate in the United States as a whole is 2.0, at population replacement level, primarily because of the high birthrate among immigrants. In many countries in the developed world, however, the birthrate has dropped to below-replacement levels as women continue to delay or forgo childbearing in order to pursue educational and employment opportunities. The *New York Times* recently reported, "There is no longer a single country in Europe where people are having enough children to replace themselves when they die. Italy recently became the first nation in history where there are more people over the age of 60 than there are under the age of 20. This year Germany, Greece, and Spain will probably all cross the same eerie divide" (July 10, 1998: A1, A6). In the Italian city of Bologna, with more highly educated women than any other place in Italy, the birthrate was 0.8 in 1997; the proportion of the city's aged population is rapidly growing, with 1,500 people now turning seventy-five every year. With its rapidly aging population and sharply reduced birthrate, Europe will face even sooner the issues that are posed for the United States in this chapter.

2. Some New England towns had a high proportion of elderly precisely because the young migrated out. In Hampton, New Hampshire, for example, the proportion of sixty-year-olds in the population increased from 4 percent in 1656 to 6.3 percent in 1680 (Demos 1978: 253). The elderly population of established New England communities was between 4 and 7 percent, whereas commercial centers, such as Boston and Newport, had a smaller proportion of elderly because of the steady flow of young newcomers into these cities (Manheimer 1994: 8)

3. In the mid-1960s, family historians launched a major research effort that also started from a critique of modernization theory. The first research overturned the

claim that extended families became nuclear as a result of industrialization. Historical demographers reconstructed households in the past and found that the nuclear form had predominated in preindustrial Western societies (Laslett 1965; Wrigley 1966, 1969; Laslett and Hall 1972) and that, occasionally, extended families resulted as a response to industrialization (Anderson 1980). Studies of attitudes, ideologies, and meanings in family life have also shaped the field of family history. As the history of old age takes off with a similar trajectory, it is worth reminding scholars in this new field that many of the best studies in family history trace attitudes and social structures as interdependent rather than mutually exclusive areas of inquiry.

6

Conclusion

Are children more at risk today than ever before? Are adolescents beyond the reach of parental control and more at odds with the traditional values of family life? Are adults more selfish, allowing their own needs and desires to weaken long-term commitment to stable marriage and family responsibility? Are the elderly needier and more isolated from family life than in the past? All of these questions and others like them that go to the heart of American family life are a familiar part of contemporary public discourse. Anyone and everyone feels capable of talking about "The Family" in the broadest terms because it is an institution we all feel we know so intimately. In the course of writing this book, I learned to listen very carefully to what people thought I was studying when I mentioned "American family patterns" or "family values." Unlike many academic studies, which can sound mystifying to the nonspecialist, this one always brought a quick nod of recognition. "How interesting," most people would say, with only the barest snippet of descriptive information about the nature of my project. And then they would just as quickly launch into their own interpretation of the American family drawn from their reading of politics, popular culture, and personal experience—invariably choosing vastly different topics and themes as the crucial ones to be considered in any overview of the family.

The problem, of course, is that our own experience is always too narrow to serve as the lens for full analysis of any social institution. What we see with our own eyes is determined by where we're looking, and when. And the social environment that surrounds our experience, that invisible world of powerful social forces that sociologists attempt to make more visible, creates economic, political, cultural, and historical blinders, in addition to those created by our personal biases. American family patterns have changed in dramatic ways in the course of American history. To have the broader picture, it is necessary to step beyond the immediacy of one's own experience.

The task of understanding family life is complicated by the seemingly universal nature of growing up in a family context. The developmental stages of life have always held a fascination for social observers, and they appear to have a timeless quality. Shakespeare defined the seven ages of man as that of the infant "mewling and puking in his nurse's arms," the whining schoolboy "creeping like a snail unwillingly to school," the lover "sighing like a furnace," the soldier "seeking the bubble reputation even in the cannon's mouth," the justice "full of wise saws and modern instances," the old man "a world too wide for his shrunk shank," and, finally, "second childishness and mere oblivion" (*As You Like It,* 2.7.139–166). Nowhere in this schema is there mention of the family roles—husbands and wives, parents and children, brothers and sisters, grandparents and grandchildren—that have come to play such an important part in the stages of American life since the colonial era. What appears universal in the human life cycle is, in fact, shaped by the other social and historical forces that give very particular meaning to our lives at different times and in different cultural contexts.

The family in American history has always been at the center of social life and has served to refract many social concerns. Because it has played such an important role in organizing individual lives and the larger social order, it is not surprising that there is such concern about its present and future status and such nostalgia for its past. Much of that nostalgia needs a social context and a more visible historical thread to make it understandable, as I have suggested throughout this book. But it is a mistake to discredit the sense of longing that many have for a more vital family life simply as a conservative political stance or empty nostalgia. Two analysts of contemporary American political and social life have argued that it is familism, rather than The Family, that many yearn for—"the reciprocal sense of commitment, sharing, cooperation, and intimacy that is taken as the defining bonds between family members. . . . Familism embraces solicitude, unconditional love, personal loyalty, and willingness to sacrifice for others. Familism makes the home a base to which you can always return when your independent endeavors fail or prove unsatisfactory" (Dizard and Gadlin 1990: 6–7). Although traditionally the setting for an ethic of familism, American families are less and less able to provide for all of our material and emotional needs and social desires for attachment and community.

The model of the family as a protected haven from the outside world, with a woman as guardian of the domestic sphere and a man as sole breadwinner, autonomous yet embedded in a network of mutually supportive kin, epitomizes the symbol of the traditional American family. Such a model was built on a strict division of gender roles that was separate but not equal, on an ethos of self-sacrifice rather than self-fulfillment, and on an expanding industrial economy still relatively small in scale. It is a family model that no longer easily fits the contours of the social and economic world of the late twentieth century. Increased longevity, the massive movement of women into the labor force, and new values about autonomy and independence have changed the old rules in important and often unpredictable ways. Dizard and Gadlin suggest that the key question is whether Americans will continue to insist that families bear the sole burden of familism or to insist that the qualities of familism be embodied in the public realm as well (1990: 223–224). That is the challenge for this era of transition. The entrenched politics of the family ensure that the debate will continue to engage a broad audience and that the rhetoric will be impassioned because the expectations placed on the family are so high. American families have always been resilient, but our understanding of the uses and meanings and possibilities of this institution less so. Finding secure anchors in a rapidly changing world is a continuing problem for Americans and others in the modern era. It is in a search for those anchors that the shape and substance of family life become sources of longing—and a moment when we will either continue to follow old paths or use the opportunity of these unsettled times to construct new kinds of social ties and commitments.

References

Achenbaum, W. Andrew. 1978. *Old Age in the New Land: The American Experience Since 1790.* Baltimore: Johns Hopkins University Press.

_____. 1986a. "The Elderly's Social Security Entitlements as a Measure of Modern American Life." In *Old Age in a Bureaucratic Society,* ed. David Van Tassel and Peter N. Stearns. New York: Greenwood Press.

_____. 1986b. *Social Security: Visions and Revisions.* Cambridge: Cambridge University Press.

Acland, Charles R. 1995. *Youth, Murder, Spectacle: The Cultural Politics of "Youth in Crisis."* Boulder, Colo.: Westview Press.

The Alan Guttmacher Institute. 1994. *Sex and America's Teenagers.* New York and Washington, D.C.: The Alan Guttmacher Institute for Reproductive Health Research, Policy Analysis, and Public Education.

Alexander, Ruth M. 1992. "'The Only Thing I Wanted Was Freedom': Wayward Girls in New York, 1900–1930." In *Small Worlds: Children and Adolescents in America, 1850–1950,* ed. Elliott West and Paula Petrik. Lawrence: University of Kansas Press.

_____. 1995. *The "Girl Problem": Female Sexual Delinquency in New York, 1900–1930.* Ithaca, N.Y.: Cornell University Press.

American Sociological Association. 1998a. "Sociologists Differ About Family Textbooks' Message," *Footnotes* (January): 7–12.

_____. 1998b. "Public Forum," *Footnotes* (February): 8.

Anderson, Michael. 1980. *Approaches to the History of the Western Family, 1500–1914.* London: Macmillan Press.

Ariès, Philippe. 1962. *Centuries of Childhood: A Social History of Family Life.* Trans. Robert Baldick. New York: Knopf.

Arlen, Michael J. 1979. *Thirty Seconds.* New York: Farrar, Straus, and Giroux.

Ashby, Leroy. 1985. "Partial Promises and Semi-Visible Youths: The Depression and WWII." In *American Childhood: A Research Guide and Historical Handbook,* ed. Joseph M. Hawes and N. Ray Hiner. Westport, Conn.: Greenwood Press.

Bailey, Beth. 1989. *From Front Porch to Back Seat: Courtship in Twentieth-Century America.* Baltimore, Md.: Johns Hopkins University Press.

Baird, Robert M., and Stuart E. Rosenbaum, eds. 1997. *Same-Sex Marriage: The Moral and Legal Debate.* Amherst, N.Y.: Prometheus Books.

Bane, Mary Jo. 1976. *Here to Stay: American Families in the Twentieth Century.* New York: Basic Books.

Beales, Ross. 1975. "In Search of the Historical Child: Miniature Adulthood and Youth in Colonial New England," *American Quarterly* 27: 379–398.

Bellah, Robert N., Richard Madsen, William M. Sullivan, Ann Swidler, and Steven M. Tipton. 1985. *Habits of the Heart: Individualism and Commitment in American Life.* Berkeley: University of California Press.

Berkner, Lutz K. 1973. "The Stem Family and the Developmental Cycle of the Peasant Household: An 18th-Century Austrian Example." In *The American Family in Social-Historical Perspective*, ed. Michael Gordon. New York: St. Martin's Press.

Bernard, Jessie. 1972. *The Future of Marriage.* New Haven, Conn.: Yale University Press.

_____. 1981. "The Good Provider Role," *American Psychologist*, 36, no 1 (January): 1–12.

Berrol, Selma. 1985. "Ethnicity and American Children." In *American Childhood: A Research Guide and Historical Handbook*, ed. Joseph M. Hawes and N. Ray Hiner. Westport, Conn.: Greenwood Press.

Best, Joel. 1990. *Threatened Children: Rhetoric and Concern about Child-Victims.* Chicago: University of Chicago Press.

Billingsley, Andrew. 1992. *Climbing Jacob's Ladder: The Enduring Legacy of African American Families.* New York: Simon and Schuster.

Blankenhorn, David. 1995. *Fatherless America: Confronting Our Most Urgent Social Problem.* New York: Basic Books.

Blankenhorn, David, Steven Bayme, and Jean Bethke Elshtain, eds. 1990. *Rebuilding the Nest: A New Commitment to the American Family.* Milwaukee, Wisc.: Family Service America.

Blankenhorn, David, and Stephanie Coontz. 1995. "Can We Talk? The Marriage Strategy," *Mirabella*, March: 82–88.

Bloch, Ruth. 1978. "American Feminine Ideals in Transition: The Rise of the Moral Mother, 1785–1815," *Feminist Studies* 4, no. 2 (June): 101–126.

Boyer, Paul. 1978. *Urban Masses and Moral Order in America, 1820–1920.* Cambridge: Harvard University Press.

Boyer, Paul, and Stephen Nissenbaum. 1974. *Salem Possessed: The Social Origins of Witchcraft.* Cambridge: Harvard University Press.

Brandt, Allan M. 1987. *No Magic Bullet: A Social History of Venereal Disease in the United States Since 1880.* New York: Oxford University Press.

Breines, Wini. 1992. *Young, White, and Miserable: Growing Up Female in the Fifties.* Boston: Beacon Press.

Brenzel, Barbara M. 1983. *Daughters of the State: A Social Portrait of the First Reform School for Girls in North America, 1856–1905.* Cambridge: MIT Press.

Brodie, Janet Farrell. 1994. *Contraception and Abortion in Nineteenth-Century America.* Ithaca, N.Y.: Cornell University Press.

Brooks-Gunn, Jeanne, and Frank F. Furstenberg, Jr. 1989. "Adolescent Sexual Behavior," *American Psychologist* 44, no. 2 (February): 249–257.

_____. 1990. "Coming of Age in the Era of AIDS: Puberty, Sexuality, and Contraception," *The Milbank Quarterly* 68, no. 1: 59–84.

Burgess, Ernest W., Harvery J. Locke, and Mary Margaret Thomas. 1945. *The Family: From Institution to Companionship.* New York: American Book.

Burnett, John. 1982. *Destiny Obscure: Autobiographies of Childhood, Education, and Family from the 1820s to the 1920s*. London: A. Lane Publishers.

Burnham, John C. 1993. *Bad Habits: Drinking, Smoking, Taking Drugs, Gambling, Sexual Misbehavior, and Swearing in American History*. New York: New York University Press.

Calhoun, Arthur W. 1917. *A Social History of the American Family, from Colonial Times to the Present*. Cleveland: Arthur H. Clark.

Cancian, Francesca. 1987. *Love in America: Gender and Self-Development*. New York: Cambridge University Press.

Caplow, Theodore, Howard M. Bahr, Bruce A. Chadwick, Rubin Hill, and Margaret Holmes Williamson. 1982. *Middletown Families: Fifty Years of Change and Continuity*. Minneapolis: University of Minnesota Press.

Chafe, William H. 1986. *The Unfinished Journey: America Since World War II*. New York: Oxford University Press.

Chauncey, George. 1994. *Gay New York: Gender, Urban Culture, and the Makings of the Gay Male World, 1890–1940*. New York: Basic Books.

Cherlin, Andrew J. 1978. "Remarriage as an Incomplete Institution." *American Journal of Sociology* 84 (November): 634–650.

_____. 1990. "The Strange Career of the 'Harvard-Yale Study.'" *Public Opinion Quarterly* 54 (Spring): 117–124.

_____. 1992. *Marriage, Divorce, Remarriage*, revised edition. Cambridge: Harvard University Press.

_____. 1998. "By the Numbers," *New York Times Magazine*, April 5, 1998, Section 6, pp. 39–41.

Cherlin, Andrew J., ed. 1988. *The Changing American Family and Public Policy*. Washington, D.C.: Urban Institute Press.

Cherlin, Andrew J., and Frank F. Furstenberg, Jr. 1986. *The New American Grandparent: A Place in the Family, A Life Apart*. New York: Basic Books.

Children's Defense Fund. 1995. "The State of American Children." Washington, D.C.: Children's Defense Fund.

Chodorow, Nancy. 1978. *The Reproduction of Mothering: Psychoanalysis and the Sociology of Gender*. Berkeley: University of California Press.

Chudacoff, Howard P. 1989. *How Old Are You?: Age Consciousness in American Culture*. Princeton, N.J.: Princeton University Press.

Clarke-Stewart, Alison. 1993. *Daycare*, revised edition. Cambridge: Harvard University Press.

Clausen, John A. 1993. *American Lives: Looking Back at the Children of the Great Depression*. Berkeley: University of California Press.

Clement, Priscilla Ferguson. 1985. "The City and the Child, 1860–1885." In *American Childhood: A Research Guide and Historical Handbook*, ed. Joseph M. Hawes and N. Ray Hiner. Westport, Conn.: Greenwood Press.

_____. 1997. *Growing Pains: Children in the Industrial Age, 1850–1890*. New York: Twayne Publishers.

Cohen, Ronald. 1985. "Child-Saving and Progressivism, 1885–1915." In *American Childhood: A Research Guide and Historical Handbook*, ed. Joseph M. Hawes and N. Ray Hiner. Westport, Conn.: Greenwood Press.

Coontz, Stephanie. 1988. *The Social Origins of Private Life: A History of American Families, 1600–1900.* London: Verso.

_____. 1992. *The Way We Never Were: American Families and the Nostalgia Trap.* New York: Basic Books.

_____. 1997. *The Way We Really Are: Coming to Terms with America's Changing Families.* New York: Basic Books.

Coser, Rose, ed. 1974. *The Family: Its Structures and Functions.* New York: St. Martin's Press.

Cott, Nancy F. 1977. *The Bonds of Womanhood: Woman's Sphere in New England, 1780–1835.* New Haven, Conn.: Yale University Press.

_____. 1979a. "Eighteenth-Century Family and Social Life Revealed in Massachusetts Divorce Records." In *A Heritage of Her Own: Toward a New Social History of American Women,* ed. Nancy F. Cott and Elizabeth H. Pleck. New York: Simon and Schuster.

_____. 1979b. "Passionlessness: An Interpretation of Victorian Sexual Ideology, 1790–1850." In *A Heritage of Her Own: Toward a New Social History of American Women,* ed. Nancy F. Cott and Elizabeth H. Pleck. New York: Simon and Schuster.

Cowan, Philip A., and E. Mavis Hetherington, eds. 1991. *Family Transitions.* Hillsdale, N.J.: L. Erlbaum Associates.

Cuber, John F., and Peggy B. Harroff. 1966. *Sex and the Significant Americans: A Study of Sexual Behavior Among the Affluent.* Baltimore, Md.: Penguin Books.

Davis, Natalie Zemon. 1975. *Society and Culture in Early Modern France.* Palo Alto, Calif.: Stanford University Press.

Degler, Carl N. 1980. *At Odds: Women and the Family in America from the Revolution to the Present.* New York: Oxford University Press.

DeLone, Richard H. 1979. *Small Futures: Children, Inequality, and the Limits of Liberal Reform.* New York: Harcourt Brace Jovanovich.

D'Emilio, John, and Estelle B. Freedman. 1988. *Intimate Matters: A History of Sexuality in America.* New York: Harper and Row.

Demos, John. 1970. *A Little Commonwealth: Family Life in Plymouth Colony.* New York: Oxford University Press.

_____. 1978. "Old Age in Early New England." In *Turning Points: Historical and Sociological Essays on the Family,* ed. John Demos and Sarane Spence Boocock. Chicago: University of Chicago Press.

_____. 1979. "Images of the American Family, Then and Now." In *Changing Images of the Family,* ed. Virginia Tufte and Barbara Myerhoff. New Haven, Conn.: Yale University Press.

_____. 1986. "The Rise and Fall of Adolescence." In *Past, Present, and Personal.* New York: Oxford University Press.

Demos, John, and Virginia Demos. 1969. "Adolescence in Historical Perspective," *Journal of Marriage and the Family* 31: 632–638.

DiMaggio, Paul. 1982. "Cultural Entrepreneurship in Nineteenth-Century Boston: The Creation of an Organizational Base for High Culture in America." *Media, Culture, and Society* 4, no. 1: 33–50.

Dizard, Jan E., and Howard Gadlin. 1990. *The Minimal Family.* Amherst: University of Massachusetts Press.

Dorgan, Charity Anne, ed. 1996. *Statistical Record of Older Americans,* 2nd edition. Detroit: Gale Research.

Douglass, Frederick. [1892, rev. ed.] 1962. *Life and Times of Frederick Douglass: His Early Life as a Slave, His Escape from Bondage, and His Complete History, Written by Himself.* Hartford, Conn.: Park Publishing.

Dublin, Thomas. 1979. *Women at Work: The Transformation of Work and Community in Lowell, Massachusetts, 1826–1860.* New York: Columbia University Press.

Ehrenreich, Barbara. 1983. *The Hearts of Men: American Dreams and the Flight from Commitment.* Garden City, N.Y.: Anchor Press/Doubleday.

Ehrenreich, Barbara, Elizabeth Hess, and Gloria Jacobs. 1986. *Remaking Love: The Feminization of Sex.* New York: Anchor Press.

Elder, Glen H., Jr. 1999. *Children of the Great Depression: Social Change in Life Experience,* 25th anniversary edition. Boulder, Col.: Westview Press.

Elder, Glen H. Jr., John Modell, and Ross D. Parke, eds. 1993. *Children in Time and Place: Developmental and Historical Insights.* Cambridge: Cambridge University Press.

Elkind, David. 1981. *The Hurried Child: Growing up Too Fast, Too Soon.* Reading, Mass.: Addison-Wesley Publishing.

Epstein, Joseph. 1974. *Divorced in America: Marriage in an Age of Possibility.* New York: E. P. Dutton.

Erenberg, Lewis A. 1984. *Steppin' Out: New York Night Life and the Transformation of American Culture, 1890–1930.* Chicago: University of Chicago Press.

Erikson, Erik H. 1965. *The Challenge of Youth.* New York: Anchor Books.

Ewen, Elizabeth. 1985. *Immigrant Women in the Land of Dollars: Life and Culture on the Lower East Side, 1890–1925.* New York: Monthly Review Press.

Faderman, Lillian. 1991. *Odd Girls and Twilight Lovers: A History of Lesbian Life in 20th Century America.* New York: Columbia University Press.

Faludi, Susan. 1991. *Backlash: The Undeclared War Against American Women.* New York: Crown Publishers.

Farrell, Betty. 1993. *Elite Families: Class and Power in Nineteenth-Century Boston.* New York: State University of New York Press.

Fass, Paula S. 1977. *The Damned and the Beautiful: American Youth in the 1920s.* New York: Oxford University Press.

_____. 1997. *Kidnapped: Child Abduction in America.* New York: Oxford University Press.

Fein, Ellen, and Sherrie Schneider. 1995. *The Rules: Time-Tested Secrets for Capturing the Heart of Mr. Right.* New York: Warner Books.

Feldman, Shirley S., and Glen R. Elliott, eds. 1990. *At the Threshold: The Developing Adolescent.* Cambridge: Harvard University Press

Findlay, John M. 1992. "Sun City, Arizona: New Town for Old Folks." In *Magic Lands: Western Cityscapes and American Culture After 1940.* Berkeley: University of California Press.

Fineman, Martha Albertson. 1995. *The Neutered Mother, the Sexual Family and Other Twentieth-Century Tragedies.* New York: Routledge.

Finkelstein, Barbara. 1985. "Casting Networks of Good Influence: The Reconstruction of Childhood in the U.S., 1790–1870." In *American Childhood: A Re-*

search Guide and Historical Handbook, ed. Joseph M. Hawes and N. Ray Hiner. Westport, Conn.: Greenwood Press.

Fischer, David Hackett. 1977. *Growing Old in America*. New York: Oxford University Press.

FitzGerald, Frances. 1986. *Cities on a Hill: A Journey Through Contemporary American Cultures*. New York: Simon and Schuster.

Fliegelman, Jay. 1982. *Prodigals and Pilgrims: The American Revolution Against Patriarchal Authority, 1750–1800*. Cambridge: Cambridge University Press.

Foucault, Michel. 1978. *The History of Sexuality: Volume 1, An Introduction*. New York: Vintage.

Fox, Vivian C. 1977. "Is Adolescence a Phenomenon of Modern Times?," *Journal of Psychohistory* 5: 271–290.

Fox, Vivian C., and Martin H. Quitt. 1980. *Loving, Parenting, and Dying: The Family Cycle in England and America, Past and Present*. New York: Psychohistory Press.

Franklin, Donna L. 1997. *Ensuring Inequality: The Structural Transformation of the African-American Family*. New York: Oxford University Press.

Friedan, Betty. 1963. *The Feminine Mystique*. New York: Norton.

Frith, Simon. *Sound Effects: Youth, Leisure, and the Politics of Rock 'n' Roll*. New York: Pantheon, 1981.

Furstenberg, Frank Jr., and Andrew J. Cherlin. 1991. *Divided Families: What Happens to Children When Parents Part*. Cambridge: Harvard University Press.

Furstenberg, Frank F. Jr., and Gretchen A. Condran. 1988. "Family Change and Adolescent Well-Being: A Reexamination of U.S. Trends. In *The Changing American Family and Public Policy*, ed. Andrew J. Cherlin. Washington, D.C.: Urban Institute Press.

Furstenberg, Frank F. Jr., Jeanne Brooks-Gunn, and S. Philip Morgan. 1987. *Adolescent Mothers in Later Life*. Cambridge: Cambridge University Press.

Gaines, Donna. 1991. *Teenage Wasteland: Suburbia's Dead End Kids*. New York: HarperCollins.

Gallagher, Maggie. 1996. *The Abolition of Marriage: How We Destroy Lasting Love*. Washington, D.C.: Regnery.

Garfinkel, Irwin, and Sara S. McLanahan. 1986. *Single Mothers and Their Children: A New American Dilemma*. Washington, D.C.: Urban Institute Press.

Giddings, Paula. 1984. *When and Where I Enter: The Impact of Black Women on Race and Sex in America*. New York: William Morrow.

Gilligan, Carol. 1982. *In a Different Voice: Psychological Theory and Women's Development*. Cambridge: Harvard University Press.

Gillis, John R. 1997. *A World of Their Own Making: Myth, Ritual, and the Quest for Family Values*. Cambridge: Harvard University Press.

Giroux, Henry S. 1996. *Fugitive Cultures: Race, Violence, and Youth*. New York: Routledge.

Glenn, Norval. 1997a. "Closed Hearts, Closed Minds: The Textbook Story of Marriage." New York: Institute for American Values.

_____. 1997b. "Marriage Is Not a Dirty Word," *Los Angeles Times*, September 16, 1997.

Goldscheider, Frances K., and Linda J. Waite. 1991. *New Families, No Families?: The Transformation of the American Home*. Berkeley: University of California Press.

Goode, William J. 1963. *World Revolutions and Family Patterns*. New York: Free Press.

———. 1993. *World Changes in Divorce Patterns*. New Haven, Conn.: Yale University Press.

Goodman, Paul. 1960. *Growing up Absurd: Problems of Youth in the Organized System*. New York: Random House.

Gordon, Linda. 1976. *Woman's Body, Woman's Right: A Social History of Birth Control in America*. New York: Grossman/Viking.

———. 1982. "Why Nineteenth-Century Feminists Did Not Support 'Birth Control' and Twentieth-Century Feminists Do: Feminism, Reproduction, and the Family." In *Rethinking the Family: Some Feminist Questions*, ed. Barrie Thorne. New York: Longman.

———. 1988. *Heroes of Their Own Lives: The Politics and History of Family Violence: Boston, 1880–1960*. New York: Viking.

———. 1994. *Pitied but Not Entitled: Single Mothers and the History of Welfare*. New York: Free Press.

Gordon, Linda, and Sara McLanahan. 1991. "Single Parenthood in 1900," *Journal of Family History* 16: 97–116.

Gordon, Michael. 1973. *The American Family in Social-Historical Perspective*. New York: St. Martin's Press.

Graebner, William. 1980. *A History of Retirement: The Meaning and Function of an American Institution, 1885–1978*. New Haven, Conn.: Yale University Press.

Graff, Harvey J. 1995. *Conflicting Paths: Growing Up in America*. Cambridge: Harvard University Press.

———, ed. 1987. *Growing Up in America: Historical Experiences*. Detroit: Wayne State University Press.

Gratton, Brian. 1986. "The New History of the Aged: A Critique." In *Old Age in a Bureaucratic Society*, ed. David Van Tassel and Peter N. Stearns. Westport, Conn.: Greenwood Press.

Gravens, Hamilton. 1985. "Child-Saving in the Age of Professionalism, 1915–1930." In *American Childhood: A Research Guide and Historical Handbook*, ed. Joseph M. Hawes and N. Ray Hiner. Westport, Conn.: Greenwood Press.

Gray, John. 1992. *Men Are from Mars, Women Are from Venus: A Practical Guide for Improving Communication and Getting What You Want in Your Relationships*. New York: HarperCollins.

Greven, Philip J. 1970. *Four Generations: Population, Land, and Family in Colonial Andover, Massachusetts*. Ithaca, N.Y.: Cornell University Press.

———. 1973. *Child-Rearing Concepts, 1628–1861; Historical Sources*. Itasca, Ill.: F. E. Peacock Publishers.

———. 1977. *The Protestant Temperament: Patterns of Child-Rearing, Religious Experience, and the Self in Early America*. New York: Knopf.

———. 1991. *Spare the Child: The Religious Roots of Punishment and the Psychological Impact of Physical Abuse*. New York: Knopf, distributed by Random House.

Grossberg, Michael. 1985. *Governing the Hearth: Law and the Family in Nineteenth-Century America*. Chapel Hill: University of North Carolina Press.

Groves, Ernest R. 1928. *The Marriage Crisis*. New York: Longmans, Green.

Groves, Ernest R., and William F. Ogburn. 1928. *American Marriage and Family Relationships*. New York: H. Holt.

Grubb, W. Norton, and Marvin Lazerson. 1988. *Broken Promises: How Americans Fail Their Children*. Chicago: University of Chicago Press.

Gutman, Herbert. 1976. *The Black Family in Slavery and Freedom*. New York: Pantheon.

Haber, Carole. 1983. *Beyond Sixty-Five: The Dilemma of Old Age in America's Past*. Cambridge: Cambridge University Press.

Haber, Carole, and Brian Gratton. 1994. *Old Age and the Search for Security: An American Social History*. Bloomington: Indiana University Press.

Hall, G. Stanley. 1904. *Adolescence: Its Psychology and Its Relations to Anthropology, Sex, Crime, Religion, and Education*. New York: D. Appleton.

Hareven, Tamara K. 1982. "The Life Course and Aging in Historical Perspective." In *Aging and Life Course Transitions: An Interdisciplinary Perspective*, ed. Tamara K. Hareven and Kathleen J. Adams. New York: Tavistock Publications.

_____. 1986. "Life-Course Transitions and Kin Assistance in Old Age: A Cohort Comparison." In *Old Age in a Bureaucratic Society*, ed. David Van Tassel and Peter N. Stearns. Westport, Conn.: Greenwood Press.

_____. 1994. "Aging and Generational Relations: A Historical and Life Course Perspective." *Annual Review of Sociology* 20: 437–461.

Hareven, Tamara K., and Peter Uhlenberg. 1995. "Transition to Widowhood and Family Support Systems in the Twentieth Century, Northeastern United States." In *Aging in the Past: Demography, Society, and Old Age*, ed. David I. Kertzer and Peter Laslett. Berkeley: University of California Press.

Hareven, Tamara K., and Maris A. Vinovskis. 1978. *Family and Population in Nineteenth-Century America*. Princeton, N.J.: Princeton University Press.

Hawes, Joseph M., and N. Ray Hiner. 1991. *Children in Historical and Comparative Perspective: An International Handbook and Research Guide*. New York: Greenwood Press.

Hawes, Joseph M., and N. Ray Hiner, eds. 1985. *American Childhood: A Research Guide and Historical Handbook*. Westport, Conn.: Greenwood Press.

Hawes, Joseph M., and Elizabeth I. Nybakken, eds. 1991. *American Families: A Research Guide and Historical Handbook*. New York: Greenwood Press.

Hayden, Dolores. 1984. *Redesigning the American Dream: The Future of Housing, Work, and Family Life*. New York: W. W. Norton.

Hernandez, Donald J. 1993. *America's Children: Resources from Family, Government, and the Economy*. New York: Russell Sage Foundation.

Hetherington, E. Mavis. 1989. "Coping with Family Transitions: Winners, Losers, and Survivors," *Child Development* 60: 1–14.

_____. 1992. "Coping with Marital Transitions: A Family Systems Perspective." In *Coping with Marital Transitions: A Family Systems Perspective*, ed. E. Mavis Hetherington and W. Glenn Clingempeel. Monograph of the Society for Research in Child Development: serial 227, vol. 57, nos. 2–3.

Hetherington, E. Mavis, and Josephine D. Aresteh, eds. 1988. *The Impact of Divorce, Single Parenting, and Stepparenting on Children.* Hillsdale, N.J.: Lawrence Erlbaum Associates.

Hetherington, E. Mavis, K. A. Camara, and D. L. Featherman. 1983. "Achievement and Intellectual Functioning of Children in One Parent Households." In *Achievement and Achievement Motives,* ed. J. T. Spence. San Francisco: W. H. Freeman.

Hetherington, E. Mavis, Martha Cox, and Roger Cox. 1978. "The Aftermath of Divorce." In *Mother-Child, Father-Child Relations,* ed. Joseph H. Stevens and Marilyn Mathews. Washington, D.C.: National Association for the Education of Young Children Press.

Hetherington, E. Mavis, Richard M. Lerner, and Marion Perlmutter. 1988. *Child Development in Life-Span Perspective.* Hillsdale, N.J.: Lawrence Erlbaum Associates.

Heyn, Dalma. 1992. *The Erotic Silence of the American Wife.* New York: Penguin.

Higonnet, Anne. 1998. *Pictures of Innocence: The History and Crisis of Ideal Childhood.* New York: Thames and Hudson.

Hiner, N. Ray. 1975. "Adolescence in Eighteenth-Century America," *History of Childhood Quarterly* 3: 253–280.

Hiner, N. Ray, and Joseph M. Hawes, eds. 1985. *Growing Up in America: Children in Historical Perspective.* Urbana: University of Illinois Press.

Hobson, Barbara Meil. 1987. *Uneasy Virtue: The Politics of Prostitution and the American Reform Tradition.* New York: Basic Books.

Hochschild, Arlie. 1983. *The Managed Heart: Commercialization of Human Feeling.* Berkeley: University of California Press.

_____. 1989. *The Second Shift: Working Parents and the Revolution at Home.* New York: Viking.

Hunt, Morton M. 1966. *The World of the Formerly Married.* Greenwich, Conn.: Fawcett Publications.

_____. 1969. *The Affair: A Portrait of Extra-Marital Love in Contemporary America.* New York: New American Library/World Publishing.

Illouz, Eva. 1997. *Consuming the Romantic Utopia: Love and the Cultural Contradictions of Capitalism.* Berkeley: University of California Press.

Irvine, Janice M., ed. 1994. *Sexual Cultures and the Construction of Adolescent Identities.* Philadelphia: Temple University Press.

Jenks, Chris. 1996. *Childhood.* London: Routledge.

Johnson, Fenton. 1996. "Wedded to an Illusion: Do Gays and Lesbians Really Want the Right to Marry?" *Harper's* (November): 43–50.

Kanter, Rosabeth Moss. 1972. *Commitment and Community: Communes and Utopias in Sociological Perspective.* Cambridge: Harvard University Press.

Kantner, John F., and Melvin Zelnik. 1972. "Sexual Experience of Young, Unmarried Women in the U.S.," *Family Planning Perspectives* 4: 9–18.

Kasson, John F. 1978. *Amusing the Million: Coney Island at the Turn of the Century.* New York: Hill and Wang.

Katzman, David M. 1978. *Seven Days a Week: Women and Domestic Service in Industrializing America.* Urbana: University of Illinois Press.

Keniston, Kenneth. 1965. *The Uncommitted: Alienated Youth in American Society.* New York: Dell.

_____. 1971. *Youth and Dissent: The Rise of a New Opposition.* New York: Harcourt Brace Jovanovich.

_____. 1977. *All Our Children: The American Family Under Pressure.* New York: Harcourt Brace Jovanovich.

Kephart, William M. 1987. *Extraordinary Groups: An Examination of Unconventional Life Styles,* 3rd edition. New York: St. Martin's Press.

Kerber, Linda. 1980. *Women of the Republic: Intellect and Ideology in Revolutionary America.* Chapel Hill: University of North Carolina Press.

Kertzer, David I., and Peter Laslett. 1995. *Aging in the Past: Demography, Society, and Old Age.* Berkeley: University of California Press.

Kessler-Harris, Alice. 1982. *Out to Work: A History of Wage-Earning Women in the United States.* New York: Oxford University Press.

Kett, Joseph. 1977. *Rites of Passage: Adolescence in America, 1790 to the Present.* New York: Basic Books.

King, Wilma. 1995. *Stolen Childhood: Slave Youth in Nineteenth-Century America.* Bloomington: Indiana University Press.

Kinsey, Alfred S., Wardell B. Pomeroy, and Clyde E. Martin. 1948. *Sexual Behavior in the Human Male.* Philadelphia: Saunders.

_____. 1953. *Sexual Behavior in the Human Female.* Philadelphia: Saunders.

Ladd-Taylor, Molly. 1993. "'My Work Came Out of Agony and Grief': Mothers and the Making of the Sheppard-Towner Act." In *Mothers of a New World: Maternalist Politics and the Origins of Welfare States,* ed. Seth Koven and Sonya Michel. New York: Routledge.

_____. 1994. *Mother-Work: Women, Child Welfare, and the State, 1890–1930.* Urbana: University of Illinois Press.

Landers, Ann. 1998. *Boston Globe:* February 13, 1998; March 12, 1998.

Laqueur, Thomas. 1990. *Making Sex: Body and Gender from the Greeks to Freud.* Cambridge: Harvard University Press.

Laslett, Peter. 1965. *The World We Have Lost: England Before the Industrial Age.* New York: Charles Scribner's Sons.

Laslett, Peter, and Richard Hall. 1972. *Household and Family in Past Time.* Cambridge: Cambridge University Press.

Laumann, Edward O., John H. Gagnon, Robert T. Michael, and Stuart Michaels. 1994. *The Social Organization of Sexuality: Sexual Practices in the United States.* Chicago: University of Chicago Press.

Lawson, Annette. 1988. *Adultery: An Analysis of Love and Betrayal.* New York: Basic Books.

Lévi-Strauss, Claude. 1974. "Reciprocity: The Basis of Social Life." In *The Family: Its Structures and Functions,* ed. Rose Coser. New York: St. Martin's Press.

Levy, Barry. 1988. *Quakers and the American Family: A British Settlement in the Delaware Valley.* New York: Oxford University Press.

Lewis, Jan. 1983. *The Pursuit of Happiness: Family and Values in Jefferson's Virginia.* Cambridge: Cambridge University Press.

Luker, Kristin. 1996. *Dubious Conceptions: The Politics of Teenage Pregnancy.* Cambridge: Harvard University Press.

Lynd, Robert Staughton, and Helen Merrell Lynd. 1929. *Middletown, A Study in Contemporary American Culture.* New York: Harcourt, Brace.
_____. 1937. *Middletown in Transition: A Study in Cultural Conflicts.* New York: Harcourt, Brace.
Lystra, Karen. 1989. *Searching the Heart: Women, Men, and Romantic Love in Nineteenth-Century America.* New York: Oxford University Press.
Maddox, George L., ed. 1995. *The Encyclopedia of Aging.* 2d ed. New York: Springer Publishing.
Males, Mike A. 1996. *The Scapegoat Generation: America's War on Adolescents.* Monroe, Maine: Common Courage Press.
Malinowski, Bronislaw. 1974. "Parenthood, the Basis of Social Structure." In *The Family: Its Structures and Functions,* ed. Rose Coser. New York: St. Martin's Press.
Manheimer, Ronald J., ed. 1994. *Older Americans Almanac: A Reference Work on Seniors in the United States.* Detroit: Gale Research.
Martin, Teresa Castro, and Larry L. Bumpass. 1989. "Recent Trends in Marital Disruption," *Demography* 26 (February): 37–51.
Masnick, George, and Mary Jo Bane. 1980. *The Nation's Families, 1960–1990.* Cambridge, Mass.: Joint Center for Urban Studies of MIT and Harvard University.
Mason, Mary Ann, Arlene Skolnick, and Stephen D. Sugarman, eds. 1998. *All Our Families: New Policies for a New Century.* New York: Oxford University Press.
May, Elaine Tyler. 1980. *Great Expectations: Marriage and Divorce in Post-Victorian America.* Chicago: University of Chicago Press.
_____. 1988. *Homeward Bound: American Families in the Cold War Era.* New York: Basic Books.
_____. 1995. *Barren in the Promised Land: Childless Americans and the Pursuit of Happiness.* Cambridge: Harvard University Press.
Mayerson, Charlotte. 1996. *Goin' to the Chapel: Dreams of Love, Realities of Marriage.* New York: Basic Books.
McKnight, Thomas W., and Robert A. Phillips. 1993. *More Love Tactics: How to Win That Special Someone.* Garden City Park, N.Y.: Avery Publishing Group.
McLanahan, Sara, and Gary Sandefur. 1994. *Growing Up with a Single Parent: What Hurts, What Helps.* Cambridge: Harvard University Press.
Medrich, Elliott A. 1982. *The Serious Business of Growing Up: A Study of Children's Lives Outside School.* Berkeley: University of California Press.
Michael, Robert T., John H. Gagnon, Edward O. Laumann, and Gina Kolata. 1994. *Sex in America: A Definitive Survey.* Boston: Little, Brown.
Michel, Sonya. 1993. "The Limits of Maternalism: Policies Toward American Wage-Earning Mothers During the Progressive Era." In *Mothers of a New World: Maternalist Politics and the Origins of Welfare States,* ed. Seth Kovan and Sonya Michel. New York: Routledge.
Mink, Gwendolyn. 1995. *The Wages of Motherhood: Inequality in the Welfare State, 1917–1942.* Ithaca, N.Y.: Cornell University Press.
Mintz, Steven. 1983. *A Prison of Expectations: The Family in Victorian Culture.* New York: New York University Press.

_____. 1991. "New Rules: Postwar Families (1955-Present)." In *American Families: A Research Guide and Historical Handbook*, ed. Joseph M. Hawes and Elizabeth I. Nybakken. New York: Greenwood Press.

Mintz, Steven, and Susan Kellogg. 1988. *Domestic Revolutions: A Social History of American Life*. New York: Free Press.

Mnookin, Robert, ed. 1985. *In the Interest of Children: Advocacy, Law Reform and Public Policy*. New York: W. H. Freeman.

Modell, John. 1980. "Normative Aspects of American Marriage Timing Since World War II," *Journal of Family History* 5, no. 2 (Summer): 210–234.

_____. 1989. *Into One's Own: From Youth to Adulthood in the United States, 1920–1975*. Berkeley: University of California Press.

Modell, John, Frank F. Furstenberg, Jr., and Theodore Hershberg. 1976. "Social Change and Transitions to Adulthood in Historical Perspective," *Journal of Family History* 1: 7–33.

Modell, John, Frank F. Furstenberg Jr., and Douglas Strong. 1978. "The Timing of Marriage in the Transition to Adulthood: Continuity and Change, 1860–1975." In *Turning Points: Historical and Sociological Essays on the Family*, ed. John Demos and Sarane Spence Boocock. Chicago: University of Chicago Press.

Modell, John, and Madeline Goodman. 1993. "Historical Perspectives." In *At the Threshold: The Developing Adolescent*, ed. S. Shirley Feldman and Glen R. Elliott. Cambridge: Harvard University Press.

Moore, Susan, and Doreen Rosenthal. 1993. *Sexuality in Adolescence*. London: Routledge.

Morgan, Edmund S. 1966. *The Puritan Family: Essays on Religion and Domestic Relations in Seventeenth-Century New England*. New York: Harper and Row.

Morgan, Marabel. 1975. *The Total Woman*. New York: Pocket Books.

Morgan, S. Philip, Antonio McDaniel, Andrew T. Miller, and Samuel H. Preston. 1993. "Racial Differences in Household and Family Structure at the Turn of the Century." *American Journal of Sociology* 98, no. 4 (January): 798–828.

Moynihan, Daniel Patrick. 1965. "The Negro Family: The Case for National Action." Washington, D.C.: Office of Planning and Research, U.S. Department of Labor.

Nardi, Peter M. 1996. "Saying 'I Do' to Broadening the Debate." *Los Angeles Times*, February 5, 1996: B5.

Nardi, Peter M. 1997. "Friends, Lovers, and Families: The Impact of AIDS on Gay and Lesbian Relationships." In *In Changing Times: Gay Men and Lesbians Encounter HIV/AIDS*, ed. Martin P. Levine, Peter M. Nardi, and John H. Gagnon. Chicago: University of Chicago Press.

Nasaw, David. 1985. *Children of the City: At Work and at Play*. Garden City, N.Y.: Anchor Press/Doubleday.

_____. 1993. *Going Out: The Rise and Fall of Public Amusements*. New York: Basic Books.

Nathanson, Constance A. 1991. *Dangerous Passage: The Social Control of Sexuality in Women's Adolescence*. Philadelphia: Temple University Press.

Nava, Michael, and Robert Dawidoff. 1994. *Created Equal: Why Gay Rights Matter to America*. New York: St. Martin's Press.

Norton, Mary Beth. 1980. *Liberty's Daughters: The Revolutionary Experience of American Women, 1750–1800*. Glenview, Ill.: Scott, Foresman.

_____. 1996. *Founding Mothers and Fathers: Gendered Power and the Forming of American Society*. New York: Alfred A. Knopf.

Odem, Mary E. 1995. *Delinquent Daughters: Protecting and Policing Adolescent Female Sexuality in the United States, 1885–1920*. Chapel Hill: University of North Carolina Press.

Ogburn, W. F. 1933. "The Family and Its Functions." In *Recent Social Trends in the United States*. Washington, D.C.: Report of the President's Research Committee on Social Trends.

Ogburn, W. F., and M. F. Nimkoff. 1955. *Technology and the Changing Family*. Boston: Houghton Mifflin

Ogden, Annegret. 1988. "Tar Flat Tots: The Voice of Kate Douglas Wiggin (1856–1923)." *The Californians* (November-December): 14–15; 55.

Palladino, Grace. 1996. *Teenagers: An American History*. New York: Basic Books.

Parsons, Talcott. 1974. "The Incest Taboo and Family Structure." In *The Family: Its Structures and Functions*, ed. Rose Coser. New York: St. Martin's Press.

Parsons, Talcott, and Robert F. Bales. 1955. *Family, Socialization and Interaction Process*. Glencoe, Ill.: Free Press.

Patterson, Orlando. 1997. *The Ordeal of Integration: Progress and Resentment in America's "Racial" Crisis*. Washington, D.C.: Civitas/Counterpoint.

Peiss, Kathy. 1986. *Cheap Amusements: Working Women and Leisure in Turn-of-the-Century New York*. Philadelphia: Temple University Press.

Peterson, Peter G. 1996. "Will America Grow Up Before It Grows Old?," *Atlantic Monthly* (May): 55–86.

Pleck, Elizabeth H. 1979. *Black Migration and Poverty, Boston, 1865–1900*. New York: Academic Press.

_____. 1987. *Domestic Tyranny: The Making of American Social Policy Against Family Violence from Colonial Times to the Present*. New York: Oxford University Press.

Pollock, Linda. 1983. *Forgotten Children: Parent-Child Relations from 1500 to 1900*. New York: Cambridge University Press.

_____. 1987. *A Lasting Relationship: Parents and Children over Three Centuries*. Hanover, N.H.: University Press of New England.

Popenoe, David. 1996. *Life Without Father*. New York: Free Press.

Popenoe, David, Jean Bethke Elshtain, and David Blankenhorn, eds. 1996. *Promises to Keep: Decline and Renewal of Marriage in America*. Lanham, Md.: Rowman & Littlefield Publishers.

Poster, Mark. 1978. *Critical Theory of the Family*. New York: Seabury.

Postman, Neil. 1982. *The Disappearance of Childhood*. New York: Delacorte Press.

Preston, Samuel H. 1984. "Children and the Elderly: Divergent Paths for America's Dependents," *Demography* 21, no.4 (November): 435–457.

Preston, Samuel H., and Michael R. Haines. 1991. *Fatal Years: Child Mortality in Late Nineteenth-Century America*. Princeton, N.J.: Princeton University Press.

Preston, Samuel H., and John McDonald. 1979. "The Incidence of Divorce Within Cohorts of American Marriages Contracted Since the Civil War," *Demography* 16 (February): 1–25.

Prothrow-Stith, Deborah. 1991. *Deadly Consequences.* New York: HarperCollins.

Purdy, Laura M. 1992. *In Their Best Interest?: The Case Against Equal Rights for Children.* Ithaca, N.Y.: Cornell University Press.

Quadagno, Jill S. 1986. "The Transformation of Old Age Security." In *Old Age in a Bureaucratic Society,* ed. David Van Tassel and Peter N. Stearns. New York: Greenwood Press.

_____. 1988. *The Transformation of Old Age Security: Class and Politics in the American Welfare State.* Chicago: University of Chicago Press.

Rainwater, Lee, and William L. Yancey, eds. 1967. *The Moynihan Report and the Politics of Controversy.* Cambridge: MIT Press.

Reinier, Jacqueline S. 1996. *From Virtue to Character: American Childhood, 1775–1850.* New York: Twayne Publishers.

Reiss, Ira L. 1967. *The Social Context of Sexual Permissiveness.* New York: Holt, Rinehart and Winston.

Richardson, Laurel. 1985. *The New Other Woman: Contemporary Single Women in Affairs with Married Men.* New York: Free Press.

Riley, Glenda. 1991. *Divorce: An American Tradition.* New York: Oxford University Press.

Rodman, Hyman, Susan H. Lewis, and Saralyn B. Griffith. 1984. *The Sexual Rights of Adolescents: Competence, Vulnerability, and Parental Control.* New York: Columbia University Press.

Rodriguez, Luis J. 1993. *Always Running: La Vida Loca, Gang Days in L.A.* Willimantic, Conn.: Curbstone Press.

Rosenheim, Margaret K., and Mark F. Testa, eds. 1992. *Early Parenthood and Coming of Age in the 1990s.* New Brunswick, N.J.: Rutgers University Press.

Rotello, Gabriel. 1996. "To Have and to Hold: The Case for Gay Marriage." *The Nation,* June 24, 1996, 11–18.

Rothman, Barbara Katz. 1989. *Recreating Motherhood: Ideology and Technology in a Patriarchal Society.* New York: W. W. Norton.

Rothman, David. 1971. *The Discovery of the Asylum: Social Order and Disorder in the New Republic.* Boston: Little, Brown.

Rothman, Ellen K. 1984. *Hands and Hearts: A History of Courtship in America.* New York: Basic Books.

Rothman, Sheila M. 1978. *Woman's Proper Place: A History of Changing Ideals and Practices, 1870 to the Present.* New York: Basic Books.

Rowe, John W., and Robert L. Kahn. 1998. *Successful Aging.* New York: Pantheon.

Rubin, Gayle. 1975. "The Traffic in Women." In *Toward an Anthropology of Women,* ed. Rayna R. Reiter. New York: Monthly Review Press.

_____. 1984. "Thinking Sex: Notes for a Radical Theory of the Politics of Sexuality." In *Pleasure and Danger: Exploring Female Sexuality,* ed. Carol Vance. Boston: Routledge.

Rubin, Lillian B. 1990. *Erotic Wars: What Happened to the Sexual Revolution?* New York: Farrar, Strauss & Giroux.

Ruggles, Steven. 1994a. "The Origins of African American Family Structure," *American Sociological Review* 59, no. 1 (February): 136–151.

_____. 1994b. "The Transformation of American Family Structure," *American Historical Review* 99, no. 1 (February): 103–128.

Rutman, Darrett B., and Anita H. Rutman. 1984. *A Place in Time: Middlesex County, Virginia, 1650–1750.* New York: W. W. Norton.

Ryan, Mary P. 1979. *Womanhood in America: From Colonial Times to the Present,* 2nd edition. New York: New Viewpoints.

_____. 1981. *Cradle of the Middle Class: The Family in Oneida County, New York, 1790–1865.* Cambridge: Cambridge University Press.

Sanchez, George J. 1993. *Becoming Mexican American: Ethnicity, Culture and Identity in Chicano Los Angeles, 1900–1945.* New York: Oxford University Press.

Schur, Edwin M. 1988. *The Americanization of Sex.* Philadelphia: Temple University Press.

Scott, Joan W. 1979. "Review Essay: The History of the Family as an Affective Unit," *Social History* 4: 509–516.

Seltzer, Judith A. 1994. "Consequences of Marital Dissolution for Children," *Annual Review of Sociology* 20: 235–266.

Skocpol, Theda. 1992. *Protecting Soldiers and Mothers: The Political Origins of Social Policy in the United States.* Cambridge: Harvard University Press.

Skolnick, Arlene. 1991. *Embattled Paradise: The American Family in an Age of Uncertainty.* New York: Basic Books.

_____. 1998. "Solomon's Children: The New Biologism, Psychological Parenthood, Attachment Theory, and the Best Interests Standard." In *All Our Families,* ed. Mary Ann Mason, Arlene Skolnick, and Stephen D. Sugarman. New York: Oxford University Press.

Skolnick, Arlene, and Stacey Rosencrantz. 1994. "The New Crusade for the Old Family," *American Prospect* 18: 59–65.

Smith, Daniel Blake. 1980. *Inside the Great House: Planter Family Life in Eighteenth-Century Chesapeake Society.* Ithaca, N.Y.: Cornell University Press.

Smith, Daniel Scott. 1972. "The Demographic History of Colonial New England," *Journal of Economic History* 32: 165–183.

_____. 1973a. "The Dating of the American Sexual Revolution: Evidence and Interpretation." In *The American Family in Social-Historical Perspective,* ed. Michael Gordon. New York: St. Martin's Press.

_____. 1973b. "Parental Power and Marriage Patterns: An Analysis of Historical Trends in Hingham, Massachusetts," *Journal of Marriage and the Family* 35: 419–428.

_____. 1974. "Family Limitation, Sexual Control, and Domestic Feminism in Victorian America." In *Clio's Consciousness Raised: New Perspectives on the History of American Women,* ed. Mary S. Hartman and Lois Banner. New York: Harper and Row.

_____. 1977. "Child Naming Patterns and Family Structure Change: Hingham, Mass., 1640–1880," *The Newberry Papers in Family and Community History.* Paper 76–5 (January). Chicago: Newberry Library.

_____. 1978. "Old Age and the 'Great Transformation': A New England Case Study." In *Aging and the Elderly: Humanistic Perspectives in Gerontology,* ed.

Stuart F. Spicker, Kathleen M. Woodward, and David Van Tassel. Atlantic Highlands, N.J.: Humanities Press.

_____. 1986. "Accounting for Change in the Families of the Elderly in the United States, 1900-Present." In *Old Age in a Bureaucratic Society*, ed. David Van Tassel and Peter N. Stearns. Westport, Conn.: Greenwood Press.

_____. 1995. "The Demography of Widowhood in Preindustrial New Hampshire." In *Aging in the Past: Demography, Society, and Old Age*, ed. David I. Kertzer and Peter Laslett. Berkeley: University of California Press.

Smith, Daniel Scott, and Michael S. Hindus. 1975. "Premarital Pregnancy in America, 1640–1971: An Overview and Interpretation," *Journal of Interdisciplinary History* 5: 537–570.

Solinger, Rickie. 1992. *Wake up Little Susie: Single Pregnancy and Race Before Roe V. Wade*. London: Routledge.

Spigel, Lynn. 1992. *Make Room for T.V.: Television and the Family Ideal in Postwar America*. Chicago: University of Chicago Press.

Stacey, Judith. 1990. *Brave New Families: Stories of Domestic Upheaval in Late Twentieth Century America*. New York: Basic Books.

_____. 1996. *In the Name of the Family: Rethinking Family Values in the Postmodern Age*. Boston: Beacon Press.

Stack, Carol B. 1974. *All Our Kin: Strategies for Survival in a Black Community*. New York: Harper and Row.

Stansell, Christine. 1987. *City of Women: Sex and Class in New York, 1789–1860*. Urbana: University of Illinois Press.

Steckel, Richard H. 1986. "A Dreadful Childhood: The Excess Mortality of American Slaves," *Social Science History* 10, no. 4 (Winter): 427–465.

Stone, Lawrence. 1977. *The Family, Sex, and Marriage in England, 1500–1800*. New York: Harper and Row.

Sullivan, Andrew, ed. 1997. *Same-Sex Marriage: Pro and Con, A Reader*. New York: Vintage/Random House.

Sweet, James A., and Larry L. Bumpass. 1987. *American Families and Households*. New York: Russell Sage Foundation.

Swidler, Ann. 1980. "Love and Adulthood in American Culture." In *Themes of Work and Love in Adulthood*, ed. Neil J. Smelser and Erik H. Erikson. Cambridge: Harvard University Press.

Szasz, Margaret Connell. 1985. "Native American Children." In *American Childhood: A Research Guide and Historical Handbook*, ed. Joseph M. Hawes and N. Ray Hiner. Westport, Conn.: Greenwood Press.

Tannen, Deborah. 1990. *You Just Don't Understand: Women and Men in Conversation*. New York: Morrow.

Taylor, Ella. 1989. *Prime Time Families: Television Culture in Postwar America*. Berkeley: University of California Press.

Tentler, Leslie Woodcock. 1979. *Wage-Earning Women: Industrial Work and Family Life in the United States, 1900–1930*. New York: Oxford University Press.

Thorne, Barrie, and Marilyn Yalom. 1982. *Rethinking the Family: Some Feminist Questions*. 2d ed., 1992. New York: Longman.

Tocqueville, Alexis de. 1969. *Democracy in America*, ed. J. P. Mayer. Garden City, N.Y.: Anchor Books/Doubleday.

Uhlenberg, Peter. 1978. "Changing Configurations of the Life Course." In *Transitions: The Family and the Life Course in Historical Perspective*, ed. Tamara K. Hareven. New York: Academic Press.

_____. 1980. "Death and the Family," *Journal of Family History* 5 (Fall): 313–320.

Uhlenberg, Peter, and David Eggebeen. 1986. "The Declining Well-Being of American Adolescents," *The Public Interest* 82: 25–38.

Ulrich, Laurel Thacher. 1982. *Good Wives: Image and Reality in the Lives of Women in Northern New England, 1650–1750*. New York: Knopf.

U.S. Advisory Board on Child Abuse and Neglect. 1995. "A Nation's Shame: Fatal Child Abuse and Neglect in the United States," 5th report. Washington, D.C.: Department of Health and Human Services, Administration for Children and Families.

U.S. Bureau of the Census. 1975. *Historical Statistics of the United States, Colonial Times to 1970, Bicentennial Edition, Part I*. Washington, D.C.: U.S. Bureau of the Census.

_____. 1997. *Statistical Abstract of the United States: 1997*, 117th edition. Washington, D.C.

Vaughan, Diane. 1986. *Uncoupling: How Relationships Come Apart*. New York: Vintage.

Veroff, Joseph, Elizabeth Douvan, and Richard A. Kulka. 1981. *The Inner American: A Self-Portrait from 1957 to 1976*. New York: Basic Books.

Vinovskis, Maris A. 1988. *An "Epidemic" of Adolescent Pregnancy? Some Historical and Policy Considerations*. New York: Oxford University Press.

Waite, Linda. 1995. "Does Marriage Matter?," *Demography* 32, no. 4: 483–507.

Wall, Helena M. 1990. *Fierce Communion: Family and Community in Early America*. Cambridge: Harvard University Press.

Waller, Willard. 1937. "The Rating and Dating Complex," *American Sociological Review* 2 (October): 727–734.

Wallerstein, Judith S., and Sandra Blakeslee. 1989. *Second Chances: Men, Women, and Children a Decade After Divorce*. New York: Ticknor and Fields.

_____. 1995. *The Good Marriage: How and Why Love Lasts*. Boston: Houghton Mifflin.

Wallerstein, Judith S., and Joan B. Kelly. 1980. *Surviving the Breakup: How Children and Parents Cope with Divorce*. New York: Basic Books.

Walzer, John F. 1974. "A Period of Ambivalence: Eighteenth Century American Childhood." In *The History of Childhood*, ed. Lloyd DeMause. New York: Harper and Row.

Ware, Susan. 1982. *Holding Their Own: American Women in the 1930s*. Boston: Twayne Publishers.

Weeks, Jeffrey. 1985. *Sexuality and Its Discontents: Meanings, Myths, and Modern Sexualities*. London: Routledge and Kegan Paul.

_____. 1986. *Sexuality*. New York: Methuen.

Weiss, Robert R. 1975. *Marital Separation*. New York: Basic Books.

Wells, Robert V. 1982. *Revolutions in Americans' Lives: A Demographic Perspective on the History of Americans, Their Families, and Their Society*. Westport, Conn.: Greenwood Press.

Welter, Barbara. 1966. "The Cult of True Womanhood, 1820–60," *American Quarterly* 18 (Summer): 151–174.

West, Elliott, and Paula Petrik, eds. 1992. *Small Worlds: Children and Adolescents in America, 1850–1950*. Lawrence: University of Kansas Press.

Weston, Kath. 1991. *Families We Choose: Lesbians, Gays, Kinship*. New York: Columbia University Press.

Wexman, Virginia Wright. 1993. *Creating the Couple: Love, Marriage, and Hollywood Performance*. Princeton, N.J.: Princeton University Press.

Whitehead, Barbara Defoe. 1993. "Dan Quayle Was Right," *Atlantic Monthly*, April, 47–84.

_____. 1994. "The Failure of Sex Education," *Atlantic Monthly* October, 55–80.

_____. 1996. *The Divorce Culture: Rethinking Our Commitments to Marriage and Family*. New York: Vintage.

Wilson, William Julius. 1987. *The Truly Disadvantaged: The Inner City, the Underclass, and Public Policy*. Chicago: University of Chicago Press.

Winn, Marie. 1983. *Children Without Childhood*. New York: Penguin.

Wishy, Bernard. 1972. *The Child and the Republic: The Dawn of Modern Child Nurture*. Philadelphia: University of Pennsylvania Press.

Wrigley, E. A. 1966. *An Introduction to English Historical Demography*. London: Weidenfeld and Nicolson

_____. 1969. *Population and History*. New York: World University Library.

Wyatt-Brown, Bertram. 1986. *Honor and Violence in the Old South*. New York: Oxford University Press.

Zelizer, Viviana A. 1985. *Pricing the Priceless Child: The Changing Social Value of Children*. New York: Basic Books.

Zelnik, Marvin, John F. Kantner, and Kathleen Ford. 1981. *Sex and Pregnancy in Adolescence*. Beverly Hills: Sage.

Index